Hands-On Nature:

Information and Activities for Exploring the Environment with Children

Edited by Jenepher Lingelbach

Illustrated by Edward Epstein

Vermont Institute of Natural Science
Woodstock, Vermont 05091

Design by The Laughing Bear Associates
Illustrations by Edward Epstein
Typeset by Quad Left Graphics
Photography: Peter S. Hope (page 4); Barbara Kashanski
(page 16); Andrew Kline (page 68); Jenepher Lingelbach
(page 118); Cecil B. Hoisington (page 166).

Snowflake designs on page 187 are derived from "Snow
Crystals" by W.A. Bentley and W.J. Humphreys; 1962; Dover
Publications.

Library of Congress Cataloging-in-Publication Data

Lingelbach, Jenepher, 1935-
  Hands-on nature.

  Bibliography: p.
  Includes index.
  1. Natural history—Study and teaching.
2. Environmental education. 3. Nature study.
I. Title.
QH51.L56   1986   372.3'57   86-28268
ISBN 0-9617627-0-5

Published by Vermont Institute of Natural Science,
Woodstock, Vermont 05091

Copies of *Hands-On-Nature: Information and Activities for
Exploring the Environment with Children* may be obtained
from Vermont Institute of Natural Science, Woodstock, Vermont 05091, 802-457-2779.

ACKNOWLEDGMENTS

There was a child went forth every day
And the first object he look'd upon,
  that object he became,
And that object became part of him for the
  day or a certain part of the day,
Or for many years or stretching cycles
  of years.

Walt Whitman
from "Autumn Rivulets"
in **Leaves of Grass**

It is impossible to acknowledge all the people who have helped in so many ways to produce this book.

Hands-On Nature would not have been written without Mary Holland Richards, whose love for the natural world and desire for excellence nurtured the development of these workshops at the Vermont Institute of Natural Science. Along the way, creative and committed staff left their indelible prints; Judith Irving Hastings, Marsha Guzewich, Larry Prussin, Janni Mark, Wendy Vogt, Michael Caduto, Sharon Behar. The present staff, Margaret Barker, Beth Ann Howard, and Bonnie Ross, prepared the bibliographies, critiqued each stage of the manuscript and gave caring support and advice to the editor. Also vital were the thousands of Vermont volunteers who taught these workshops to children in their communities and gave valuable feedback and suggestions.

The transition from successful Vermont program to a national book could not have happened without the help of many. VINS Director, Sally Laughlin, and VINS Trustees encouraged the project, and VINS members endorsed it with financial support. Special thanks are given to the following major contributors: Raymond G. Ankner, Ada A. Brown, Thomas A. Kiley, June H. McKnight, Mrs. William G. Nightingale, Mr. and Mrs. William Peabody, Plumsock Foundation, Polaroid Foundation, Wilson Foundation. My sister, Barbara Kashanski, read through each draft wielding her red pen with care and incisiveness. Professors and teachers at the 1985 NSF Workshop for Elementary Science Teachers, held at the University of Wyoming, gave helpful suggestions. Thanks to scientific advisors, Dr. Ross Bell, Michael Caduto, Marc Des Meules, Rick Drutchas, Tom French, Peter Hope, Sally Laughlin, Nancy Martin, and Colonel Harold O'Brien, and to Mary Lou Webster for preparing the glossary.

Bob Nuner and Mason Singer, at Laughing Bear Associates, were wonderfully supportive throughout, and Susan Mesner of Kailyard Associates was perceptive and sensitive in her editing. But there is one person whose sign on my wall, "Yea we did it!" summarizes her dedication — the typist, Terry Kenison.

Finally, my thanks to those closest to me whose love, patience, and support gave me strength and freedom to complete this dream.

Jenepher Lingelbach
Jenepher Lingelbach

Table of Contents

Chapter IV - Designs Of Nature 167

INTRODUCTION

66 *The exploratory drive is perhaps the most powerful form of motivation in childhood. The child learns because he must.* 99

Alice Yardley
Discovering the Physical World

Citation Press NY 1973

Purpose of the Book

Hands-On Nature invites children and those who teach them to discover a world of simple wonders. One needn't travel far to see a leaf with exquisite veining patterns or to watch a bustling insect, miraculously coordinating its six legs.

The purpose of this book is twofold: to enable novice leaders to teach nature subjects successfully and to offer creative new approaches to experienced environmental educators. Ultimately, we hope to encourage children's curiosity and concern about their natural world and to give them experiences from which they can gain an understanding of the way it functions. What they learn and how much they care will affect us all.

How This Book Came into Being

Hands-On Nature is an outgrowth of the successful environmental education/natural science program designed and taught by the Vermont Institute of Natural Science (VINS) located in Woodstock, Vermont. Initially responding to a request from parents who wished to teach natural science in the local elementary school, VINS devised this hands-on workshop method to introduce children to the natural world. Called the ELF (Environmental Learning for the Future) program, these workshops have been presented to tens of thousands of teachers, community volunteers, and children in elementary schools throughout Vermont over the past thirteen years with notable success. One elementary school principal described ELF's effect as follows: "I hear students asking, 'What is it?,' or saying, 'Be careful,' and 'Let me see.' The other day after the snowstorm several students asked, 'When do we have ELF? We missed it yesterday.' That type of question is a good evaluation of the program because no one mentioned missing gym or art or music or reading or recess."

The enthusiasm of teachers and volunteers has spread the word about ELF workshops far beyond VINS' capacity to teach them. Requests for ELF materials have come in from all parts of the country, which helped us decide to publish the workshops. It is with great pleasure that we now offer them to nature leaders, classroom teachers, and outdoor-loving adults throughout North America.

Philosophy of Teaching

Children, like adults, learn best when they're actively engaged in the learning process and feeling good about themselves and each other. These workshops involve the children in many kinds of activities from creative arts, to sorting and classifying, to roleplaying, to using their senses, with the hope that every child will feel the joy of success no matter what his or her particular skills and abilities.

In designing these workshops there were a number of do's and don'ts that guided us through the labyrinth of possible activities and competing approaches.

Do focus each workshop topic so the information and activities clearly relate to each other, and so the children will understand the focus.

Don't rob the children of their own discoveries by over-teaching and over-directing.

Do include an outdoor field excursion, preferably nearby.

Don't emphasize identification. Answering the "what is it?" questions too soon seems to inhibit rather than enhance curiosity.

Do encourage care for the environment by setting examples such as releasing all creatures and rarely picking plants.

Who Can Use This Book?

Anyone who works with children and/or who wants to learn more about the natural world can use this book. Initially the workshops were designed for parent volunteers to use in their children's classrooms. Since then usage has expanded to include the following:

• Teachers — preschool, elementary, junior high, even senior high
• Nature Center Leaders
• Scout Leaders
• Camp Counselors
• Sunday School Teachers and Church Camps
• Garden Club Leaders
• Outdoor Education Center Staff
• 4-H Leaders
• Community Volunteers
• Parents
• School Districts for In-service Training
• Colleges or Universities for Pre-service Teacher Training

The activities were designed for children at the K-6 level. However, they have been selectively used or adapted for older and younger children as well. Because of the variety of cognitive and affective learning approaches, there have been reports of many kinds of children who do well with these workshops. Special education teachers say the hands-on way of presenting information allows their children to internalize and express their new-found knowledge. Gifted students are challenged because each activity calls for the best an individual can bring to it. Skills, competencies, concepts, facts are all presented in such a way that every child will gain some knowledge, according to his or her abilities.

HOW TO USE THIS BOOK

The format of this book is designed to be simple, clear, and consistent. There are, however, many components that can be utilized in a variety of ways. Our hope is that it will encourage creative teaching and spirited learning.

Overall Design

The workshops are grouped into four separate chapters: Adaptations, Habitats, Cycles, and Designs of Nature, with each workshop relating directly to its chapter's concept. Within the chapters, the workshops are arranged in seasonal order, starting with fall, which reflects their origins as elementary school teaching units. However, many of the workshops are appropriate for more than one season; some may be used year round.

Workshop Layout

Within each workshop there are two main parts: an informational essay, and an activity section. The informational essay is written with the workshop's focus in mind and covers basic facts and concepts needed to teach the workshop. Words set in boldface are defined in the Glossary at the end of the book. In a few cases, there is an additional fact sheet or chart included after the activities. For some this will be enough background information. Others will wish to read further in suggested reference books listed at the end of each essay. The activities follow, arranged in sequence to offer a logical progression of information from introductory to concluding activity.

The Many Options

The workshops are designed to be thematically connected, in seasonal sequence, and with a logical order to the activities. However, there are multiple ways the book can be used. Each workshop can stand by itself or can fit in as a supplement to other natural science programs. The order of the activities within a workshop may be changed, activities can be added or deleted. Some prefer to set up a series of activity stations and rotate groups of children through them rather than lead all the children simultaneously through each activity. An individual activity could be lifted from any workshop to use as a nature game or to enhance a course of study.

The information sections include pertinent facts, basic concepts and interesting tidbits. By themselves, they make interesting and informative natural history reading.

Activity Section Format

The activities are the heart of *Hands-on Nature* and were designed to encourage hands-on learning. There are a number of teaching hints included in each activity section that should help leaders and teachers use the book to its fullest. For clarity's sake, they are described here in order of appearance.

Seasons — legend in the upper right hand corner of activity page designating appropriateness for: spring (SP), summer (S), fall (F), winter (W)

Focus — a brief statement explaining the central theme of the workshop

Initial question — a broad question to start the children thinking about the topic and give them a chance to tell what they already know

Objective — an explanation of what each activity aims to teach or accomplish

Activity instructions — a step-by-step explanation of how to set up and teach each activity

Materials — a list of needed equipment or materials

Follow-up activities — suggestions to extend the scope of the workshop

Skills list — a summary of the Science Process Skills and the Integrated Curriculum Skills promoted by the activities

Suggested reading for children — a short list of good children's books relating to the topic

Teaching aids (such as puppet show script) — as needed to carry out the listed activities

Teaching hints that are not included:

Suggested grade levels (occasionally included) We have found children to be responsive to a far wider range of hands-on experiences than most experts advise.

Length of time — the time it takes to complete an activity or a workshop varies greatly depending on the leader, the children, and time limitations. Each workshop *can* be completed in an hour; one and a half to two hours is average.

Equipment And Materials

Most of the supplies called for in the activities of *Hands-On Nature* are deliberately simple to find or easy to procure: crayons, paper, pipecleaners, leaves, cups, cones to name a few. Appendix B at the end of the book lists materials and equipment that may be more difficult to obtain and suggests either ways to make them or places to find them.

Special Features

Puppet Shows

A word about puppet shows. As introductory activities, they are excellent vehicles for setting the focus and communicating information to all ages. From kindergarteners to high school teachers, it has been proven time and again that the audience really remembers what it learns in a puppet show. Whether adults put the shows on for the children, or the children put them on for each other, puppet shows are effective teaching tools. For the actual puppets we use simple cardboard cut-outs glued on to paint sticks. If a character is a plant, we often use the actual plant, such as Mary Milkweed. The stage is likely a table turned on its side or a movable bookcase.

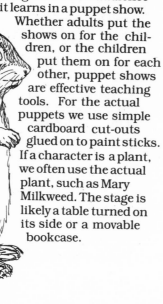

Suggested Reading for Children

A list of recommended books for children appears at the end of each activity section. Compiling this bibliography was a great challenge, as there are many more children's books than we could possibly obtain and review. The lists given represent the recommendations of the VINS staff, as well as teachers, librarians, and other environmental educators who offered their suggestions. We have tried to give brief descriptive comments for those books that we ourselves have seen and recommend. We also give a general age level designation for most books: younger-y (grades k-2); older-o (grades 3-6). These should be interpreted very loosely, as there is much overlap. You as the teacher/leader should determine the best use of any book. Many may be helpful for adult reference.

We invite your comments and suggestions for other good books.

Evaluation

The goals of *Hands-on Nature* are to spark children's curiosity about the natural world, to increase their awareness of the many interrelationships within it, and to foster a positive attitude towards it.

There are many ways to evaluate the degree to which the goals are met. Teachers, leaders, and parents can be asked to indicate on a check list the changes they notice in the children's interest, awareness, and attitude after *Hands-on Nature* experiences.

The objectives for reaching these goals are to give children *skills* they can use to help them learn and discover and *knowledge* of basic natural science concepts and facts. How well the objectives are reached is easier to measure.

The skills are divided, for convenience sake, into two categories: science process skills and integrated curriculum skills. The regular use of *Hands-On Nature* activities has been credited with raising the science scores in some Vermont elementary schools. The children's effective use of a particular science process or integrated curriculum skill could be plotted on a 1 (low) to 5 (high) scale. If this were done with each successive workshop, it would become clear whether or not the children were acquiring or increasing competence in the listed skills. (Not all skills are applicable to all workshops, but every skill is utilized several times throughout the book.)

To verify what basic natural science concepts and facts were learned, the initial question asked at the beginning of each workshop could be asked again days, weeks, or months after the workshop. Often children summarize what they've learned by drawing pictures like "monster mouthfuls" in Thorns and Threats. Ask parents whether their children relay information or activities to them or to their siblings. In a school situation, a questionnaire might be used, although formal testing is anathema to the joy and excitement we want children to feel. How much the children have learned and remember is also indicated by the frequency with which they refer to information from previous workshops.

YOU AS ENVIRONMENTAL EDUCATOR

Be A Role Model

"Do as I say, not as I do."

This exhortation rarely works. You are the leader and the children will follow your example. Your attitude toward the environment will register clearly with them as you carefully replace a log rolled over for investigation, or pick up trash left by people there before you.

How you feel about nature should and will come through to the children — when you stop suddenly to listen to a favorite bird song or pause to watch an ant laboring under a heavy load. Curiosity and caring are contagious.

Everyone is Afraid Of Something

Most people fear, or "hate," some things in nature. To lessen those fears by learning more about the object of them is a worthwhile goal, for our own sakes and for the sake of the children we influence.

Should one express fear or conceal it from the children? You will have to be a very good actor to hide your fear of snakes when you're startled by one during a field trip. So you might as well be honest. When the situation arises, explain that you are afraid of snakes, or spiders, or mice, and that you are trying to increase your knowledge about them so you will become less fearful. This admission may lead to a good discussion in which children can admit their fears and be encouraged to realize they need not be trapped forever by them. Many leaders who hated spiders have come away from the Spider Webs workshop still wary but with admiration and curiosity to know more.

Some fears are too deep-seated to deal with immediately. Some are valid for safety reasons, but many can be dispelled by accurate information, simply explained. What a favor you will have done for a child if you can dispel a fear.

Sense of Humor

Children learn best when they're having a good time; your playfulness and sense of humor will keep them on their toes. Children seem to relish corny jokes and ridiculous riddles — they will laugh at yours and feel great when you laugh at theirs. Keep some jokes up your sleeve for times when things drag a bit or children are tired.

A witty remark can turn a mistake or a minor accident (like losing a shoe in the mud) into a comical situation. Laughter is good for the soul as well as for the brain.

Expected Behavior

Whether indoors or out, a respect for each other helps engender a respect for nature.

We all have different tolerances for commotion, but none of us need tolerate meanness or thoughtless infringement on the rights of others. Most important is for you to be clear in your own mind which behaviors are acceptable and which are not and to explain your expectations to the children. Encourage them to discuss their expectations of each other. Then when you have to discipline a child, you are reviewing behavior codes, not initiating them. Reasonable behavior translates into a lot more fun for everyone.

Boundaries

Outdoor activities often erupt into a joyous explosion of energy and dispersal into the far reaches of an outdoor area.

Before you give the children their final activity instructions or equipment and send them off, clearly define the boundaries beyond which they may not explore. It may be specific limits like a fence; it may be more general like within sight of your red kerchief or within earshot of your whistle.

Children are usually more secure, and thus freer to concentrate on finding, looking, investigating, when they know the boundaries.

Running Wild

Exuberance and pent-up energy, especially for children who have just emerged from a school bus or a classroom, can be channeled. Your plans may call for a sit-down discussion or a controlled scavenger hunt, but if you feel the lid about to pop, stop and organize a relay race or a red light game or a "hop like a _____" tour.

Then when the kinks are out, you can go over your behavior expectations. Children who egg each other on should be separated. Occasionally one may have to be sent indoors; the other children have the right not to be distracted or misled.

Running wild evokes images of ponies galloping on the plains, manes and tails streaming behind them. Sometimes children, too, have the need to stretch out, try their speed, express their joy at being let loose. The trick is knowing when to let it happen.

Don't Pick

Collecting is one of the hardest natural inclinations to regulate. Children love to pick, catch, keep what they find. Most of the scavenger hunts in this book say "find" rather than "collect," hoping to encourage children to leave their discoveries where they found them.

You, as leader, will have to decide when it is ok to collect and when it isn't. A general rule of thumb is that it's ok when there are so many you couldn't possibly count them. Once you've decided, make sure the children understand.

If they may collect, set firm guidelines on how big and how many: one leaf from a plant, one flowerhead, or one insect. When living creatures are collected, a release ceremony at the end of the session is very helpful. The leader can give a brief farewell address and then all children release their creatures simultaneously, back to the places in which they were found. Our feeling is that no child should be allowed to keep a creature found during a group expedition; possibly the leader may decide to keep one temporarily for group study and observation.

Limiting Stories

Sometimes a question is asked because the child is curious to know the answer, but often questions are actually lengthy stories and anecdotes. Even carefully planned discussions with the children may open a Pandora's box of tales from their own or their family's experiences.

It feels mean to cut short a child's story, but children understand time limitations. If you explain there will not be enough time to go outdoors or play thus and such a game, they will be willing to move on. Tell the children they will have a chance to tell you after the workshop. Don't forget to give them the chance; often, however, they will have forgotten what they wanted to say.

Add a Slice of Silence

Children's lives frequently feel as hectic as our own. If you can inject a little serenity into their time with you, you will help them enjoy and understand both the natural world and themselves a little better.

Our noisy intrusion into a field or forest or wetland brings natural activity to a temporary halt as creatures freeze or scurry into hiding. Encourage the children to be silent and still occasionally, wherever they are, and let the natural flow of life resume around them.

PREPARING TO GO OUTDOORS

Why Go Out?

Simply stated, outdoors is where a child can become part of the natural world, watching it and wondering about it. It's where one can see tracks in the dust, hear a dragonfly's wings, smell honeysuckle or sage or balsam fir. Curiosity, caring, discovery, and sharing are experiences that happen outdoors to nurture an inquiring mind.

Taking children outdoors to learn about nature can be a challenge. It is little wonder that school teachers hesitate to go outside with twenty to thirty children. In this book, the outdoor scavenger hunts and explorations suggested with almost every workshop have enough specific tasks for the children to do that being outside is not only manageable, but fun. Additional adult support can often alleviate some pressure; ask parents to come along for the outdoor portions.
(See Appendix A)

Which Activities to Do Outdoors

The Obvious Ones

Most of the workshops have at least one activity that invites the children outdoors to investigate. Some suggest field trips to special places such as to a forest or a pond. Scavenger hunts, included in a great many workshops, are excellent ways to challenge the children while focusing their searches. Certain active games requiring a lot of space are much more fun if played outside. Just as important as all the above are the outdoor sensory experiences — sitting with eyes closed by a pond or lying on the forest floor.

The "Why Not If The Weather Is Ok" Ones

The joy and sense of well-being that can come from being outdoors are feelings this book hopes to engender in children; the more time spent outdoors the more likely this is to happen. There are very few activities that cannot be done outdoors. Role-playing and other games are often more realistic and less inhibited when conducted outside. Show and tell activities work well if there's a good place to sit, look, and listen. Creative projects become more imaginative, but materials need to be accessible and organized. If it's very windy, either find a lot of stones to weight things down or retreat indoors. The weather, the chemistry of the group, and the available outdoor facilities will all help determine how much to do outside.

Where to Go

Usually one need go no further than the backyard, school yard, or nearby open areas. There are two reasons for encouraging such proximity: minimal cost and complication of travel arrangements, and the message to children that nature explorations can and should happen right outside their own back doors.

If a trip further afield is planned, make a point of scouting it out ahead of time so you will know where the children can find what they're looking for, how long they will need to spend, the best route, and the time it will require to get there and back. It also helps to plan the food and rest stops.

Preparing the Children for the Trip

Anticipation is half the fun, or it can be. Whether walking fifty yards across the way or driving twenty miles to a park, include the children in some of the planning, and brief them enough to spark their interest. If pocket money, special clothing (like an extra pair of shoes), or picnic lunches are needed, sending notes home to parents may help the children come prepared. Parents can better support your outdoor efforts if they know what you're doing. Some parents might even be willing to go along to help.

Preparing Yourself for the Trip

The Girl Scouts have good advice when they say "Be prepared." Some of the things to organize ahead of time include: equipment needed for the exploration such as task cards and hand lenses, field guides or other reference books, minimum first aid supplies, and a couple of surprises like a snack or a mystery object. Finally, consider what you would do in case of emergency — who would help take charge.

The Trip Itself

Have a good time. Be flexible. Often the unplanned happenings and the spur-of-the-moment inspirations turn out to be the best parts of the trip. But stay on schedule. It's better to stop while they're having fun than to prolong a trip and risk ending up with restless, oversaturated children.

CHAPTER I — ADAPTATIONS

Why do ducks have webbed feet and rose bushes have thorns? Adaptations in the natural world are structural or behavioral responses to the environment. If the response is appropriate, the organism is more likely to survive.

Picture a desert fox with enormous heat-releasing ears in contrast to an Arctic fox with tiny furry ones. Over time, as foxes spread across the continents, the ears adapted successfully to extreme environments. White-tailed deer are said to have altered their feeding times from day to night, a behavioral adaptation to avoid human activity.

The workshops in this concept will introduce many different adaptations of plants and animals and will also encourage children to think about how particular physical adaptations relate to important skills and behaviors, and ultimately to survival. A duck's webbed feet enable it to swim, to spend much of its time in the comparative safety of water. A rose bush protects itself with its thorns.

The study of adaptations invites a child to ask the question Why? As such, it offers an exciting introduction to the world of science.

Insects: Amazingly Adapted and Adaptable

There are more insects than any other group of animals in the world. They live on top of mountains, in underground caves, in deserts and rivers, and in fields and forests. Their numbers are enormous, with over 900,000 species identified. There is great diversity within this large population, but all insects have the same basic structure, with each species adapted to meet the demands of its own particular environment.

Insects are **arthropods** — related to spiders, crabs, and lobsters, and like these cousins they have jointed legs and an exterior skeleton. An insect's body consists of three main parts: head, **thorax,** and abdomen. The head contains the eyes, one pair of **antennae**, and mouthparts. The antennae are finely tuned sense organs, capable of feeling, tasting, smelling, detecting temperature, and receiving chemical stimuli. Some are long and slender, some quite feathery, and others club-like. The mouth of the insect is adapted to the food it eats. Thus a grasshopper's mouthparts are adapted for biting and chewing, a house fly's for lapping, a butterfly's for sucking, and a mosquito's for piercing and sucking. A few species, such as the mayfly, live as adults only long enough to mate and have no mouthparts with which to eat.

The middle section, or thorax, has three pairs of legs and usually two pairs of wings (sometimes one and occasionally none). For this reason, many muscles are located in the thorax. Insect musculature is highly specialized in many species — grasshoppers have about 900 muscles compared to humans' 800, and an ant can carry 50 times its own weight. Legs are adapted in as many ways as mouthparts. The grasshopper has hind legs specialized for jumping; the house fly has sticky pads on its feet, allowing it to walk up vertical walls; honeybees have specialized hairs on their hind legs that form "baskets" in which to carry pollen. The wings may be long, short, narrow, wide, leathery, or quite delicate depending on the type and amount of flying the insect does.

The abdomen is divided into many segments and contains the heart, the digestive system, and the reproductive organs. On females of some species, the egg-laying device (the ovipositor) protrudes noticeably from the end of the abdomen.

Breathing is done through holes (spiracles) in the abdomen leading to the tubes that carry air throughout the body. (There are also some spiracles on the thorax.) Air is pumped in and out by the swelling and relaxing of the abdomen.

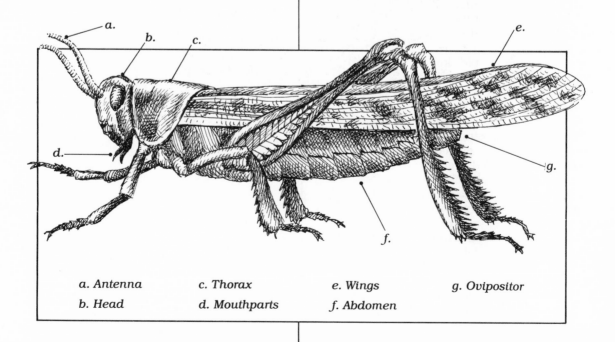

a. Antenna   c. Thorax   e. Wings   g. Ovipositor

b. Head   d. Mouthparts   f. Abdomen

The challenge of breathing under water has produced some remarkable adaptations, including the breathing tube of the mosquito larva, gills of immature caddisflies, damselflies and mayflies, and a system for carrying an air bubble used by certain water beetles.

For at least a third of a billion years, insects have been adapting to their environment. Of great importance to their flexibility in coping with harsh seasonal variations is the evolution of **complete metamorphosis**, resulting in the utilization of new habitats and food sources. (See information for Insect Life Cycles, p. 120.)

The success of insects as a group is due to their having several major assets: flight, adaptability, external skeleton, small size, metamorphosis, and the ability to produce multiple offspring rapidly.

Flight has given insects an advantage over landbound animals in being able to search actively for their mates, forage widely for food, escape from their enemies, and leave areas that no longer provide for their needs.

Insects are remarkable in their ability to adapt so well to extreme living conditions. With short life cycles and rapid reproduction, insects can change, if necessary, in a relatively short time to meet the requirements of a changing environment. For instance, when smoke from the Industrial Revolution darkened buildings and vegetation in England, one light-colored species of moth that had a few dark individuals born by chance in each generation could adapt to the new landscape by eventually producing generations of the darker moths. The lighter moths were visible to predators and did not survive.

The external skeleton is vital to insects as a suit of protective armor. Its essential ingredient is **chitin**, which is flexible, lightweight, tough, and very resistant to most chemicals. A growing insect simply sheds its old skeleton or skin and the new one inside quickly dries and hardens.

The small size of insects acts to their advantage. The speck of food that is a feast for an insect is usually much too small to be noticed by a larger animal. Being small, most insects can readily find shelter, even in tiny cracks, thus escaping detection and predation.

Timing is important for insect survival. Insect eggs are timed to hatch when the proper food and living conditions are available for the young. Also, with metamorphosis, the immature insect can use one food supply while the adult nourishes itself on something completely different.

Insects are fun to study and exciting to watch. There are far too many to be able to identify, but a close look can reveal remarkable adaptations.

Suggested References:

Burton, Maurice. *Insects and Their Relatives*. New York: Facts on File, 1984.

Farb, Peter. *The Insects*. New York: Time-Life Books, 1968.

Frost, S. W. *Insect Life and Insect Natural History*. New York: Dover Publications, 1959.

Sharp, David. *Insects*. New York: Dover Publications, 1970.

Zim, Herbert, and Clarence Cottam. *Insects*. New York: Golden Press, 1956.

Focus: *Insects share a basic structural design, but their adaptations allow for great diversity among them.*

ACTIVITIES	MATERIALS
Initial Question: What adaptations do insects have that help them survive?	

PUPPET SHOW

Objective: To illustrate some different kinds of tasks insects can perform with their various adaptations.

Perform, or have the children perform, the puppet show. Discuss the adaptations mentioned in the story.

- *script, p. 22*
- *puppets*

MAKE AN INSECT

Objective: To familiarize students with the basic body structure of insects.

Using pictures or a made-in-advance egg carton insect, discuss the basic structure of an insect. Using three connected egg sections of an egg carton, have each child fashion an insect with three body parts — one head with two antennae, two eyes, and mouthparts; one thorax with two pairs of wings and three pairs of legs; and one abdomen with spiracles (for breathing) and possibly an ovipositor. Each insect should be named and introduced by its maker, who should explain its special adaptations.

- *styrofoam egg cartons*
- *sharpened pencils to puncture holes*
- *pipe cleaners*
- *glue*
- *tape*
- *scissors*
- *assorted leaves, grasses, and seed heads*

INSECT SCAVENGER HUNT

Objective: To find a variety of insects outdoors.

Divide the children into pairs or small groups and give them Insect Scavenger Hunt cards with the following instructions:

- Listen for three different insect noises. Describe each.
- Look for a flying insect. Follow it. How many times does it land? What does it land on?
- Find a flower with three different kinds of insects on it.
- Inspect a patch of grass, look at the earth under the blades of grass to see how many minibeasts you can find.
- Watch a grasshopper. Does it have wings?
- Look for a honeybee or bumblebee and notice whether yellow or orange pollen has collected on its legs.
- Find a cricket. If it has 3 tail appendages it is a female.
- Find an ant. Is it carrying anything? Where is it going?
- If you can find a stone or a log, roll it over and see what minibeasts are under it. Replace exactly as you found it.
- Catch an insect. Put it in a container for the next activity.

Explain boundaries and time limit, then send them off to look. Small groups with a leader to read the cards work best with younger children.

- *Insect Scavenger Hunt cards*
- *hand lenses*
- *baby food jars or bug boxes* to contain captured insects

ACTIVITIES	MATERIALS

INSPECT AN INSECT

Objective: To look closely at one insect to see its body parts and how it moves.

• *questionnaires and pencils* for grades 4-6

Ask the children to inspect their insects, varying the instructions according to age.

(Grades 1-3) Look at it closely. Imitate how it moves.

(Grades 4-6) Look at your insect through a hand lens and fill out the following questionnaire:

1. What do you notice first?
2. Can you see wings?
3. Can you see legs? How many pairs can you see? Are all legs the same length? Which, if any, are longer?
4. Is its shell shiny?
5. Are there hairs on the insect's body?
6. Does it have antennae? How long are they?
7. Look at its eyes. Do they seem made up of hundreds of dots?
8. Can you see its mouthparts?
9. Is any part of the insect moving? Which part(s)?

Have the children draw their insect.

RELEASE CEREMONY

Objective: To return the insects to their proper homes by letting them all go at once.

Return by groups to the places where the insects were found. All at once, with the leader(s) reading the following poem, the children should release their insects.

Fly away, crawl away, run away, hop
You're free to go — I'm not going to stop
You from living your life
You deserve to be free
Thanks for sharing this time with me.

MINIBEASTS PUPPET SHOW

Characters: Bruno Bear
Rocky Raccoon
Tammy Termite
Fannie Fly
Betsy Butterfly

Bruno Bear: Boy, am I tired. Being king of the forest is no easy job. One problem after another.

Rocky Raccoon: Bruno Bear, Bruno Bear!

Bruno: Oh boy, not another problem. What is it, Rocky Raccoon? I hope it's nothing too awful.

Rocky: Oh, it is, it is. I saw a human pick the forget-me-not that grows by the edge of our forest. Dug it up, roots and all.

Bruno: Oh no, this *is* terrible. A forget-me-not flower only brings good luck to a forest *as long as* no one forgets about it. Now that it's gone, we'll no longer have good luck.

Rocky: What can we do Bruno?

Bruno: If only we knew where this man lived, we could try to get the flower back. It wasn't any of those humans out there in the audience, was it?

Rocky: Hmmm, let's see (looks over audience). No, I don't see him. But I know where he lives. I followed him back to his house.

Bruno: Perhaps we should tell all the other animals of the forest what has happened and where this man lives. Maybe someone will come up with a plan for rescuing our forget-me-not. (Both leave; Rocky appears again with Tammy Termite)

Tammy Termite: Rocky Raccoon, where are you running off to?

Rocky: Hi, Tammy Termite. I'm just spreading the bad news.

Tammy: What bad news?

Rocky: Some man has picked our forget-me-not.

Tammy: Oh my, that is bad news. What are we going to do?

Rocky: Well, I know where he lives. His house is all locked up, but I looked through the window. The man is sleeping on a couch next to a table. On the table is a vase of flowers. The poor forget-me-not is so little, it has fallen to the very bottom of this long vase. I don't know how we'll ever get it without waking up the man.

Tammy: I could easily sneak into his house without him hearing me. I'd just chew through his front door.

Rocky: Insects can chew through wood? I never knew that.

Tammy: Well, not all insects. But some of us, like termites, have special mouthparts made for chewing.

Rocky: But the forget-me-not is way down in the bottom of a long, skinny glass vase. You can't chew through glass, can you?

Tammy: No, I'm afraid not. Sorry I can't be of more help Rocky. Be sure and let me know if there's anything I can do. (Tammy Termite leaves)

Rocky: Oh, this is terrible. We'll never get the forget-me-not back. (Fanny Fly appears)

Fanny Fly: What's wrong, Rocky Raccoon? You look pretty upset.

Rocky: Oh, hello Fanny Fly. I am very upset. Our one and only forget-me-not is in the bottom of some man's glass vase, and there's no way for us to rescue it.

Fanny: If I had a way to get into the house, I could walk down the sides of the glass vase and rescue it.

Rocky: But you're a fly. How can you walk, especially on glass?

Fanny: Flies have special pads on their feet that let out a sticky fluid. That sticky fluid helps us stick to walls and windows so we can walk on them. It's no problem at all for me to walk down the side of a glass vase.

Rocky: Well, Tammy Termite has a special mouthpart for chewing through wood. She could make a hole for you to fly through and get in the house. Then, with your special legs you could walk down to the bottom of the vase and get the forget-me-not. Audience, do you think it will work? (pause)

Fanny: There's only one problem. I bet that forget-me-not is lying in water, and I can't swim. If there's water in that vase there's no way I'll crawl down. I could drown.

Rocky: Oh dear me. If only we could get rid of the water.

Fanny:	Well, let me know if you do need me. I'll be glad to help, as long as I don't have to swim. (Fanny Fly leaves)
Rocky:	Boy, I thought we had it solved. If we only had a way to get the water out of the vase. (Betsy Butterfly flies in)
Betsy Butterfly:	I could get rid of it easily.
Rocky:	Betsy Butterfly! You could, how?
Betsy:	I have a special mouthpart just like Tammy Termite. Only my mouthpart isn't made for chewing through wood, it's made for sucking up nectar from flowers.
Rocky:	You mean it's kind of like a straw?
Betsy:	That's right. If I can suck up nectar from a flower, I'm sure I can suck up water from a vase.
Rocky:	Oh, that's wonderful. You think this will work, audience? (pause) We'll try it. Let's go get Tammy Termite and Fanny Fly. Together, the three of you will be able to rescue the forget-me-not and bring good luck back to our forest. Let's go. (both leave)
Rocky:	Bruno Bear, cheer up. The forget-me-not is back growing in the ground.
Bruno:	Rocky, how did you ever do it?
Rocky:	I didn't do it. The insects did it.
Bruno:	The insects! How did they do it?
Rocky:	Well, insects have all sorts of special parts for doing special things. Tammy Termite used her special mouth to chew right through the man's front door. Then Betsy Butterfly went in and used her special mouth to suck the water out of the vase so that Fanny Fly could crawl down the side of the vase and rescue the flower. There were no problems at all, except when the man woke up.
Bruno:	The man woke up! I hope he didn't hurt any of the insects.
Rocky:	Well, he started chasing them, but then Maggie Mosquito came by.
Bruno:	Maggie Mosquito? What did she do?
Rocky:	What else? She bit him on the belly button!
Bruno:	Ha, ha. Those insects sure are well equipped. Let's go have a big celebration.
Rocky:	In honor of the forget-me-not?
Bruno:	Oh no, in honor of the insects of course.
Rocky:	Good idea. Let's go.

FOLLOW-UP ACTIVITIES

1. Quiet Watch
Encourage the children to sit quietly in a place where they've noticed insects, and watch them at work. They could report orally or write down what they saw, using a Field Guide for identification if desired.

2. Invite an Entomologist
Invite someone with an insect collection or special knowledge about insects to talk about insect adaptations, their usefulness to the environment, and some of the problems they can cause.

3. Ant Farm
Set up an ant farm and ask the children to notice which tasks need performing and whether all ants seem to do all tasks. Experiment by offering different kinds of food to see which their favorites are and how they harvest and store them.

Skills
Science Process: Observing, Inferring, Communicating, Predicting, Comparing, Experimenting, Recording Data

Integrated Curriculum: Art, Drama, Social Studies, Reading, Writing, Language Arts, Math

Suggested Reading For Children:

Armour, Richard. *Insects All Around Us*. New York: McGraw-Hill, 1981. (y/o — informative poems about 10 insects)

Blough, Glenn Orlando. *Discovering Insects*. New York: McGraw-Hill, 1957. (o)

Brouillette, Jeanne S. *Insects*. Chicago, IL: Follett, 1963. (o — good information and pictures)

Cole, Joanna. *An Insect Body*. New York: William Morrow, 1984. (y/o — pop-up book)

Fields, Alice. *Insects*. New York: Franklin Watts, 1980. (y/o — appealing illustrations)

Griffin, Elizabeth. *A Dog's Book of Bugs*. New York: Atheneum, 1967. (y — fun picture book)

Hutchins, Ross E. *The Travels of Monarch X*. Chicago, IL: Rand McNally, 1966. (y/o — life cycle, migration; also filmstrip)

Oxford Scientific Films. *Mosquitoes*. New York: J.P. Putnam's Sons, 1982. (y/o — excellent photos, life cycle)

Selden, George. *The Cricket in Times Square*. New York: Ariel, 1960. (o — classic story)

Selsam, Millicent E. *Backyard Insects*. New York: 4 Winds, 1981. (y — good photos, camouflage)

Selsam, Millicent, and Joyce Hunt. *A First Look at Insects*. New York: Walker and Co., 1974. (y — good pictures, fun mysteries)

Seymour, Peter. *Insects: Close Up Look*. New York: MacMillan, 1984. (y/o — pop-up book)

White, Florence M. *Your Friend the Insect*. New York: Knopf, 1968. (o — ten helpful insects)

Ingenious Ways to Get Away

Anyone who has blown the fluffy seeds from a ripe dandelion or tossed an apple core onto the ground has unwittingly contributed to one of the most important missions in the plant world — seed dispersal. For without the dispersal of seeds to new locations, young seedlings would be competing with their parent plants, often unsuccessfully, for sunlight, soil, water, and nutrients, and the plant's success as a species could well be endangered.

Seed production and dispersal may not seem especially significant to those of us whose favorite part of a plant's life cycle is the flowering stage, but for the plant it is the ultimate goal. Flowers are just one step in the process; they are the plant's way of conceiving, fertilizing, and nurturing the tiny plant embryos as they develop into seeds.

Seeds are well adapted to house the plant's next generation because they provide both nourishment and protection for the infant plant. An inner layer, surrounding the embryo, stores enough food to nourish the tiny plant when it first sprouts until its roots can take nutrients from the soil and its leaves can produce their own food.

The outer seed coat protects the embryo from drying out, freezing, and being destroyed by some animals. An apple seed is apt to be eaten, but its seed coat is relatively smooth and hard, so it passes through an animal's digestive system intact. Each kind of seed, no matter how tiny, has its own distinctive seed coat. A hand lens will reveal the ridges, indentations, and sometimes tiny hairs that give a seed its characteristic markings.

The formation of viable seeds is a plant's primary goal; their dispersal to a favorable location is the next assignment. Plants don't move, so how can seeds travel? Among flowering plants, it is at this stage that the seed container plays a vital role, whether it be an apple, an acorn, or a coconut. Plants package their seeds in whatever way best guarantees dispersal. Biologically, the seed is a fertilized, ripened **ovule** and its container, the ripened ovary. The technical name for flowering plants is **angiosperm**, which translates to seed in a vessel.

Some seed containers serve as foods for humans or animals who eat them and either discard the seeds or, in storing them, carelessly leave some behind. Squirrels hide acorns and forget to retrieve them all. Cherry seeds pass unharmed through the birds that eat them. Since the time when humans began tilling the soil and traveling to all corners of the earth, we have become the primary dispensers of many seeds.

There are ingenious seed containers. Some have wings or blades to propel them through the air whichever way the wind takes them. Maple, ash, elm, and basswood trees have such seeds. Some grow parachutes or fluffy hairs, which enables the wind to sweep their seeds aloft. Airborne dandelion and poplar tree seeds can travel long distances. Other seeds have sharp hooks or barbs that attach to passersby. Burdocks and beggar ticks are well-known hitchhikers. There are even seed containers with seams that burst open with such force the seeds explode from the parent plant. Jewelweed gets its nickname touch-me-not from the sudden expulsion of seeds that follows touching a ripened pod. A few seed containers are buoyant and carry their seeds on the water to new destinations. Coconuts are perhaps best known for this, although the seeds of many plants that grow along waterways are at least in part dispersed by water.

Thus dispersal of seeds is accomplished in a variety of ways, but they all attempt to achieve a common objective — distribution of the ripened seeds far enough away from the parent plant to reduce competition.

Suggested References:

Harlow, William M. *Fruit Key and Twig Key to Trees and Shrubs*. New York: Dover Books, 1941.

Peterson, Maude Gridley. *How to Know Wild Fruits*. New York: Dover Publications, 1973.

Stefferud, Alfred. *The Wonders of Seeds*. New York: Harcourt, Brace, 1956.

Symonds, George W. D. *The Tree Identification Book*. New York: William Morrow, 1958.

Focus: *Seeds are effectively adapted in a variety of ways to travel away from their parent plants to new locations.*

ACTIVITIES	MATERIALS
Initial Question: What are some of the ways seeds travel away from their parent plants?	

PUPPET SHOW

Objective: To introduce different mechanisms used to disperse seeds.

Perform or have the children perform the puppet show. Which dispersal method did the children like best?

- *script, p. 28*
- *puppets*

FOUND A PEANUT

Objective: To discover the parts of one seed.

Give each child an unshelled peanut. Open the shell (the ripened ovary) and look at the nuts inside (the seeds). Discuss the different parts including the brown papery seed coat, the bulk of the nut, which is food stored (a) for the plant when it is first germinating, and the tiny leaflets (b) between the two halves of the nut. Then eat them!

- *unshelled peanuts*
- *hand lenses*

a.

b.

MIX AND MATCH

Objective: To encourage thinking about where some familiar seeds come from and how they are dispersed.

Have the children match seeds to their parent fruits, looking closely at the shapes and designs of both. Briefly discuss how each type of seed might be dispersed.

- *sets of cards* each with a seed taped on it (e.g., apple seed, milkweed seed, burdock seed)
- *parent fruit* (e.g., apple, milkweed pod, burdock seed head)

ACTIVITIES	MATERIALS

SEED SCAVENGER HUNT

Objective: To discover what seeds can be found outside and how they are dispersed.

Send teams to find the following items listed on the Seed Hunt card:

- Two different seed containers that look good enough to eat. (Don't eat them yourself!)
- Two different seeds that travel a distance of three feet when you blow on them.
- Two different seeds that have hooks to stick to fur. (Put a wool sock on over one shoe and periodically check to see what seeds are hitchhiking a ride.)
- Two seed heads that have more than 20 seeds on them. Which one has the most?
- If there are trees nearby, look for two different seeds that are carried by wind; two seeds that animals might eat.
- Look at some different seeds through a hand lens. Are they smooth? rough? hairy? Describe one.

They should collect only if there is a very large area with many seed-producing plants. At the end of the hunt, have each group introduce a seed they found interesting. Discuss its means of dispersal.

Materials:
- *Seed Hunt cards — 1 for each team*
- *bags for collecting*
- *old wool socks*
- *hand lenses*

MILKWEED RACE

Objective: To have fun and see how far a seed can travel with a little hot air.

Give each child a milkweed seed. Have the children see how far they can make the seed go without letting it drop to the ground or using their hands.

Materials:
- *milkweed seeds*

FRUIT CUP

Objective: To enjoy a fruit snack while learning about seeds.

Bring in a collection of common and exotic fruits and dissect them with the children. Examine and discuss where the seeds are and how people contribute to seed dispersal. Then eat them!

Materials:
- *variety of fruit banana, apple, orange, grapes, nuts, kiwis, pomegranates*

SEED DISPERSAL PUPPET SHOW

Characters: Mary Maple Seed (fastened to the top of a dowel or pencil so she can be spun)
Ma Maple
Polly Parachute Seed
Carol Coconut
Charlie Chipmunk

Prop: Sign saying Next Spring

Mary Maple Seed: Mom, what am I gonna be when I grow up?

Ma Maple: A maple tree, just like me, dear.

Mary: Well, where am I gonna live, Mom?

Ma: I don't know, dear, but someplace far enough away from me so that your roots will have space to grow and your leaves can get all the sunshine they need.

Mary: How am I going to get there?

Ma: I'm not sure. You might fly or float in water or be carried by an animal.

Mary: Boy, that sounds exciting! I wonder which I'll do. Do all seeds fly, float, and get carried away from their parents?

Ma: No dear. Some seeds have such special designs they travel only one way. I'm sure you'll meet many different kinds on your journey.

Mary: (big wind noises) Yikes! I guess I'm going by air. Bye Mom. Wow, I'm getting dizzy spinning around like this.
(spin dowel; Ma Maple exits; Polly enters)

Polly Parachute Seed: You poor thing. I'm glad I don't spin that way. I'm so well-rounded, I just float along like a parachute.

Mary: You sure do Polly Parachute. Me? I'm like a helicopter propeller spinning out of control until I crash land somewhere.

Polly: Well, I'll be drifting along. Goodbye.
(Polly leaves; Mary stops spinning)

Mary: Hey, where am I? I've stopped spinning. I must have landed in a river. It's a good thing I can float. Wow, I'm really moving fast. Ouch! That rock hurt.
(Carol Coconut enters)

Carol Coconut: It doesn't hurt if you're built like me. I have such a tough coat that bumping into things doesn't hurt at all. We coconuts float so well we've travelled thousands of miles, even across oceans.

Mary: Gosh, you are a *really* good floater. Do coconuts always travel by water?

Carol: Usually, but sometimes human beings pick us up for food or take us home as souvenirs. That's how I got here. Someone brought me home and dropped me into the water to see if I could float, and I floated away, like I'm doing right now. Oops. Here I go! Goodbye.
(Carol leaves)

Mary: She sure is better adapted for water travel than I am. I'd like to get out of here. (bobs up and down, higher and higher) This is pretty rough. (pause, stops moving) Whew! Lucky thing that a big wave just shoved me onto the shore. But now what? (sobs a little) I don't want to live here. It's cold and damp. How can I move on to a good place to live, like my mom said.
(Charlie Chipmunk enters, bustling back and forth)

Charlie Chipmunk: Gotta hurry. Gotta hurry. Have to collect all my seeds before winter. Gotta hurry.

Mary: Goodness, who is that? I wish he'd slow down. He makes me nervous.

Charlie: Hello Mary Maple. I'm Charlie Chipmunk, out collecting seeds.

Mary: Well, that's funny. I thought I just saw you getting rid of seeds. Weren't you rubbing against that rock to scrape off some seeds?

Charlie: Yes. You're right. I was. But those weren't the kind I want to collect. Those were sticky seeds that try to hitchhike. But, *you* look good. Want to come home with me? I'll give you a lift over to my secret hiding place. (Secretly to the audience) I won't bother telling her that she's next winter's dinner!

Mary: Sure. I need a ride if I'm going to get to a good place to grow up. Where are we going?

Charlie: You'll see shortly. (Charlie picks up Mary, runs across stage, and puts her down) Here we are. A nice cozy hole in the ground. I'll just leave you with these other seeds. Catch ya later.
(Charlie leaves)

Mary: My goodness there are lots of seeds here. I wonder why. I seem to be way over on the side. I wonder if that matters?

Charlie:	Here I am back again, in time for dinner. A couple of maple seeds will taste mighty good. (munch, munch) Off again, more to collect. (Charlie leaves)
Mary:	Whew! That was close. *Now* I know why the chipmunk brought me here. I'm sure glad I was dropped way over on the edge of this hole. If I'm lucky, he'll forget about me. (Mary leaves; sign saying NEXT SPRING appears; Mary enters with two leaves sprouting from her)
Mary:	Hooray! I made it through the winter, and here I am starting to grow. It'll take a long time for me to grow as big as my mom, but I'm off to a good start. Bye, everybody.

FOLLOW-UP ACTIVITIES

1. Seed Mural
The class can make a mural and glue on the seeds collected during the scavenger hunt to show where they were found. They should also indicate how the seeds were dispersed.

2. Seed Journey
Ask the children to pretend they are seeds. Have them describe their travels from the mother plant to the place where they might land and start to grow.

3. Plant a Seed
Have the children save some seeds found during the Scavenger Hunt. Plant half and see whether they grow. Put the other half in a sheltered place outdoors for a few months, then plant them. Any difference in how many grow?

Skills
Science Process: Observing, Inferring, Brainstorming, Communicating, Comparing, Sorting and Classifying

Integrated Curriculum: Art, Drama, Social Studies, Reading, Writing, Language Arts, Math

Suggested Reading for Children:

Johnson, Sylvia A. *Apple Trees.* Minneapolis, MN: Lerner Publication, 1983. (y/o — seed & fruit development)

Jordan, Helene J. *Seeds by Wind and Water.* New York: Crowell, 1962. (y — simple text)

Lauber, Patricia. *Seeds Pop, Stick, Slide.* New York: Crown, 1981. (y/o — nice information and photographs)

Overbeck, Cynthia. *How Seeds Travel.* Minneapolis, MN: Lerner Publication, 1982. (o — photographs, general information)

Petie, Haris. *The Seed the Squirrel Dropped.* Englewood Cliffs, NJ: Prentice-Hall, 1976. (y)

Selsam, Millicent E. *Seeds and More Seeds.* New York: Harper, 1959. (y — good author)

_____. *Milkweed.* New York: William Morrow, 1967. (nice photographs, easy text)

_____. *Peanut.* New York: William Morrow, 1969. (y/o — photographs, life cycle details)

Adapted to Survive All Seasons

The ancestors of the white-tailed deer (**Odocoileus virginianus**) were not native to America, but emigrated from Asia by crossing the land bridge millions of years ago. The white-tailed deer evolved as a species in North America and, because of its ability to adapt to changing conditions, continues to thrive.

As a **prey** animal, the deer is well suited to detect and avoid its predators. A phenomenal sense of smell plus acute hearing warns a deer of trouble often before the predator, man or beast, knows of the deer's presence. Its eyesight is also very good, quick to notice the slightest movement. Once a predator has been detected, the deer may choose to run, hide, or fight. It is well-equipped to do any of these; in short bursts a deer may run faster than 30 mph, leap more than twenty-five feet over obstacles as high as eight feet. Its uncanny ability to hide comes partly from an intimate knowledge of every nook and cranny in the approximate square mile it inhabits, plus the camouflage of a bark-colored, brown-gray coat for the non-summer months. As a fighter, a deer can attack with very sharp front hooves.

The deer's digestive system also contributes to its ability to avoid predators. As a **ruminant**, with a four-chambered stomach, it can eat and run, storing the food in its first stomach. Later, when there is quiet time, the deer will regurgitate it, chew it as cud, and pass it on through the last three stomachs for final digestion.

The life cycle of the deer is closely related to seasonal changes. Fawns are born in late spring after a 200 day gestation period. A healthy doe will give birth to one fawn her first year and usually twins from then on if she has adequate food. Within minutes the fawns can walk, suckle, hear and react to noises, and lie absolutely still when commanded to do so by their mothers. With their spotted coats and absence of odor for the first few weeks, they are almost undetectable unless they move. Fawns grow rapidly on the rich doe milk, which has almost twice the solids of cow's milk and nearly three times the protein and fat. By fall, at the age of about four months, they are weaned, and only their somewhat smaller size and absence of antlers distinguish them from adult does and bucks.

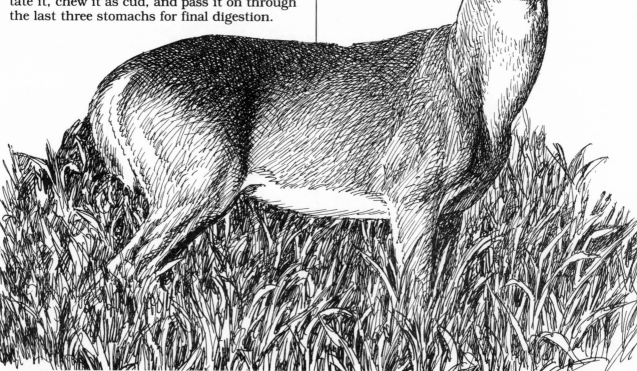

For three seasons of the year deer can usually find plenty of food. But winter in the north is a difficult time. Cold, snow, and a diminished food supply are the chief problems confronting deer in winter.

The cold is dealt with in two ways. First, long, hollow, air-filled hairs replace the scanty short summer ones and fine inner hairs grow close to the skin, thus providing double insulation. Second, deer often seek shelter in large groves of conifers that help block the bitter winds.

Snow presents a travel problem for deer. When more than twenty inches of snow are on the ground, it is difficult for them to get through it and they must use a disproportionate amount of energy to do so. At this time they confine their movements to a relatively small area called a deer yard, usually on a south-facing slope or in protected lowlands, where some melting from the winter sun, plus the interception of much of the snow by the conifer boughs, results in relatively shallow snow. As snow accumulates, the deer regularly tramp down paths throughout the area so travel remains possible within the yard.

This leads to the critical question of food supply. An adult deer is said to need a minimum of two and one half pounds of browse per day to stay healthy, although recently it has been observed that deer become semi-dormant for short periods (up to a few days), which reduces their expenditure of energy and thus their food requirements during that time. Deer can safely lose up to 30 percent of their body weight, but in a severe winter when deer cannot go beyond the yard's confines, they may use up the food supply, gradually absorb their own body fat and protein, and finally face starvation.

There is a definite dominance pattern in feeding when food is scarce; bucks feed first, then does, then finally fawns. The fawns are already at a disadvantage because their summer's food has gone into growth with little to spare for fat reserves. Thus, they are the first to succumb to starvation. In a mild winter, when they can easily move about, deer prefer buds and twigs from white cedar, hemlock, and red and striped maple, the fruits and nuts from apple, beech, and oak trees, and young poplar sprouts.

The effect of winter hardships on deer is often not sufficiently recognized. A deer herd is healthiest when its numbers relate favorably to availability of winter food and habitat. In some areas of the country with sizeable deer populations, efforts are being made to protect and increase winter habitat for deer, and in many states, Fish and Wildlife Departments monitor the size of the deer population and regulate the deer hunting seasons and quotas accordingly.

Whether one considers deer a natural resource, a symbol of natural beauty, or a garden nuisance, one has to admire their ability to adapt to the many challenges they face.

Note: Additional information may be found in Deer Facts, p. 34.

Suggested References:

Godin, Alfred. *Wild Mammals of New England.* Baltimore, MD: The John Hopkins Univ. Press, 1977.

Hall, L.K. (ed.). *White-tailed Deer: Ecology and Management.* Harrisburgh, PA: Stackpole Books, 1984.

Rue, Leonard Lee, III. *The Deer of North America.* New York: Crown, 1978.

_____. *The World of the White-tailed Deer.* Philadelphia, PA: J.B. Lippincott, 1962.

Focus: *A white-tailed deer is successfully adapted to escape predators and to survive northern winters.*

ACTIVITIES	MATERIALS

Initial Question: What special adaptations does a white-tailed deer have to help it survive?

MEET A DEER

Objective: To introduce the adaptations and life cycle of the white-tailed deer.

Using pictures or slides, introduce the special adaptations and the life cycle of a deer.

Note: State Fish and Wildlife Departments, which manage deer herds in their states, may have slides to loan.

- *pictures or slides*

SHOW AND TELL

Objective: To give the children a chance to look closely at certain deer adaptations.

Divide the children into four groups. Give each group one of the deer parts and have the children investigate it closely and think about how this part is a useful adaptation. Then pass the part on to the next group. Once each group has its original part back again, hand out the fact sheets, and have each group present its object to the others, telling about its adaptations and uses.

Note: Deer hunters, Fish and Wildlife Departments, or private collectors are usually willing to lend deer parts.

- *a deer skull, hoof, hair, and antlers*
- *fact sheets, p. 34*
- *hand lenses*

POPULATION PUZZLE

Objective: To illustrate the problems of over-population in an area of limited food supply, such as a deer yard.

Show the *minimum* amount of actual food (2½ pounds of browse) needed each day by each deer to remain alive. Divide participants into groups of twos, threes, and fours. Give each group a pile of 8 pretzels. Explain that each person needs a *minimum* of one pretzel per day to remain alive. Each pile is to last the group for three days. Then announce Day 1, Day 2, Day 3, pausing between each for the children to eat their pretzels, or, if none remain, to collapse of starvation. At the end, compare survival roles. Discuss whether deer are polite the way people tend to be, which deer eat first, which deer starve first. Is there adequate winter habitat for deer in your state?

- *2½ pounds of deer browse* (enough twigs to fill a grocery bag)
- *pretzel sticks* divided into piles of 8

ACTIVITIES	MATERIALS

EAT AND RUN

Objective: To show the dilemma deer face when they must browse for many hours daily yet also be on the alert for danger.

Ask each child to kneel down. Put a piece of paper with cereal on it in front of each. Tell the children that they are deer, grazing in an open field. They should put their heads down like deer and eat. Appoint one deer to walk among them and act as a lookout. When it senses danger (leader could flash a picture of a predator), the lookout deer raises his white tail flag, and the feeding deer must stop eating and flee to SAFETY (designated spot with SAFETY sign on it). Another child then becomes the lookout. After they have tried it, discuss how deer are better adapted to be aware of potential danger, and why it is advantageous for the deer to be a ruminant. (See information, p. 30)

- *papers*
- *cereal*
- *SAFETY sign*
- *White flag* (made to look like a deer's tail)

ROOM AND BOARD

Objective: To learn what makes a suitable winter habitat for deer.

Divide the children into groups of three and give each group their Room and Board cards with the following instructions:

FOOD
You must find some shrubs and trees that you can reach when on your knees.

PATHS
Tramp down paths both to and fro so deer can follow through the snow.

BEDS
Where to sleep or where to rest? A wind-free, sheltered place is best.

The groups then spread out within a given area, and each should find a good place to winter as deer, deciding together which place is most suitable for Food, Paths, and Beds. Get back together to discuss the various winter habitats found.

- *Room and Board packets* with one card each for Food, Paths, Beds

THE SKULL

Eyes

Are a deer's eyes large or small and why?

A deer's large eyes are sensitive to even tiny movements, but don't notice objects that don't move. This excellent eyesight is important for spotting danger.

Why is there a bony framework around the eyes?

To protect them from sticks and branches that could hurt the eyes, as the deer runs through the forest.

What are the openings on the front rim of the eye socket?

These are tear ducts, for the tears that are important in washing dust, pollen, or other particles out of the deer's eyes.

Jaw

Where are the teeth missing?

The deer's upper jaw is missing its front teeth. Live deer would have a hard pad there. The back rows of teeth are used for chewing and grinding their food.

How might the teeth indicate the age of a deer?

Very worn and smooth teeth would indicate that the jaw or skull belonged to an older deer, whereas rougher, sharp-edged teeth would show the deer was younger.

Ears

Where are the openings for the ears?

The opening is funnel-shaped and surprisingly small, up and behind the eye socket.

Are the deer's ears large or small?

The large ear we see is an excellent funnel to collect even the slightest sound and send it through the small opening to the ear drum. Kidney-shaped bones on the underside of the skull act as sound chambers.

THE ANTLERS

Sex of the Deer

Do all deer grow antlers?

It is usually the male deer (buck) that grows antlers, though occasionally a female (doe) will grow them.

What are the antlers used for?

The bucks use the antlers during the rutting, or breeding, season to defend their territories and their does against other bucks and/or to challenge a rival buck for a doe.

Formation

What are antlers made of?

Antlers, which grow and are shed every year, are made of bone and grow right from the skull bone. Horns, which look like antlers, are permanent and are made from a hair-like substance over a bony core.

What do the antlers look like while they are growing?

Each year the antlers start growing as little "buttons" on the skull, three or four months after the old pair falls off in January. They then grow to their full size covered with "velvet."

What does the velvet do?

This velvet, or fuzzy, coating on the antlers is really skin and is filled with blood vessels, which provide nutrients for the growing antlers. While the antlers are covered with velvet they are very sensitive and can easily be hurt and damaged. When they have finished growing, the deer rubs them against trees and shrubs and scrapes the dried velvet skin off in shreds.

Size

What does the size of a deer's antlers show about the deer?

The size indicates how healthy the deer is and whether or not it has had enough nutritious food to eat. Ill-nourished deer have smaller antlers than well-nourished deer of the same age. Thus a buck's age, other than a single-spiked yearling, cannot be determined by its antlers.

Shedding

When and how do deer lose their antlers?

They may be knocked off prematurely, but normally they fall off in early winter.

Antlers are rarely found in the woods. Where do they disappear to?

Deer antlers are recycled. Animals, like mice, squirrels, and porcupines, like to chew on the antlers, which have calcium and other minerals the rodents need.

THE HAIR

Color

Why is the gray color of the winter coat an advantage?

The reddish-brown summer hair would show up in leafless winter woods more easily than the gray hair, which is a good camouflage color against the bare tree trunks.

Where does a deer have white hair?

White hairs are found on the underside of the tail, in a bib on the throat, inside the legs, and on the lower chest and belly.

Texture

Is there a difference in texture between the summer coat and the winter coat?

Summer hairs are solid, fine, and short to help the deer stay cool. Winter hairs are long, coarse, wavy, and hollow. In addition, short, fuzzy underfur helps insulate. A winter hair bends like straw, leaving a crinkle mark.

Warmth

How would hollow hairs benefit a deer in winter?

Long, hollow hairs trap much more body heat than short, fine hairs. Dead air spaces within and between the hairs provide excellent insulation even in the coldest weather.

HOOVES

Shape

How is the hoof shaped?

The hoof is divided into two separate halves. Each half is actually a toe. These two toes were once the third and fourth toes on the foot of ancient deer relatives. The first toe or thumb disappeared, and the second and fifth toes are now the dew claws. The deer hoof is far less clumsy than its 5-toed predecessor.

Where are the dew claws? How might they help the deer?

These two toenail remnants, which are behind and slightly above the main toes, occasionally leave round dents behind the main hoof imprints in a deer track. They could help keep a deer's foot from slipping or getting caught in a crack.

Advantages

What are some possible advantages and disadvantages of hooves for the deer?

Small hooves enable the deer to bound surefootedly over tangled, uneven terrain. But in winter, the small hooves can be a disadvantage, easily breaking through snow or ice crusts, because the deer's weight presses down so hard on each tiny hoof. It is similar to a person wearing skis who can stay on top of the snow because his weight is distributed along the ski, but who without skis would sink into the snow.

Structure

How is the sole of the hoof different from the outer covering?

Soft, leathery pads (dried up on a specimen) fit into the hard frame of the hoof.

How would these pads help or harm the deer?

The pads help keep the deer from slipping when it walks over rocks and ledges.

How might the hard outer covering help the deer?

The covering of the hoof is made of keratin, like fingernails. It cuts into the earth to give sturdy footing. It also makes the hoof a dangerous weapon — one sharp blow from a deer's forefoot can crush a dog's skull. In winter it can be slippery, making it almost impossible for a deer to get up after it has fallen on the ice.

FOLLOW-UP ACTIVITIES

1. Storytime
Read the children the story "Lightfoot, Blacktail, and Forkhorn" from *The Burgess Animal Book for Children* by Thornton W. Burgess. (New York: Grosset & Dunlap)

2. Resources
Invite a Game Warden into the school to talk about the deer population.

3. Personal Experiences
Have the children talk with someone who has watched deer and write about that person's experience. If the children have seen deer, they should write about their own observations.

Skills
Science Process: Observing, Inferring, Brainstorming, Communicating, Predicting

Integrated Curriculum: Drama, Social Studies, Reading, Writing, Language Arts, Math

Suggested Reading for Children:

Eberle, Irmengarde. *Fawn in the Woods.* New York: Crowell, 1962. (o — story format, good information)

George, Jean Craighead. *The Moon of the Deer.* New York: Crowell, 1969. (y)

Hurd, Edith T. *The Mother Deer.* Boston, MA: Little, Brown, 1972. (y — story format)

Jenkins, Marie M. *Deer, Moose, Elk and Their Family.* New York: Holiday House, 1979. (adaptations, life cycles)

Zoo Books 2. *The Deer Family.* (Vol. 1, #10). San Diego, CA: Wildlife Education Ltd., 1985. (o — adaptations of many species)

Predator and Prey: A Complex Relationship

Every animal on this earth shares a common problem. It must get enough nourishment to keep its body going or else face death. **Herbivores**, the hunted, are animals that depend on plants for their food. **Carnivores**, the hunters, largely depend on herbivores to supply their food, and **omnivores** eat both plant and animal matter. The problems of getting enough food to eat are quite different for herbivores and carnivores. An herbivore's food source is stationary and often fairly abundant; the challenge is how to get enough of it while avoiding attack by a hunter. Carnivores have to work harder to find and catch their food. However, meat is a more concentrated food source and, therefore, hunters do not have to eat as often. Adaptations, both structural and behavioral, have evolved in both hunters (**predators**) and hunteds (**prey**), which help them meet the challenge.

Escape is the most important defense for the hunted or preyed-upon species. Their sense of hearing is usually well developed and their ears often large, to catch the sound waves. A white-tailed deer will hear the approach of something long before it can be seen. The eyes of most hunted animals are placed towards the sides of their heads to enable them to get a broader view of their surroundings, but often they will not notice an object until it moves. Their sense of smell is also well developed. The ability to escape rapidly is obviously helpful; some prey, especially those in flocks or herds, take off, but most dive for protective covering.

Hunted animals often find safety in numbers, especially when feeding. One sign of fear from any member will be enough to set them all fleeing. Many prey animals also bear numerous offspring, which increases the chances that at least a few will survive.

For several species of prey animals, a speedy escape is not a reasonable alternative. Instead, many other protective devices have evolved over time. (See information for Thorns and Threats, p. 55 and for Camouflage, p. 201.) It is important to keep in mind that no prey species has a perfect defense. As the prey improves its defense, the predator often adapts accordingly and improves its attack.

A hunter's or predator's orientation to survival is entirely different from its prey's unless it suddenly becomes something else's prey. Predators tend to be curious rather than afraid of strange phenomena. They must investigate every possible channel that might yield food. A predator's movements are often quick, restless, energetic, and alert. Most predators have a well-developed sense of smell. The trails of animals provide a map full of valuable information to the sensitive nose. A predator's sight is also important; slight movements in the grass may reveal an errant mouse to the fox. All carnivores have their eyes placed

towards the front of their heads, providing three-dimensional, binocular vision essential for the capture of prey.

Once a prey is located, speed and quickness are important. Of course predators also need strong jaws and sharp teeth. (See information p. 43.)

The adaptations of both predator and prey are successful only if they enable adequate numbers to survive. However, in order for a predator to live, a prey must die. This might seem contradictory at first, but this interaction between predator and prey, the hunter and the hunted, is a vital part of the checks and balances in the natural world. Neither the hunter nor the hunted is right or wrong, evil or good.

Predation is an absolute necessity in the scheme of nature, and is as important to the prey species as to the predator. Hunters go for the easiest prey they can find, so they often weed out the fringe members of a species — the old, the very young, the diseased, and the injured.

66 To understand the value of predation it is important to remember that among all animals the fiercest competition is between members of the same species — between muskrats and muskrats — rather than between members of different species — mink and muskrats. Animals of the same kind need exactly the same kind of food, shelter, nesting areas, mates, and these resources are limited. When there are more animals trying to live in an area than there are resources available, the competition between them becomes disastrous. Some will die of starvation, as one takes food from another. Others will die of exposure, driven from protected territories by their own kind....Finally, overpopulation and severe competition seem to create social problems. Surrounded by too many of their own kind, animals become abnormally aggressive, irritable, may not mate readily, bear fewer and weaker young, sometimes fail to care for their litters, or may even destroy them. (Bil Gilbert, *The Weasels*, p. 61) **99**

An awareness of the remarkable adaptations of the hunter and the hunted, and of the important relationship between them, is central to understanding the natural world.

Suggested References:

Carrington, Richard. *The Mammals*. New York: Time-Life Books, 1965.

Eckart, Allan W. *Wild Season*. Boston, MA: Little, Brown, 1967.

Gilbert, Bil. *The Weasels — A Sensible Look at a Family of Predators*. New York: Pantheon Books, 1970.

Whitfield, Dr. Philip. *The Hunters*. New York: Simon & Schuster, 1978.

Focus: *Animals that hunt for their food, and animals that are hunted, have special adaptations to meet their own particular challenges, many of which are common to both groups.*

ACTIVITIES	MATERIALS
Initial Question: What are some differences between animals that hunt and those that are hunted?	• *pictures of hunter and hunted animals* or mounted specimens

WHAT'S THE DIFFERENCE

Objective: To start children thinking about adaptations that are: 1) special to either hunter or hunted animals, or 2) common to both.

Divide into two groups. Using pictures or mounted specimens, have one group study hunters and the other group study hunteds. Each group should make a list of words that describe adaptations of their hunter or hunted. Compare lists. You might ask the children in one group to read an adaptation and the children in the other group to then read an adaptation that would counter it.

Note: Introduce the terms *predator* and *prey*.

SUPER HUNTER

Objective: To show how predators must be adapted to catch their prey.

• *crayons*
• *paper*
• *cards*

All hunting animals must be adapted successfully to catch their food or prey. Otherwise starvation is just around the corner. Pass out cards describing prey and where it can be found:

• Fish in fast-flowing stream
• Spider hiding in the rocks
• Turtle eggs buried in sand
• Deer in wooded part of an island
• Snake sunning on a stone
• Ducks swimming about in a marsh
• Termite in a house
• Porcupine inside of a hollow tree
• Bats hanging on walls of a cave
• Chickens in a chicken coop
• Ants inside tunnels of an ant hill
• Fly on a lily pad in a pond
• Green frog in a grassy swamp
• Snail in a rotten log
• Mouse in a barrel of grain in a barn

(Grades K-2) One card for each group of children. Either leader or children might draw habitat and prey, then children draw their own imaginative predators after a discussion to point out some of the special problems in catching that particular prey. (Grades 3-6) Ask children, in pairs, to devise and draw a picture of a "successful" predator (an imaginative creature) catching the assigned prey in its habitat.

ACTIVITIES	MATERIALS

RABBITS AND FOXES

Objective: To gain an appreciation of the interdependency and delicate balance between predators and their prey.

Read Rabbits and Foxes story aloud and portray the characters on felt board with cut-outs. Discuss the story and then ask the children what might happen next in the story.

Note: Read through beforehand and mark where rabbits, foxes, and tree leaves go on and come off the felt board.

- *felt board*
- *cut-outs* of 15 rabbits, 10 foxes, tree, leaves
- *cotton balls*
- *masking tape* (if paper cut-outs)
- *story*, p. 41

EARS AND NOSES

Objective: To appreciate firsthand the importance of senses to the survival of wild animals.

These activities may be done simultaneously after the children have been divided into two groups.

Ears — Select two children to stand in the center of a circle formed by the rest of the children. One is a fox, the other is a mouse; both are blindfolded. By listening to each other, the fox tries to tag the mouse and the mouse tries to stay away from the fox.

Note: Two boxes of thumbtacks may be handy to rattle if the game is played on a carpet or on grass.

Noses —While the Ears follow sounds, the Noses are each given a length of paper tape, a cotton ball, and a scent. Securing their tapes with stones (or taping them to the floor if inside), the children dab their scents regularly along their tapes, almost like tracks. Tapes from different children may crisscross depending upon the degree of difficulty desired. When all are ready, each NOSE pairs up with an EAR who will play the part of a hunter using its nose to find its prey. The hunter is blindfolded, led to the start of the appropriate scent trail, given a whiff of the cotton ball, told to get down on hands and knees, and to sniff along the trail. When the hunter reaches the end of the trail, the trail-maker should be waiting, ready with congratulations. (Perhaps a snack would be a good ending.)

- *blindfolds*
- *adding tape*
- *cotton balls*
- *blindfolds*
- *scents:*
  flavorings
  Worcestershire sauce
  after-shave lotion

SHARING CIRCLE

Objective: To have everyone participate by considering a specific animal's adaptation.

Have each child complete the sentence, "I would like to be a _____ (animal). I need _____ (adaptation) to help me survive."

RABBITS AND FOXES

This is a story of Faraway Woods, a young fox named Freddie, and a young rabbit named Roberta. (The children listen and watch as felt rabbits, foxes, and leaves appear and disappear from the feltboard, as the story dictates).

Our story starts during the summer on a warm and sunny day. Freddie and Roberta are both youngsters. They were born this spring and are beginning to learn how to find their own food.

There are lots of good things to eat all summer long. Roberta has a wonderful summer. (start putting up lots of rabbits) She has lots of brothers and sisters, aunts and uncles, cousins and grandparents, and there's also plenty of food for all of them. The only thing Roberta worries about is THE BIG DANGER. In the middle of the field is a fox hole (put up 3 or 4 foxes) and she's been told many times to be careful of the new fox family that lives there.

Meanwhile Freddie is learning how to catch grasshoppers, pick berries, lunge after mice, and keep his nose open for any sign of rabbits. He's been told many times that the very best thing for dinner is a nice young rabbit.

Things start changing around Faraway Woods come October. The days get shorter, it gets chilly, leaves fall off the trees, and food is harder to find. (remove leaves) Some rabbits have been forced far away from home to look for food. (remove a few rabbits) They often bring back very bad news; it seems like there isn't much food anywhere, and there is another fox family in the area. (add foxes)

Meanwhile Freddie is ready to leave his home. He decides not to go too far away from the area since there are so many nice juicy rabbits around that would make good meals all winter long. If only he could catch one!

One day in late fall after spending many hours looking for something to eat, Freddie catches the scent of a rabbit. Crouching down, he slowly approaches a low bush. There, nibbling, is an older rabbit. Freddie feels a little scared since he'd rather try catching a little one for his first try. But his hungry stomach pushes him on. He moves in quickly and springs. Surprisingly, the rabbit is caught unaware and Freddie manages to kill it. It turns out to be a very old, weak rabbit, but it's food to Freddie. His first successful rabbit hunt!

Winter finally moves in, (add cotton here and there) covering Faraway Woods with a layer of white fluffy stuff, something completely new to Freddie and Roberta. Life becomes much more difficult for the rabbits. Food is much harder to find. The farther they have to look for food, the harder it is and the more dangerous.

Traveling in the snow isn't much fun either. More and more often another report comes in that a rabbit has been taken by a fox. (remove a few rabbits)

Freddie, of course, can't find berries and nuts to eat any more, but there are plenty of mice and squirrels and, best of all, rabbits to keep him going. He has become quite a pro at catching his own food. (remove a few rabbits)

By the time spring rolls around, (cotton off, leaves on) the rabbit colony is not in very good shape. Luckily for our story, Roberta has survived, but everyone is pretty thin. In fact, some rabbits have even died of starvation. Not very many baby rabbits are born this spring. (add a few rabbits)

Freddie and the rest of the foxes have had a great winter dining on rabbits. All are well fed and nice litters of two or three kits are being born. (add a lot of foxes)

The summer goes well for everybody. All the young foxes grow up eating lots of good mice, berries, and grasshoppers. The older foxes notice that there are not as many rabbits this summer as there were last year. The young ones, usually so easy to catch, are few and far between. But right now it doesn't matter.

Roberta and the rabbits are recovering from their difficult winter. All look a lot better and are getting enough to eat now. They are extra wary of the foxes; there are so many around these days.

All the animals are surprised at how soon winter comes this year. (leaves off, cotton on) By Thanksgiving there is snow on the ground. As winter continues, it becomes obvious that there are too many foxes. Freddie and his friends find themselves fighting over hunting territories. Many of the foxes are even forced to leave Faraway Woods. (remove quite a few foxes) If only there were as many rabbits as last year.

As spring slowly begins to return, (leaves on, cotton off) Roberta notices that almost all the rabbits are alive and well. There may not be too many, but the ones who are there are well fed and looking forward to all the litters of baby rabbits that will soon be born.

On the last day of our story, Freddie is lying on a sun-warmed rock looking over the field. He notices how few foxes survived the winter. But as he looks over to the far end of the field, he sees lots of small rabbits hopping around. (add lots of rabbits) "Hmm," he says, "Look at all those tasty little rabbit meals over there waiting for me. Maybe things aren't going to be so bad after all."

FOLLOW-UP ACTIVITIES

1. Reading from *The Weasels* by Bil Gilbert
Read Bil Gilbert quote from information on p. 38 and discuss.

2. Write a Story
Tell the children to pretend to be a hunter or a hunted. Write a story about how it feels to be hunting or hunted.

3. State Agencies as a Resource
Suggest to the children they write a letter to the Fish and Wildlife Commission and ask about hunting laws pertaining to animals they are concerned about.

Skills

Science Process: Observing, Inferring, Brainstorming, Communicating, Predicting, Comparing

Integrated Curriculum: Art, Drama, Social Studies, Reading, Writing, Language Arts, Math

Suggested Reading for Children:

Freedman, Russell. *Tooth and Claw.* New York: Holiday House-Scholastic Book Services, 1980. (y/o — photographs)

Freedman, Russell, and James E. Morriss. *Animal Instincts.* New York: Holiday House, 1970. (y)

Hungerford, Harold R. *Ecology: The Circle of Life.* Chicago, IL: Children's Press, 1971. (o)

Lane, Margaret. *The Fox.* New York: Dial Press, 1982. (y)

Laycock, George. *Wild Hunters: North American Predators.* New York: McKay, 1978. (o)

Ryden, Hope. *The Wild Pups.* New York: G.P. Putnam's Sons, 1975. (y/o — coyotes)

Dentition Determines the Diet

For those who possess them, teeth play a vital part in the game of success and survival. Over time, a clear plan and pattern for their size, shape, position, number, and distribution, related closely to each animal's diet, has developed. In fact, dentition (tooth arrangement) is so distinctive that it is a clear key to identification of a particular mammal species.

Creatures have a variety of food preferences ranging from the extremely limited food choices of the pandas, which eat mainly bamboo, to the general diets of opossums, skunks, and humans, who can and will consume just about anything. Dentition is a clear reflection of these eating habits.

In relation to their diets, animals can generally be broken into four main groups: **carnivores**, eating meat; **herbivores**, eating plants; **insectivores**, eating insects; and **omnivores**, eating a variety of foods. Specific kinds of teeth are correspondingly arranged and shaped to fit the needs of individuals in each of these groups: **incisors**, in the front of the mouth, used for cutting, dagger-like **canines**, next to the incisors, used for tearing and shredding meat, and **molars**, in the back of the mouth, used for grinding.

Omnivores have a mixture of all three kinds of teeth, none of which is particularly specialized. While humans and opossums both belong to this group, human teeth (thirty-two adult teeth) are considerably less effective than those of the opossum (who has an impressive mouthful of fifty sharp ones). By cooking their food and using sharp utensils to cut it, humans have, over time, become less dependent on their teeth.

Carnivores, who are largely meat eaters, depend only marginally on their incisors for nipping and biting. Their success as hunters is attributable to sharpened molars for cutting and tearing their food and dagger-like canines for grabbing, puncturing, and holding onto their **prey**. Powerful sets of muscles control the jaws and provide the force for the use of these specialized sharp teeth. All members of the cat family are carnivorous, from the Meow-Mix-loving domestic cats to the great lions, as are most members of the dog family.

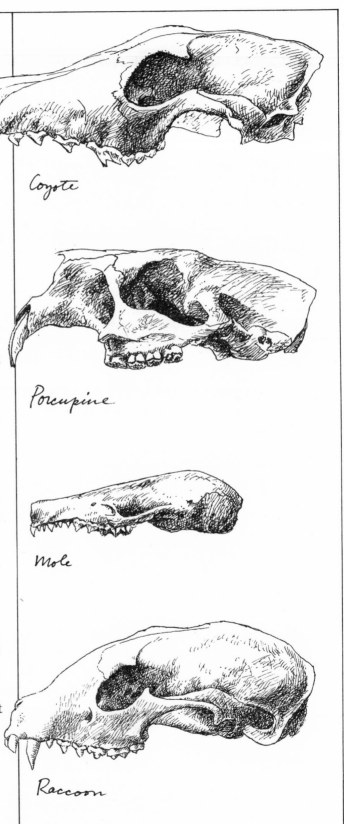

Coyote

Porcupine

Mole

Raccoon

43

On the other side of the dietary coin are the plant eaters, or herbivores. These animals often serve as food for the carnivores and are an important link in the **food chain.** They include a wide variety of animals from deer, cows, horses, sheep, and goats to the smaller mice, rats, woodchucks, rabbits, and beavers. They lack canines entirely and possess only clipper-like incisors and grinding molars with which to bite off their food and grind it up. Squirrels and other nut-eating rodents use their incisors as a vice to grip and pressure open or to puncture the hard shells of nuts.

The beaver, whose work may be seen in the pointed, chewed-off stumps of trees cut down for dam building and food, is the most exceptional of the rodents. Rodent incisors are ever growing and must be used continually to remain trimmed and sharp. The outer layer of enamel is harder than the inner layer of dentine; the dentine thus wears away faster, leaving the slightly extended enamel as the cutting edge. Situations where the upper and lower incisors do not meet, due to a broken tooth or some other malformation, allow the continual curved growth of the teeth to go unchecked, and may eventually cause the animal's death.

Moles, shrews, and bats are best known among the insectivores and have a mouthful of sharp little teeth, which are used in seizing and crushing hard-shelled insects and other small animals. Although bugs of various descriptions make up a sizeable portion of their diet, shrews are well-known for attacking and eating small mammals often larger than themselves.

Each of these animals would be lost without its teeth, particularly the wild ones who, unlike humans, cannot buy another set, nor shop for prepared foods.

Suggested References:

Burt, William. *Mammals of the Great Lakes Regions.* Ann Arbor, MI: Univ. of Michigan Press, Ann Arbor Paperbacks, 1972.

Burt, William and Richard Grossenheider. *A Field Guide to the Mammals.* Peterson Field Guide Series. Cambridge, MA: Houghton Mifflin, Riverside Press, 1964.

Hamilton, William J. Jr., and J.O. Whitaker. *Mammals of the Eastern United States.* Ithaca, NY: Cornell University Press, 1979.

Schwartz, C. W., and E. R. Schwartz. *The Wild Mammals of Missouri.* Columbia, MO: University of Missouri Press, 1981.

TOOTH TYPES

Focus: *There are different types of teeth that are shaped to get hold of and chew different kinds of food. The kind of teeth an animal has helps determine the food it eats.*

ACTIVITIES	MATERIALS
Initial Question: Why do the kinds of teeth an animal has make a difference to what it eats?	

PUPPET SHOW

Objective: To introduce tooth variations in plant-eating animals (herbivores) and meat-eating animals (carnivores).

Perform, or have the children perform, the puppet show. Discuss the terms used.

- *script*, p. 48
- *puppets*

TOOTH TYPES

Objective: To point out the kinds of teeth commonly found in different groups of mammals.

Show drawings of herbivore, carnivore, omnivore, and insectivore skulls with teeth. Discuss the kind of teeth each has and/or does not have.

- *skull drawings* of the following (showing teeth): herbivore, carnivore, omnivore, insectivore

SKULL STUDY

Objective: To notice differences in skulls, and to relate size and tooth type to animal type.

Divide the children into groups, giving each a skull to inspect closely. Try to decide which group of animals the skull might belong to. Once they have had time to investigate their skulls, each group passes on its skull to the next group. How is the new skull different? Continue passing skulls until each group has its original skull. If possible, count the number of teeth. Next, show the animal pictures and ask them to choose which one they think represents the animal whose skull they have and to explain why. Which group of animals has the least number of teeth?

Note: State Fish and Wildlife Departments, high schools or colleges will often lend skulls.

- *skulls*
- *pictures of animals* whose skulls are studied

ACTIVITIES	MATERIALS

MENU MATCHING

Objective: To show how foods eaten relate to tooth arrangement and animal type (carnivore, herbivore, omnivore, insectivore)

• *skulls & pictures* from preceding activity

Give each group from preceding activity one of the following menus:

Main Courses
1. Squirrel Stew
2. Baked Buds
3. Fried Flowers
4. Toasted Toads
5. Boiled Bats
6. Steamed Stems

Side Dishes
1. Roasted Roots
2. Toasted Tails
3. French Fried Feet
4. Grilled Grass

Drinks
1. Tadpole Tea
2. Moose Milk
3. Pond Water Punch

Desserts
1. Baked Berries
2. Chocolate Chipmunk
3. Petal Pie

Have them decide which foods their animal would choose. Ask each group to explain what their animal might pick from the menu and how its teeth are important for its eating habits.

TOOTH TOUCH

Objective: To become aware of how human teeth are adapted to eating a variety of foods.

• *crackers*
• *carrots*
• *apples*

Ask the children to feel their own teeth with their tongues. How many different kinds of teeth do they feel? Give each child something to eat. How do the different teeth help in eating? (Front incisors bite, back molars chew.) Ask the children to figure out where their canine teeth are. Can humans tear a hunk of raw meat with their canines as effectively as a carnivore?

ACTIVITIES	MATERIALS

COMPLETE A JAW

Objective: To design a set of teeth to fit a particular animal's diet.

Give each pair or group of children a cardboard jaw and some clay. They should make a set of teeth specialized to eat a diet of their choice. With younger children, a direction may help, such as "Create teeth for a meat-eating animal or a plant eater." Also, younger children may do better just drawing jaws and teeth. Jaws for a fictional animal are fine as long as the children can explain what the teeth do.

- *drawings of jaws and teeth* from tooth types
- *cardboard jaws*
- *clay*

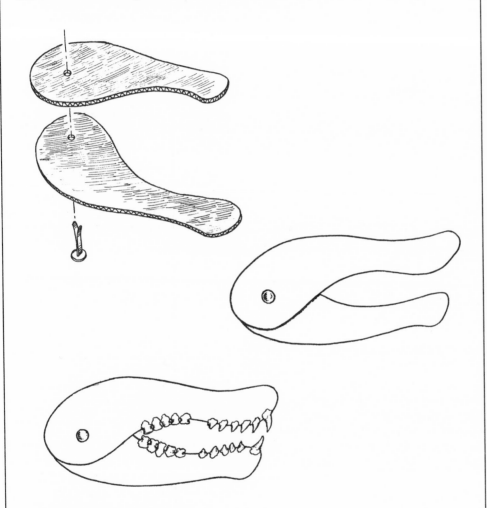

SHARING CIRCLE

Objective: To appreciate our own teeth and how we use them to eat our favorite foods.

Form a circle, and have each child finish the sentence, "My favorite food is _____, and I use my _____ teeth to eat it."

TOOTH TYPES PUPPET SHOW

Characters: Herbert Hare
Marsha Mouse
Francie Fox

Herbert Hare: Oh, it's so wonderful to munch away in this nice sunny field. (sniff, sniff) What's that funny smell? It's not the grass. (sniff, sniff)

Marsha Mouse: Don't eat me, don't eat me, *please* don't eat me! I didn't mean to come into your grassy field. I'll never bother you again if you *just* don't eat me!

Herbert: So, you're what I was smelling. Mouse smell is very different from grass smell.

Marsha: Oh yes, and mouse *taste* is different too! Mice aren't as tasty as grass.

Herbert: Well, I wouldn't know about that. I don't eat mice.

Marsha: Please spare me, don't eat. . . did you say you don't eat mice?

Herbert: Of course I don't eat mice. Why, I couldn't eat mice even if I wanted to.

Marsha: You couldn't? Why not?

Herbert: Have you ever seen a hare's teeth? They're not made for biting into mice or other animals.

Marsha: Then what are they made for?

Herbert: They're made just right for chomping on grass, leaves, and other plants.

Marsha: I never knew that. If I don't have to worry about you eating me, maybe I will come back to this field to run around.

Herbert: Oh, you're welcome to. Maybe I'll run into you another time. Bye, bye.

Marsha: So long.
(Marsha leaves)

Herbert: Gosh, maybe I should have warned that mouse about the fox that comes wandering in this field. I know that fox would love to have me for dinner. She might just like that little mouse for dessert. Perhaps I better try to find that mouse and warn her.
(Herbert leaves; mouse and fox appear on opposite sides of stage)

Marsha: Now that I don't have to worry about being eaten, I'll just stay in this field a little longer. What's that I see up there? Oh, it's a fox. I'm not afraid of her anymore. She probably can't eat me either. I'll go over and say hello.
(walks up)

Francie Fox: Hey, what are you doing walking up here. How come you're not afraid of me. I could eat you, you know.

Marsha: You couldn't eat me even if you wanted to. Herbert Hare just told me how teeth are made for munching on plants, not animals.

Francie: *His* teeth are made for munching on plants. My teeth are made for biting into animals — animals like hares and mice.

Marsha: You mmmmean you ccccould eeeat mmmme? YIKES! (runs away)

Francie: Ha, ha, ha. That little mouse is lucky. I'm not hungry right now. Imagine thinking my teeth aren't fit for eating an animal.
(walks off; Marsha and Herbert enter)

Herbert: Oh, I'm so glad I found you. I was looking for you. I have to tell you something.

Marsha: Yeah, well I have to ask *you* something. Why didn't you tell me your teeth were different than a fox's?

Herbert: I was going to tell you. Most animals know that already.

Marsha: How was I supposed to know that?

Herbert: 'Cause foxes are *carnivores* and hares are *herbivores*, that's how.

Marsha: Carnivores, herbivores. What are you talking about?

Herbert: Carnivores, like foxes, eat other animals. So their teeth are sharp and pointy, made to bite through skin. Herbivores, like us, just eat plants. We don't need sharp and pointed teeth. So, our teeth are wide and flat, perfect for chewing up leaves and grasses.

Marsha: Oh, I get it now. All I have to do is look at an animal's teeth, and then I'll know if he can eat me or not.

Herbert: Well, it might be a bit safer if you just ask me. I know my herbivores and carnivores pretty well, without looking at their teeth.

Marsha: O.K. I'll do that. But right now we both better get out of here. There's a certain fox carnivore back there that just might stick her sharp pointy teeth into us.

Herbert: Let's go!

FOLLOW-UP ACTIVITIES

1. Human Teeth
Borrow a set of human teeth from a local dentist and have the children notice what sort of teeth we have. Are we carnivores, herbivores, or omnivores? Invite a dentist to talk with the children.

2. Animal Teeth
If the children have pet animals, ask them to watch what foods they eat, what teeth they use to bite off portions, and what teeth they use to chew the food.

Skills
Science Process: Observation, Inferring, Brainstorming, Communicating, Predicting, Comparing, Sorting and Classifying

Integrated Curriculum: Art, Drama, Social Studies, Reading, Language Arts, Math

Suggested Reading For Children:

Friedman, Judi. *The Biting Book*. New Jersey: Prentice-Hall, 1975. (y — why animals bite)

Gallant, Roy A. *Me and My Bones*. Garden City, NY: Doubleday, 1971. (o — human vs. other animal bones)

Livandais, Madeline. *The Skeleton Book*. New York: Walker, 1972. (y/o — good photographs)

Merrill, Margaret W. *Skeletons That Fit*. New York: Coward, McCann & Geoghegan, 1978. (o — evolution of skeleton)

Fantastic Flying Machines

Which creature has eyes that take up nearly half of its head? What animal has a skeleton that may weigh a mere 10 percent of its body weight? And who has the warmest, strongest, lightest-weight body covering of all? Birds — remarkable creatures, uniquely adapted to fly great distances and to stay warm in extremely cold weather. Their greatest challenge is to find adequate food to give them energy for these and other demands. Especially designed beaks, feet, legs, eyes, and wings all contribute to meeting this challenge.

Beaks: Bird beaks are modified in numerous ways to adapt them for obtaining specific types of food. There are wide scoop-like bills with which ducks and geese can shovel in submerged plant and animal food. Most shore birds have rather long bills to probe the soft mud and sand for tiny **invertebrates**. The slender bills of chickadees, titmice, and nuthatches are very good at reaching insects in bark crevices, while the broader bills of flycatchers scoop insects out of the air during flight. Seed-eating birds have stout bills. Hawks, eagles, and owls all have sharp, curved beaks adapted to tearing the flesh of their prey.

Feet: Birds use their feet in numerous ways: to walk, hop, run, perch, swim, and to catch or grip their food. Actually, the term feet is misleading because a bird uses its toes to accomplish all those tasks. Most birds have four toes, with the first toe (the hallux) normally facing backward and the other three forward.

A bird's feet also hold it in place while it sleeps; the toes are actually locked on its perch. When the bird relaxes in sleep, its body slumps down on its feet. In this position, a tendon passing behind the heel is pulled tight. This draws the three forward toes and the hind toe toward each other, clamping the bird onto the twig. When the bird rises to a standing position, the clamp is released.

Swimming birds have a variety of designs to aid their propulsion through the water. Most common are webbed feet, like those of a mallard duck whose front three toes are connected by a full web of skin.

The feet of **birds of prey** — hawks, eagles, and owls — have long, sharply pointed, curved talons, or nails, designed for catching, piercing, and killing their living prey. Ospreys have rough pads on their feet that allow them to grasp slippery fish with greater ease.

Legs: What most of us consider the leg of a bird is actually its foot, with an elongated instep slanting upwards and backwards to the heel. A bird's knee, which bends forward as ours does, is usually hidden by feathers. The length and sturdiness of birds' legs, as we know them, vary according to their feeding habits.

Tails: Birds' tails have adapted in an amazing number of ways. They may be used as props, as balancers, as brakes, as rudders, as additional flight surface, or as showy displays in courtship.

Eyes: Most birds have extremely keen vision. Hawks and eagles particularly are able to sight their prey at great distances. Binocular vision and rapidly focusing eyesight enable these birds to accurately pursue their living prey.

Placement of the eyes differ according to feeding habits and the bird's vulnerability as prey. Most birds have eyes on the sides of their heads, allowing broad peripheral vision. Birds of prey have forward-facing eyes.

Wings: Many shapes and sizes of wings make it possible for birds to feed and nest in different types of habitats. Birds, like partridges and sparrows, that nest and feed in grass-covered or brush-covered areas can rise almost vertically from the ground with their short, broad wings. Birds that pursue their food on the wing usually have long, narrow, and angled wings. Vultures, eagles, and many hawks have long, broad wings that make it possible for them to soar on set wings when the air currents are right.

Knee

He

Hallux

Feathers: Feathers are unique to birds, and are the most remarkable body covering ever devised, as they contribute not only to a bird's warmth, but to its ability to fly. There are three main types of feathers.

The flight feather has a central hollow shaft running its entire length and webs on two opposite sides, which presents a lightweight, yet solid, surface for flight. Down feathers have a very short shaft with many non-interlocking barbs to create dead air spaces for good insulation. The contour feather is a smooth, surface feather that streamlines the bird and is colored and patterned to contribute to the coloration of the bird.

Feathers do not grow evenly on a bird's body but sprout from special areas of the skin called feather tracts. Small songbirds have somewhere between 3500 and 5000 feathers; waterbirds, which must stay warm in frigid waters, may have as many as 12,000 feathers. Each feather is composed of **keratin**, the same substance that forms the basis of hair and scales, and emerges from a tiny growth pit in the skin called a follicle, much like mammal hair follicles.

Each bird is uniquely adapted to survive in its own particular environment. Noticing these adaptations adds a new dimension to watching birds.

Suggested References:

National Geographic Society. *The Wonder of Birds*. Washington, DC: National Geographic Society, 1983.

Pasquier, Roger. *Watching Birds*. Boston, MA: Houghton Mifflin, 1977.

Perrins, and Middleton (ed.). *The Encyclopedia of Birds*. New York: Facts on File, 1985.

Peterson, Roger Tory. *The Birds*. New York: Time-Life Books, 1963.

Terres, John K. *Audubon Encyclopedia of North American Birds*. New York: Alfred Knopf, 1980.

Welty, Joel Carl. *The Life of Birds*. Philadelphia, PA: W. B. Saunders, 1962.

Contour

Flight

Down

Focus: *Birds have exceptional adaptations that enable them to fly, to keep warm, and to procure food.*

ACTIVITIES	MATERIALS
Initial Question: What special adaptations do birds have?	

PICTURE PARADE

Objective: To notice and think about bird adaptations.

Show the children a variety of pictures that illustrate different types of beaks, feet, legs, wings, and tails. Discuss each picture from the perspective of how each adaptation helps the bird procure and/or eat its food.

- *pictures* of different kinds of birds that emphasize one or more adaptations

MIX AND MATCH

Objective: To have the children think about how a bird's beak and feet are designed to help the bird get its food.

Give each child a picture of a bird. Spread out pictures of possible bird foods. Some possible combinations are:

- *bird pictures* from the first activity
- *pictures of foods* for the above birds

> owl — mouse
> hawk — rabbit
> eagle — fish
> sparrow — seed
> robin — worm
> crow — corn
> swallow — flying insect
> gull — mussel
> heron — crab

Have each child match its bird with appropriate food. More than one bird may eat the same kind of food. How do the different beaks and feet enable the birds to catch and eat their food?

FOCUS ON FEATHERS

Objective: To have the children learn first-hand about the structure and uses of a feather.

Barb

Barbules

Give each child a feather to examine. a) Ask them one at a time to describe some part of the feather, which the leader then draws on the blackboard to illustrate a model feather. If possible, include a flight feather and a downy feather. Use names appropriate to the grade level. Make sure to note the hollow shaft. b) Gently pull apart the web of the feather. Use a hand lens to see the tiny barbules that project from the barbs. Discuss how they help hold the web together. Try to zip the feather together by pinching and drawing your fingers along the separated barbs from the shaft to the outer edge. c) Discuss the functions of flight, warmth, and color performed by feathers.

- *feathers*
- *hand lenses*

ACTIVITIES	MATERIALS

BIRD SEARCH

Objective: To look for birds outdoors and to notice their special adaptations.

Take the children on a bird walk, visiting as many kinds of habitats as possible (e.g., a pond, a field, a beach, a bird feeder). Look for birds that:

- binoculars (handy but not necessary)

> flap their wings a lot
> glide as they fly
> fly in a flock
> fly alone
> hop on both legs
> walk or run
> climb around on the bark of trees
> swim
> have long beaks, short beaks, fat beaks
> are eating — what are they eating?
> are cleaning their feathers
> are perched on a branch
> have brightly colored feathers
> are well camouflaged

Find a favorite bird.

MAKE A BIRD

Objective: To reinforce the function of various bird adaptations.

Each child is given a Task Card with the following information:

- scissors
- string
- tape
- construction paper
- Task Cards

- You catch fish with your *beak*.
- You tear flesh with your *beak*.
- You collect nectar from deep inside flowers through your *beak*.
- You catch insects with your *beak* while you are flying.
- You crack hard seeds with your *beak*.
- You hammer holes in trees with your *beak*.
- You can spot a mouse 1/2 mile away *(eyes)*.
- You can see very well at night *(eyes)*.
- You dig for worms in the ground with your *beak*.
- You paddle around in the water with your *feet*.
- You catch mice in your *feet*.
- You catch fish in your *feet*.
- You eat bugs under the bark with your *beak*.
- You climb up and down trees with your *feet*.
- You spend a lot of time soaring in the sky *(wings)*.
- You fly after your food and must be able to change directions quickly *(wings)*.
- You use your *tail* to help support you on the trees you climb looking for insects.
- You attract a mate with your beautiful *tail*.

The child then makes a body part (large enough to wear), which is able to perform the assigned task. After making and attaching body parts, the children, in turn, act out their adaptations. Have the other children guess what the adaptation is used for.

Note: Younger children may enjoy doing this in groups rather than as individuals.

FOLLOW-UP ACTIVITIES

1. The Rest of the Story
Give each child a generic bird outline minus beak, feet, wings, and tail. Tell the children to decide what the bird eats and draw a little picture of its food. Then have them complete the drawing of the bird paying special attention to beaks and feet. They could then write stories about their birds.

2. Pick a Beak
Set foods, listed below, on a table. Put the "beaks" (fondue fork, spoon, etc.) at one end of the table. One at a time, have the children choose a "beak" and find a food for which it is adapted to eat. Are some "beaks" adapted to more than one food? What would happen if the foods that your beak is adapted for disappeared? What would happen if more than one bird was adapted to eat the same food?

Materials needed: bowl with water (for grapes), salad dressing bottle (for raisins), fondue fork, spoon, toothpicks, nutcracker, spatula, tweezers, raisins, grapes, apple squares, nuts (in shells), crackers, sunflower seeds.

3. Bird Feeders
Make and hang out bird feeders. Watch the birds that come to each and notice their beaks. Use a field guide to identify them. Be sure to keep the feeder full in cold weather.

Materials needed: plastic gallon jugs with half of one side cut away, rope, bird seed.

Skills
Science Process: Observing, Inferring, Brainstorming, Communicating, Comparing, Sorting and Classifying

Integrated Curriculum: Art, Drama, Reading, Writing, Language Arts

Suggested Reading For Children:

Cole, Joanna. *A Bird's Body.* New York: William Morrow, 1982. (y/o — photographs/ feathers and flight)

Cross, Diana H. *Some Birds Have Funny Names.* New York: Crown Publishers, 1981. (y/o — adaptations section)

Gans, Roma. *When Birds Change Their Feathers.* New York: Crowell Jr. Books, 1980. (y)

McGowen, Tom. *Album of Birds.* Chicago, IL: Rand McNally, 1982. (o — thorough coverage)

Parnall, Peter. *A Dog's Book of Birds.* New York: Charles Scribner's Sons, 1977. (y — great drawings, fun)

Selsam, Millicent E., and Joyce Hunt. *A First Look at Birds.* New York: Walker, 1973. (y — good author)

Wright, Dare. *Look at a Gull.* New York: Random House, 1967. (y — black and white photographs)

THORNS AND THREATS

Plants and Animals Share Strategic Defenses

Many plants and animals have developed surprisingly similar defenses. One of the most familiar defensive weapons found on both plants and animals are projections that might scratch or puncture. Thorns and prickles protect plants from being eaten and are especially prevalent on plants that grow in open and/or dry areas where grazing animals might otherwise threaten their survival.

Animals, too, have rather formidable projections. Horns and antlers are perhaps the most familiar. Horns, usually found on both male and female, are permanent structures that continue growing throughout the life of their bearer. (Pronghorn antelope are the exception; they lose and regrow horns every year.) Antlers, on the other hand, are temporary, annual growths of bone, and usually grow only on the male. Tusks also project from the head region, but have evolved from teeth. And finally, there are quills. These modified hairs, which so effectively protect the slow-moving porcupine, are covered with hundreds of minute diamond-shaped overlapping scales. The quills of the North American porcupines also have barbed tips at the end. When threatened, the porcupine erects these "hairs" with special muscles and either waits for the predator to attack, or turns its back to the attacker and swats with its tail. The loosely attached quills release easily on contact; the porcupine cannot throw its quills. New quills begin to grow within a few days to replace the lost ones.

A second, often deadly, defensive weapon used by plants and animals alike is poison. When people think of poisonous plants, the first that come to mind are often mushrooms. Although most mushrooms are *not* poisonous, enough are to warrant caution. There are other plants that are also toxic, especially to grazing animals. It is important to learn the ones that grow in your area.

Poison as a defensive weapon can also be found, though less frequently, among animals. Snakes are probably the most feared. Like mushrooms, most snakes are not poisonous, but one should learn to recognize those that are. Spiders are also feared by many, a far more appropriate response for insects than humans. Spiders are venomous, paralyzing their prey with venom from glands opening into fang-like appendages near the mouth. Spider venom used defensively against larger animals can cause pain or itching, but rarely death. The short-tailed shrew, a tiny mammal, is capable of poisoning its prey or its attacker. One man's account of a shrew bite described swelling, burning, and shooting pains, not death.

The third defense, used to good advantage by plants and animals, is offending the senses. Plants have developed very proficient "don't touch" deterrents. Nettles are a good example. The hairtips covering the stems and leaves of the nettle break off easily when touched and release a hypodermic injection of fluid into the passerby. A swelling, stinging rash follows almost immediately. Poison ivy causes an itching rash. Mullein with its fuzzy leaves and pasture junipers with their sharp needles are rarely eaten. Pungent odors and strong tastes of certain plants work to defend not only these particular plants but even those surrounding them.

No one except a great horned owl, which has a very poor sense of smell, is likely to risk the stink of a skunk more than once. The bombardier beetle creates an internal explosion that you can hear when it shoots its foul-smelling and bad-tasting fluid from its anal openings. Ants, toads, and other would-be pursuers are effectively deterred. Another insect with a powerful defense is the yellow jacket, which, along with many of her female wasp cousins, can inflict a painful sting.

Bad taste or at least very unpleasant mouth sensations are inflicted by a number of creatures. American toads can secrete a substance that is very irritating to mucous membranes. Dogs, for instance, froth at the mouth after picking up a toad. Monarch butterflies retain the bitter taste of milkweed from their larval stages, which renders them inedible. Experiments in Massachusetts showed that a blue jay would throw up after eating two and one half monarch butterflies.

Body posture, the pretense of looking fierce or dead so that a predator will give up, can be very effective. An opossum drops as though dead and fools predators that prefer live prey. Owls look fierce as they ruff their feathers and hunch their wings in a dorsal threat display. A threatened cat assumes a similar posture, back arched and hairs erect, which makes it look much larger than its actual size.

Tough outer covering can prevent successful attack. Most woody plants, especially trees, are protected by hard bark, which until age, disease, or accident make penetration possible, serves to deter most threats.

Animals, too, have evolved a variety of protective coats or shelters: armadillos, turtles, and snails for example. Fish scales are both tough and slippery. One characteristic shared by all **arthropods** (insects, spiders, crabs, lobsters, and so on), is their hard outer body covering, which serves both as a skeletal framework and as protection.

Finally, there is a rather remarkable defense used to advantage by plants and animals: a "take it, I don't need it" adaptation. Plant lovers who have taken cuttings from favorite plants know the regenerative powers of many plants.

In the animal kingdom there are many examples of expendable body parts. Spiders can replace a lost leg with a new smaller leg at the next molting. Crayfish can grow a new claw; lizards can grow a new tail. Ground feeding birds can relax the muscle of each tail feather, so those grabbed by a predator simply fall out. In time new ones grow back.

Despite the great variety of effective defenses used by plants and animals, some predators continue to circumvent or overcome these defenses, thus maintaining a balance in the natural world.

Suggested References:

Mason, George F. *Animal Tools*. New York: William Morrow, 1951.

———. *Animal Weapons*. New York: William Morrow, 1949.

Tinbergen, Niko. *Animal Behavior*. New York: Time-Life Books, 1965.

Went, Frits W. *The Plants*. New York: Time-Life Books, 1963.

Focus: *In order to protect themselves, many plants and animals have developed similar defenses.*

ACTIVITIES	MATERIALS
Initial Question: How do some plants and animals defend themselves?	

PUPPET SHOW

Objective: To introduce some defenses common to plants and animals.

Perform, or have the children perform, the puppet show. Then show pictures of other plants and animals with good defenses and ask the children to name the defense and tell how they help their owners survive.

- *script, p. 59*
- *puppets*
- *pictures*

CONCENTRATION

Objective: To reinforce children's awareness of common defense mechanisms used by both plants and animals.

Divide the children into a Plant Team and an Animal Team. Alternating between the two teams, a member from each team will go up to the Concentration Board, which has the following pictures or descriptive words:

Plants	**Defenses**	**Animals**
Nettles	Sting	Bee
Blackberries	Prickle	Porcupine
Milkweed	Taste Bad	Toad
Poison Ivy	Itch	Mosquito
Nuts	Hard Coat	Turtle
Cherry Twig	Smells Bad	Skunk
Mullein Leaf	Fuzzy	Woolly Bear Caterpillar

Note: Different animals and plants may be used to illustrate the defenses. Scramble plants and animals so that they are not beside their corresponding defense.

Each should try to match the defending plant or animal with its appropriate defense. If the correct match is made, the flap is removed from the plant or animal name, but *not* from the defense name. When all plants and animals have been matched, remove flaps from defenses. Discuss whether some plants and animals use more than one defense.

- *Concentration Board with flaps to cover pictures or words*

ACTIVITIES	MATERIALS

EAT ME NOT

Objective: To notice the variety of ways plants make themselves inedible or untasty, thus insuring their own survival.

Have the entire group come up with as many plant defenses as they can think of. List them on the board or on newsprint (prickly, stinky, hairy, hard, squishy, leathery, rough, slippery, tastes bad, and so on). Divide into groups of 4 or 5, tell each to choose 4 common plant defenses, and give each a paper plate, which they should divide into 4 sections and label with one of the defenses. Armed with plates and masking tape, groups go outdoors to look for plants that exemplify their chosen categories. Tape tiny samples (no bigger than a fingernail) to the appropriate plate sections. Compare findings.

- *blackboard or newsprint*
- *paper plates*
- *magic markers*
- *masking tape*

PANTOMIME PARADE

Objective: To give the children a chance to act out how some defenses might work.

Whisper to each child in turn to act out:

"You are picking a prickly rose . . . You smell a skunk . . . You are eating an onion . . . You are a frightened turtle . . . You are a cat afraid of a dog . . . You are a goat using your horns . . . You are walking through stinging nettles . . . You are a dog with porcupine quills in your nose . . . You are picking up a slippery fish . . . You have been stung by a bee . . . You are an opossum playing dead . . . You have poison ivy . . ."

MONSTER MOUTHFUL

Objective: To challenge imaginations to outdo nature.

Explain that every species of plant and animal tries to survive by defending itself against being eaten. Review the types of defenses covered in the workshop. Each person should draw an imaginary plant-animal that has such good defenses that NO ONE would try to get a monster mouthful. Each monster should be introduced.

- *paper*
- *pencils*
- *crayons*

THORNS AND THREATS PUPPET SHOW

Characters: Benjy Bear
Penelope Porcupine
Rachel Rosebush
Todd Turtle
Teddy Toad
Bonnie Bee

Benjy Bear: (yawning) Ah me, things have been awfully quiet around here lately. I think it's time for some excitement, maybe a competition of some sort. Oh, hi, Penelope.

Penelope Porcupine: Hullo. Did you say excitement? Competition? Nothing to get my blood pressure up I hope. You know what happens when somebody upsets me, gets in my way. *Swat* with my tail and the animal's nose ends up looking like a pincushion.

Benjy: That's it! Great idea!

Penelope: What d'ya mean great idea? Play stick the quill on the nose? Some animals might not like that game.

Benjy: No, no. A competition to see who has the best defenses. Survival depends on a good defense you know.

Penelope: Yes, I know all about good defenses. Mine are so good, animals almost never attack me. Saves me a lot of energy, not having to run or fight. In fact, you needn't bother with a competition. My prickles are the A number 1 best defense. (goes close to Benjy; says threateningly) *Aren't* they Benjy?

Benjy: (backing away) Yup, yup. They are good ones alright. (Penelope leaves; Rachel Rosebush appears; Benjy backs into her) Yikes! Ouch! How could I back into prickly Penelope when she just left?

Rachel Rosebush: EXCUSE ME. My name is not Penelope. It's Rachel Rosebush. I don't like folks walking all over me, and *I* let them know it.

Benjy: You sure do! Say, maybe you'd like to enter the competition.

Rachel: What competition?

Benjy: The competition to see who has the best defense.

Rachel: Well, I'll stand my ground against anyone. Wait, I'll prove it. Hey you out there in the audience, how many of you would like to walk over me, especially if you didn't have shoes on? (pause) None? See, I told you.

Benjy: Rachel, I've seen enough prickles in the last few minutes to know they get their point across. You and Penelope Porcupine want me to leave you alone, which I guess I will. Bye. (walks away from Rachel; Rachel exits; Todd enters)

Todd Turtle: Watch out, clumsy! Your big foot would have flattened me if I didn't have this hard shell.

Benjy: Sorry. That's another good one.

Todd: What d'ya mean, another good one? Do you like to go around stepping on creatures?

Benjy: No, no, Todd Turtle. You don't understand. I'm looking for good defenses, and you've got a real tough one. I'm thinking of setting up a competition.

Todd: Well, I shrink from competition myself, shrink right inside my shell, where even bears can't bug me. (leaves)

Benjy: Hmm. I'm getting hungry. I think I smell some honey. (enter Bonnie Bee)

Bonnie Bee: You can smell it Benjy, but you can't get at it.

Benjy: What? Who said that?

Bonnie: I did. You may be a big bear, and I'm a little bee, but my sisters and I can defend our honey from anyone. A few stings on that shiny black nose of yours and you'd be off at a run!

Benjy: I believe you. I've been stung once, and that's enough. Nice talking to you. I'll put your name in for the competition.

Bonnie: You're welcome to put my *name* anywhere, but you're not welcome to put *your nose* into my bees' nest.

Benjy: Ok. Ok. So long. (walks along; Bonnie leaves) I'm still hungry, hungry as a bear! What's that rustling in the leaves? Maybe a tasty treat?

Teddy Toad: (slow, drawling voice) No-o-o, Benjy. Toads are not tasty treats.

Benjy: Well, you sure look ugly, not very appetizing. But that doesn't mean you don't taste good. Do you both taste bad *and* give warts?

Teddy: I do *not* give warts. And my looks have nothing to do with my secret weapon.

Benjy: Secret weapon? Another contestant for my best defenses competition.

Teddy: No thanks, Benjy. I don't go for public appearances or competitions. I prefer to hide in damp, dark places. Keeps my skin in good shape for defending myself.

Benjy: Your skin?

Teddy: Yup. I ooze a terrible tasting fluid through my skin that makes animals like you spit me out pretty quick. Now, if you'll excuse me, it's rather bright out here and I don't want my skin to dry out.
(Teddy leaves)

Benjy: Goodbye Teddy. (pause) I don't think I'll organize a competition — too dangerous! I'm big and tough, but there sure are defenses that work, even against big strong animals like me. Maybe peace and quiet isn't so bad after all. (yawn) So long folks.

FOLLOW-UP ACTIVITIES

1. Creative Writing
Have the children write stories about their monsters.

2. Plant Defenses
Initiate a project to learn about plants in the area that have defenses that may harm people, and have the children make a chart. State agricultural extension services are good resources.

3. Animal Defenses
Suggest that the children observe their pet animals or animals in a zoo to see what defenses they use to protect themselves. How often do they really fight?

Skills
Science Process: Observing, Inferring, Brainstorming, Communicating, Comparing, Recording Data

Integrated Curriculum: Art, Drama, Social Studies, Reading, Writing, Language Arts

Suggested Reading For Children:

Bowman, John S. *On Guard: Living Things Defend Themselves.* Garden City, NY: Doubleday, 1969. (o — good information, adult)

Hornblow, Leonora, and Arthur Hornblow. *Animals Do the Strangest Things.* New York: Random House, 1965. (y — protection strategies)

Mason, George F. *Animal Clothing.* New York: William Morrow, 1955. (how coverings protect)

Miraculous Transformation

There is something irresistible about a frog. Not a thing of beauty with its bulging eyes, wide gaping mouth, and slippery skin, it nevertheless intrigues children. A visit to a pond is almost always punctuated by shrieks of "There's a frog" followed by immediate lunges to catch it or cautious efforts to sneak up on it. Usually neither is successful, and the frog slips nonchalantly or leaps suddenly into the water. Frogs are **amphibians**, cold-blooded animals that live part of their lives in water and part on land (*amphi bios* — double life). They have smooth, moist skin, and long hind legs which make them excellent jumpers and swimmers. Most have some webbing on their hind feet and are found in or near water.

For many months of the year, frogs are hidden from sight down in the mud at the bottoms of ponds or on land beneath the frost line. As cold-blooded creatures, unable to generate their own heat, they must hibernate to avoid freezing temperatures. Frogs are most apparent during the spring of the year, as they are not only visible but also quite vocal during this period of courtship. Having emerged from hibernation, adult frogs mate from early spring through summer, each species having its own particular timetable. Although capable of living as adults on land, most species demonstrate their evolutionary roots by returning to water to mate and lay their eggs.

Males arrive at the breeding ponds first and begin calling. Each species has its own distinctive call that serves to attract females of the same species to the pond. Females are usually silent. A frog makes its calls by pushing air back and forth from mouth to lungs, thereby vibrating its vocal cords. Vocal sacs in the throat region act as resonating chambers when they inflate, thus producing the loud singing sound. Males are most often vocal at night.

Although frog eggs are fertilized externally, there is quite a mating ritual with males crawling on the backs of females and grasping them around the body behind the forelegs. As the female deposits the eggs in the water, the male releases his sperm over them.

Egg-laying strategies vary. The spring peeper lays one at a time, the wood frog and bull frog lay them in masses, and the American toad lays bead-like strings of eggs. The eggs are covered by a gelatinous substance just before they are laid, and this material swells to form a thick protective coat. Some eggs float freely, others are anchored to vegetation.

The number of eggs laid varies from only a few hundred for spring peepers to over 20,000 for bullfrogs. Incubation time varies from species to species. The timing also depends somewhat on available sunshine to warm the generally dark-colored eggs, thereby speeding their development. After laying and fertilizing their eggs, most frogs abandon them.

When the eggs do hatch, tiny tadpoles or polliwogs emerge, which are very different in physical form and behavior from the adults they will become. Tadpoles have round bodies, vertically flattened tails, and gills, adaptations for a strictly aquatic existence. Most tadpoles are vegetarians, with mouths adapted for scraping algae and other tiny plants off submerged objects. How long the tadpole stage lasts depends on the species and on the weather. This is the most critical phase of the life of frogs. Of the large numbers of tadpoles that hatch, very few reach maturity. They are the prey of numerous aquatic animals, such as predaceous diving beetles, crayfish, and dragonfly **nymphs**. They also are at the mercy of the environment. Some eggs are laid in small temporary pools and puddles, and the tadpoles risk death if they do not complete their transformation to adulthood before the spring sunshine dries up the pool. In addition, amphibian eggs and **larvae** are very susceptible to water pollution. In fact, recent studies point to acid rain as a real threat, particularly for the survival of egg and larval stages.

Over time, the tadpole begins to grow hind legs. Then its front legs emerge, blocking the gill openings. Simultaneously, lungs develop that replace the gills. The eyes migrate somewhat toward the top of the head and bulge out, and the mouth changes from a tiny opening with rasping edges to a wide gap capable of catching and holding live prey. Gradually the tail is absorbed, a major source of nourishment during this transition period.

Adult frogs are primarily insectivorous, eating many insects thought to be pests by humans. While small frogs eat primarily insects, large species, like the bullfrog, are known to eat mice, small birds, and other frogs.

Adult frogs are well adapted for the lives they lead. They are efficient hunters, able to spot and capture moving prey with their extendable tongues. They are camouflaged to blend in with their surroundings. They can breathe through their skins during brumation (the physiological dormancy of amphibians) and other periods of low activity. And by laying so many eggs in the nurturing environment of water, they assure the survival of at least some of their own kind.

Suggested References:

Behler, John L., and Wayne King. The Audubon Society. *Field Guide to North American Reptiles and Amphibians*. New York: Chanticleer Press, 1979.

Conant, Roger. *A Field Guide to Reptiles and Amphibians* (2nd edition). Boston, MA: Houghton Mifflin, 1975.

Golden Nature Guide on Reptiles and Amphibians

Porter, George. *The World of the Frog and the Toad*. Philadelphia, PA: J.B. Lippincott, 1967.

Smith, Hobart. *Amphibians of North America*. New York: Golden Press, 1978.

"Voices of the Night" (record), Cornell Laboratory of Ornithology, Ithaca, NY.

Focus: *Frogs survive in a wide range of habitats and temperatures because of their unique physical adaptations and their specialized life cycles.*

ACTIVITIES	MATERIALS

Initial Question: How is a polliwog different from a frog?

PICTURE PARADE

Objective: To introduce the children to some of the special adaptations of frogs and polliwogs.

Show pictures of different kinds of frogs and have the children help you list their special adaptations. Then show a chart of frogs in their various stages of metamorphosis and describe the process to the children.

* *pictures of frogs*
* *chart* showing the stages of metamorphosis

MERRY METAMORPHOSIS

Objective: To understand the growth and development of frogs from egg to adult.

Read through the script with the children listening. Assign one child to be the diving beetle. Then have the rest of them role-play the egg, tadpole, and adult stages of a frog as you read it aloud a second time.

* *script*, p. 65

FROG OR POLLIWOG

Objective: To emphasize some of the differences between frogs and polliwogs.

Divide the children into two groups, one representing frogs, the other polliwogs. Tell them you're going to hold up pictures or words that show features of frogs, polliwogs, or neither.

Frog Features: 4 legs; webbed hind feet; big eyes on top of head; eats insects, worms, etc.; big mouth; sticky tongue; long hind legs; lungs; hops on land.

Polliwog Features: tiny round mouth; no legs; tail; tiny eyes on side of head; gills; lives entirely in water.

Neither Features: hairy; covered with feathers; has wings; has 8 legs.

If the correct group claims the feature by raising their hands, they get the card. Otherwise, through group discussion, decide which group should have the card. Play until all appropriate cards have been correctly claimed and the neither cards are weeded out. Conclude by having each team explain how its adaptations affect their animal's life.

* *cards or pictures* describing features of frogs, polliwogs, or neither

LEAP FROG

Objective: To show how much better frogs' legs are for leaping than ours are.

In small groups outside have the children try leaping like frogs. They may play leap frog to the location of the next activity. Discuss why frogs leap better than we do.

ACTIVITIES	MATERIALS

MOVING MEALS

Objective: To become aware that frogs eat only moving prey.

Explain that frogs, like most predators, eat live prey. Therefore, they don't notice non-moving prey, but are quick to catch moving insects within their reach. One child is appointed frog. The rest of the class are insects. The frog, standing with his back to the insects and about 20 feet from them, counts out "1-2-3, food for me" and turns. Any insects seen moving are "eaten" and sit down. The object is for insects to get to safety by crossing an imaginary line even with the frog.

SPRING SERENADE

Objective: To demonstrate that each species of frog has a different courtship call, which the male sings to attract the females of his species.

Divide the children into two groups. Give out like sets of calling cards to each group, one per child. The first group becomes male frogs and forms a circle around the second group, the female frogs, who are given blindfolds. At Go the males sing their assigned songs. The blindfolded females listen for their assigned sound and move toward it. When they reach a correct singer, they may remove their blindfolds. One male may attract more than one female, others may attract none (as it happens in nature).

Note: If tapes of frog songs are available, introduce the activity by playing the three songs to be used in the game.

- *calling cards* with one of the following calls: quack — wood frog peep — spring peeper jug-o-rum — bull frog (or other frog songs in your area)
- *blindfolds*

FROG HUNT

Objective: To look for frogs in any and all stages of their development.

Go to a pond or a very wet area. Have the children stay in small groups. Search along the edge of the water for eggs, tadpoles, and adult frogs. The leader may collect one specimen of each for closer examination. Ask children to point out adaptations they see.

SHARING CIRCLE

Objective: To review what's been learned and to personalize the experience.

Each child should complete the following sentence: "I would like to be a frog or a polliwog because . . ." Encourage them to think of specific adaptations to explain their choice. (e.g., I would like to be a frog because I could swim fast with my webbed feet.)

MERRY METAMORPHOSIS SCRIPT

	Action
If you look closely in a pond By chance you just may see A mighty mass of frog eggs Floating in the water free	*Group huddled together moving in different directions*
Moving with the water As it ripples here and there How nice to be a frog egg Not a worry or a care	
But then, oh no, what's that you see? Swimming all about A big fat diving beetle So you quickly yell "watch out"	*One person as the diving beetle swims towards group*
For that old diving beetle Is looking for a lunch And would really be quite happy With some frog eggs in a bunch	
But then, by luck, the wind blows strong Away the eggs do float And that beetle now must seek Another frog egg boat	*Group moves away. Diving beetle person leaves*
As days go on those frog eggs Will start to look quite strange If you look closely in that pond You're sure to see the change	
Coming from that mass of eggs Are not a bunch of frogs But rather little tadpoles Also known as polliwogs	*Group begins to separate*
They have no legs to hop with Or lungs to breathe the air For they stay under water Eating plants that grow down there	*Each child now moving about with feet together and hands at their sides*
They're sort of round up in the front Their backs have wagging tails They don't look a bit like frogs But more like tiny whales	
If you look closely in that pond And watch them every day You'll see the tadpoles start to change In yet a different way	
On each side of the wagging tail Legs will start to grow The tadpoles start to use them For swimming to and fro	*Children now shake both legs and begin moving about with legs apart (hands still at sides)*
Soon some front legs will appear And that's not even all For as they do, you'll notice The tail will get quite small	*Children can now wiggle arms from elbows down (upper arm still touching sides)*
The body shapes begin to change Both inside and out They breathe with lungs and start to eat The bugs that swim about	*Children take deep breath and then pretend to eat*
With big hind legs to hop with And a tail that's gone for good Those tiny little frog eggs Now look like they should	
For if you look closely in that pond Or on some nearby logs You'll see more than eggs and tadpoles You will see some baby frogs!	

FOLLOW-UP ACTIVITIES

1. Adopt-A-Frog

Scoop up a small mass of eggs from a pond or puddle and put into a large glass dish or fish bowl filled with pond water. An open container on a *partially* sunlit windowsill, *regularly* supplied with green pond plants will provide the hatching tadpoles all the food and oxygen they need. Watch daily as the tadpoles hatch, grow, and begin to develop into frogs. Children can keep records of significant changes. What percentage of the eggs hatch? What percentage of hatchlings mature? Once the frogs have legs, give them a stone or other landing platform, but be sure they don't escape. When the tail has mostly disappeared, they should be released, preferably near the place where the eggs were collected. The whole process of metamorphosis will take many weeks.

2. Which Is Which?

Each child chooses a species of frog to research, describe, illustrate, and perhaps write a story about. Display their work on a bulletin board.

Skills

Science Process: Observing, Inferring, Brainstorming, Communicating, Comparing, Sorting and Classifying, Experimenting, Recording Data

Integrated Curriculum: Drama, Music, Reading, Writing, Language Arts, Math

Suggested Reading For Children:

Hawes, Judy. *Why Frogs Are Wet*. New York: Thomas Crowell, 1968. (y — a lot of information)

Lane, Margaret. *The Frog*. New York: The Dial Press, 1982. (y — life cycle)

May, Charles Paul. *A Book of Reptiles and Amphibians*. New York: MacMillan, 1968. (o — reference type)

McClung, Robert M. *Peeper, First Voice of Spring*. New York: William Morrow, 1977.

Selsam, Millicent E. *A First Look at Frogs, Toads & Salamanders*. New York: Walker, 1976.

Tarrant, Graham. *Frogs*. New York: Putnam, 1983. (y — pop-up book)

Zim, Herbert S. *Frogs and Toads*. New York: William Morrow, 1950.

CHAPTER II — HABITATS

A habitat is a place where specific plants and animals can live successfully. It might be likened to a home in a child's mind — a place in which food, family, shelter, safety, and familiar plants and animals can be found. Not all of those components are present all the time, but each habitat must provide for its inhabitants the basics for survival: food, water, protection from enemies and weather, and places to raise young.

Because of the various combinations of living organisms and the differences in environmental factors such as climate, topography, and soils, each habitat is unique. A brook trout could not live in a field, nor even in a shallow pond, because it needs a habitat containing cold, clean, well oxygenated water.

Within a habitat there are many interactions among those who live there. Some of the most important are explained in terms of food chains, which pertain to the flow of energy from sun to plants to animals, and food webs, which illustrate the complex interdependencies in the "who eats what" game of survival.

In this concept, some very different kinds of habitats are introduced along with their common inhabitants. Emphasis is placed on the special characteristics of each, as well as on some of the ecological principles fundamental to all.

Who Lives There and Why?

Welcome to a field. Close your eyes and feel the heat of the sun and the coolness of the wind. A field is one of the more exposed habitats, susceptible to extremes of heat and cold, drought and storms. This quality of being exposed to the elements means that those that inhabit a field must either be especially equipped to do so or must be able to leave the field when necessary.

In most places, the fields chosen to be investigated and explored by children will be fields that have been mowed within five years. They will likely host a number of familiar plants: goldenrod, clover, yarrow, daisies, buttercups, Queen Anne's Lace, black-eyed Susan, and, of course, grasses.

Plants that withstand the drying winds and hot rays of the summer sun are amazingly varied in shape and texture. Some, like the milkweed, have stiff leaves that, with their leathery coating and thickened juices, do not dry out. Others have toothed or divided leaves, goldenrod and clover for example. And plants like yarrow have lacy leaves, allowing very little surface to be directly exposed to sun or wind.

Texture, too, protects plant leaves and stems from drying out. Examine black-eyed Susan leaves through a hand lens; its bristly black hairs prevent the sun's rays from directly hitting the surface of the leaves, illustrating another effective method to prevent excess moisture loss. Noticing the myriad designs of plants in a field helps focus on their diversity; it is not necessary to know the names to see and feel the differences.

The more diverse the plant life in a field, the wider the variety of animals that can live or feed there. Easiest to find are the insects, such as grasshoppers, ants, crickets, leaf hoppers, bees, butterflies, beetles, and their relatives the spiders and daddy longlegs. **Amphibians** — toads, frogs, and salamanders — are scarce, unless there is a damp or protected area nearby because they lose too much body moisture in sunny, dry areas. Snakes, on the other hand, can find shelter under the grasses or in rodent holes. A field is a good place for these **reptiles** to hunt for mice and other food. Most mammals cannot fill all their habitat requirements in a field, but a great many depend on the field for food. Plant eaters such as mice, woodchucks, voles, rabbits, and deer spend much of their lives in open fields, and they in turn are a food source for **predators** that visit but rarely inhabit a field: foxes, coyotes, hawks, owls.

The interdependency of plants and animals found in a field illustrates some concepts basic to all successful habitats: **food chains, food webs,** and food pyramids. Survival of plants and animals depends on their having enough energy to carry on the business of living. The transfer of energy from one organism to the next can be illustrated by a food chain. The original source of energy is the sun. Plants receive energy from the sun, which allows them to produce their own food. This process, called **photosynthesis**, enables a plant to manufacture sugars and starches from carbon dioxide and water in the presence of **chlorophyll** and sunlight. Plants are thus called **producers**. Dependent upon plants for food are the vegetarian animals, or **herbivores**, such as rabbits and mice. In the context of a food chain, they are called **primary consumers**. Then there are meat-eating animals, or **carnivores**, like foxes and hawks, which are **secondary consumers**. Because most animals have multiple food sources, they are linked in many possible food chains, which in any given habitat are interconnected in a food web.

Another term, food pyramid, describes the relative numbers or mass of each portion of a food chain. When you stop to think about life in a field, you realize that in terms of sheer mass, plants outweigh other forms of life there. As producers, they represent the base of the pyramid. When the energy flows from plants to the animals that feed on them, approximately 10 percent is actually useable to those animals, and 90 percent is lost in the transfer. This 10 percent transfer of energy, 90 percent loss is true all the way up the line from producer to primary consumer to secondary consumer. It takes 100 pounds of plant life to provide energy for ten pounds of primary consumer life to provide energy for one pound of secondary consumer life.

When one portion of a field is disturbed, there is a reaction throughout. Fire or herbicides may destroy the plants in a field, leaving the mice and grasshoppers to die without food, which in turn starves the foxes and hawks that prey upon them.

A field is a fascinating place to study because of the diversity of life to be found there and the complex relationships among those that inhabit or visit it. A field is also a beautiful place to sit quietly, listening and watching the life around you.

Suggested References:

Allen, Durward L. *The Life of Prairies and Plains.* New York: McGraw-Hill, 1967.

Andrews, William, (ed.). *A Guide to the Study of Terrestrial Ecology.* Englewood Cliffs, NJ: Prentice-Hall, 1974.

Food Pyramid

❝ ...When you stop to think about life in a field, you realize that in terms of sheer mass, plants outweigh other forms of life there. ❞

Focus: *A field is a relatively exposed habitat, which can support diverse plants and animals, many of whom depend on one another for food and shelter.*

ACTIVITIES	MATERIALS
Initial Question: Why is a field a good place for some plants and animals to live?	

PUPPET SHOW

Objective: To help the children understand the interdependence of plants and animals in a field.

- *script*, p. 75
- *puppets*

Give the puppet show. Discuss who or what is important to successful life in a field.

WHO AM I?

Objective: To think about who lives in a field.

- *signs*
  1 for each child

Make signs with a picture or the name of one of the following animals on it and the food it eats:

fox — rodents
bee — nectar
deer — grass
butterfly — nectar
snake — mice, frogs
skunk — insects, fruit
owls — mice
mole — insects, worms
coyote — small animals
rabbit — grass, plants
grasshopper — grass, plants
woodchuck — grass, plants
hawk — mice
mouse — seeds
robin — worms
cricket — plant foods
spider — insects
earthworms — dead plants

(Grades K-2) Divide the children into groups and have them sit in circles. Tape a picture or name of an animal onto the back of each. One at a time, the children stand in the center of their groups. The others give hints about the animal, and the center child tries to guess what it is. Once the animal has been identified, another child takes a turn. The leader may need to focus the hints (size, color, coat, way of moving, etc.). When all children have guessed their identities, discuss why these animals might be found in a field.

ACTIVITIES	MATERIALS

(Grades 3-6) Tape a sign to each child's back. At "go" the children should find partners, look at each other's signs, and ask each other three yes/no questions to figure out what animal they are. Leader might review helpful questions before the game starts, relating to:

Size — bigger than a lunch box?

Movement — fly? crawl? run? walk?

Coat — fur? feathers?

Food — plant eater or meat eater? (food information can be included on the animal signs)

Keep changing partners until every animal is identified. As children find out what they are, signs should be taped on the front. In turn, all should explain why they might be found in a field. (Hint: what do they eat?)

POPCORN FOOD CHAIN

Objective: To understand how the energy flows from the sun through the plants to the animals in a field.

- *yellow hat*
- *bowl of popcorn*
- *green headbands*
- *signs* from previous activity

To set up for this activity, select children to act as:

1 sun — with yellow hat and bowl of popcorn

12 plants — with green headbands

6 plant eaters — with appropriate signs from previous activity

2 meat eaters — with appropriate signs from previous activity

Have them sit or kneel (easier to manage if they're not standing) in rows, in the above order, with the plants, plant eaters, and meat eaters facing the sun. Leader explains that all living things need energy and the sun has a limitless supply. The plants get their energy from the sun, the plant eaters get their energy from the plants, and the meat eaters get their energy from the plant eaters. To begin the energy flow, each plant takes one handful of popcorn from the sun and eats some of it. (This represents using up some energy to grow and stay alive.) Next, each plant eater takes the popcorn from 2 plants, and eats some, but not all, of the popcorn energy. Finally, each meat eater takes the unconsumed popcorn from 3 plant eaters. Discuss with the children who got the energy directly from the sun, whether the plants passed on all their energy to the plant eaters, and why the meat eaters needed energy from more than one plant eater.

Note: Role-play, or ask what would happen, if all the plants were sprayed with herbicides or if some of the plant eaters died in a cold winter.

SILENT WATCH

Objective: To silently become part of life in a field.

Go out to the field, younger children in small groups with a leader, older children as individuals. Spread out so there is a feeling of being alone. Sit very still, not moving, so that life in the field resumes its activities. (This can last 2 or 3 minutes for younger children, up to 10 minutes for older ones.) What did they see? watch? enjoy?

ACTIVITIES	MATERIALS

HABITAT HUNT

Objective: To notice the diversity of plant life in the field, and to see that some plants are depended on by many for food and shelter.

Divide the children into small groups and give each a Habitat Hunt card that has the following directions on it:

Shape: Find leaves with: smooth edges, edges with tiny teeth, deeply cut edges (like dandelion leaves)

Color: Find plants with at least one shade of red, pink, orange, brown, yellow, white, purple. Find 5 shades of green. (Note: paint sample cards could be used for matching colors.)

Texture: Find things that are soft, fluffy, hairy, prickly, smooth, bumpy

Size: Find a plant as tall as your waist, knee, ankle. Find a leaf as wide as your foot, as long as your little finger. Find a flower that is as big as your fist, that is so small you can cover it with the end of your finger

Signs of animals: Look for leaves with holes in them (how did they get there?); eggs (look on undersides of leaves); an "animal" resting on a plant, or living inside a leaf or stem; a plant with many visitors on it; a flower with an insect on it gathering pollen or nectar; a hole in the ground; a path made by animals; birds flying overhead

Explain boundaries and time limits, also no-picking rules. Then send them off to search and discover. Afterwards, compare findings.

Materials:
- *Habitat Hunt cards*
- *hand lenses* (optional)

SHARING CIRCLE

Objective: To wrap up the workshop by sharing feelings about life in a field.

Each child, in turn, completes the sentence:
"If I lived in a field, I'd like to be a _____ because. . ."

LIFE IN A FIELD PUPPET SHOW

Characters: Tall piece of grass
Mouse
Fox
Sun
Little Girl

(behind stage)

Grass: (Whispery voice)
I'm going to be elected.

Mouse: (Squeaky voice)
You are not, I am the best candidate.

Fox: (Deep voice)
Neither one of you is, because *I* am going to win.

(Little Girl appears)

Little Girl: What is going on here? Who is going to win what?
(fox appears)

Fox: We are holding an election to see who is most important in the field. I, of course, am the most handsome candidate with my beautiful red coat, and I'm also the most powerful (growls a little). Look at me run (races back and forth a couple of times).

Little Girl: Well, you are handsome and quite a runner.
(fox leaves; mouse appears)

Mouse: Just a minute here. I am the most important. I am the cute, down-to-earth type. I eat lots of seeds that might grow up to be weeds. And do you know how many of my relatives there are in this field? Hundreds! Maybe even thousands! I'll get elected if all my relations vote for me.

Little Girl: You are pretty cute, Mr. Mouse. And there are so many of you, probably you will.
(mouse leaves as grass appears)

Grass: Stop right there. Don't say another word until you hear what I have to say. I will win the title of MOST IMPORTANT. Look at me. What am I children? (pause - "grass") And what grows in the fields? (pause - "grass") And what do horses, cows, rabbits, woodchucks, and deer all eat? ("grass") Can there be any doubt about it? *I* am most important. (leaves)

Little Girl: Oh dear, now I am confused. I don't know which is most important. You can't have a very good field without grass. And a good field always has lots of mice in it eating weed seeds and making grass tunnels and nests. And if there are lots of mice in the field, then there are foxes hunting them.
(fox appears)

Fox: Yes, you see how important I am. If I didn't catch some mice there would be so many you'd be standing up to your *knees* in mice right now, little girl.

Little Girl: Oh, dear, I wouldn't like that.

Fox: And they'd eat up all the grain seeds your animals need. (leaves)

Little Girl: Well, let's let the audience decide. Candidates, you may each say one sentence to explain why you are most important. Grass, you go first.

Grass: I *am* the field, providing food and shelter to all who need it.
(grass leaves; mouse appears)

Mouse: The field is my home. I help spread seeds around and eat enough seeds to help keep the field neat and clean. I even provide food for the foxes, (fox enters) though that is *not* my favorite part of the job!
(mouse leaves)

Fox: I keep things in balance by eating the extra mice. Without me, there'd be so many mice they'd eat *all* the seeds.

Little Girl: Audience, now it's up to you to decide. I'm going to say each name, grass, mouse, fox, and ask you to register your vote by applauding for the one you think is most important. OK, let's hear it for:
the grass
the mouse
the fox
(sun appears) Whoops, oh dear. Hello, Mr. Sun. We forgot to include you in the election.

Sun: That's all right. I just wanted the audience to think about how important I am to the field. Without me the grass won't grow, then the mice will have nothing to eat and nowhere to hide, and with no mice, the foxes will starve. We all work together to make a good field. I'll sing a little song to explain it.
(tune of "You are My Sunshine")

I am your sunshine, your only sunshine
I make the plants grow so all can dine
But some who eat plants are also eaten
Nature's balance is quite fine.
Now when the grass grows and goes to seed
The voles and mice have a lot of feed
Then foxes know where to find their dinner
Nature's balance is the winner!

Well, I've got to go spread some sunshine. Good-bye little girl. Bye, bye, audience. (sun leaves)

Little Girl: Good-bye Mr. Sun. I guess the sun is *most* important, but *everything* that lives in a field is important in its own way. So I'm declaring all three of you winners. So long everyone.

FOLLOW-UP ACTIVITIES

1. Collage
Have the children make a collage of bits of plants (flowers, leaves, seeds) found in a field, either free form or filling in a butterfly, grasshopper, or field landscape drawing.

2. Inventory
The children should choose a favorite place in the field. Mark it with stakes or string. Check it once a week to see which plants are in flower, have gone to seed, have died, and which creatures are active. Keep a record.

3. Imagine Yourself as an Insect
Suggest that the children write a story pretending they are small insects or animals in a big field. What do you they see above them? How do they get around? What do they do each day? Are they scared of anything?

Skills

Science Process: Observing, Inferring, Brainstorming, Communicating, Predicting, Comparing, Sorting and Classifying, Recording Data

Integrated Curriculum: Art, Drama, Music, Social Studies, Writing, Language Arts, Math

Suggested Reading for Children:

Lubell, Winifred, and Cecil Lubell. *The Tall Grass Zoo.* New York: Rand McNally, 1960. (o — many common species)

Pringle, Laurence P. *From Field to Forest: How Plants and Animals Change the Land.* New York: World Publishing, 1970. (o — black and white photos, brief text)

_____. *Chain, Webs, & Pyramids: The Flow of Energy in Nature.* New York: Crowell, 1975. (o)

Home of the Hidden Workers

The forest floor is an area bursting with invisible energy. It has been estimated that the energy expended by all the forms of life in an acre of soil would equal the amount of energy expended by 10,000 humans living and working on that acre. It is the habitat of billions of unsung heroes of our **ecosystem**, who aid in the yearly breaking down or **decomposition** of many tons of plant and animal refuse. Through decomposition, the minerals and nutrients, once useful to their plant or animal hosts, are released and recycled.

The floor of the forest is the most densely populated level. It is cool, moist, dark, free from winds, protected from extremes and sudden changes in temperature, low in oxygen and high in carbon dioxide; all in all, a very unique environment. Studies done on a July day in a mixed forest area in New England showed that the temperature and humidity remained quite constant at ground level, while at tree top level they varied considerably.

What type of life thrives in this specialized habitat, so rich in organic material? In a teaspoon of soil there may be 5 billion bacteria, a million microscopic animals, and 200,000 algae and fungi. Ninty-five percent of all insect species spend some part of their lives in the soil. Mites, springtails, and millipedes live in the top few inches of the forest floor. In a one foot square layer of soil, two inches thick, 15,000 mites and 2,000 springtails have been counted.

Since both these **arthropods** are relatively unknown, a close look at them might be in order. Mites inhabit every conceivable **niche** in the world but very little research has been done on the many types that inhabit the forest floor. They feed on plant and animal material and are therefore important decomposing agents. They are so small the Greeks considered each one to be an atom, but they are numerous enough to make up 5 percent of the life weight of forest soils.

Springtails have changed very little from the way they were 300 million years ago. Their food consists of tiny specks of plant material. They are most notable for their special method of locomotion; their folded-under tails straighten with a force that allows them to spring two feet up in the air.

A much larger form of life is the millipede, another creature scarcely touched by evolution. Millipedes feed only on certain types of dead tree leaves, each species having its own preference. They spend much of their lives inactive due to low tolerances for wetness and dryness.

Lower down in the forest floor we find the preferred habitat of the burrowers. As far down as three or four feet the soil may be honeycombed with tunnels that give the ground a soft, spongy feeling and also aerate the soil.

Supposedly, the most numerous but least often seen burrower is the shrew. This tiny mammal is known as one of the fiercest animals around because of its willingness to attack almost anything. The shrew's secret to success is a small poison gland behind its **incisors**. It must first make a wound in its prey so that poison, mixed with saliva, can enter the victim's blood stream. The shrew has the highest metabolic rate of any animal and must eat every hour, making hibernation impossible. A shrew's menu may include snails, insects, worms, mice, snakes, birds, and other small animals. The shrew is perfectly constructed for a burrower's life with its nose made of bones to serve as a plow and its body covered with velvet-like fur.

The dominant mammal on the forest floor is the mouse, who is active all year round collecting, storing, and eating the many types of nuts and seeds that land on the forest floor. The entrances and exits to mouse tunnels can be found throughout a forest.

Earthworms, "the intestines of the earth," permeate most forest and grassland soils, although they prefer areas that are not too acidic. Worms consume millions of leaves, depositing small piles of castings behind, as much as forty tons of material per acre. The material is substantially richer and less acidic than the surrounding soil, containing 45 percent more phosphorus and nitrogen and

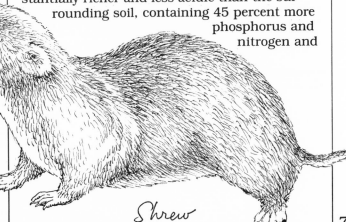

Shrew

77

50 percent more potassium. As all gardeners know, earthworms contribute immeasurably to the aeration and turning over of the soil.

The plant life of the forest floor is vital to its stability as a habitat. Leaf litter, root systems, and rotting logs, to name but a few, are important sources of shelter and food for many small animals, as well as for **fungi**. Fungi are the most widespread microorganisms on the forest floor and are responsible for initiating most of the forest decomposition. The visible mushrooms are merely the fruiting bodies of masses of underground fungal structures often seen as white threads in the soil or under the bark of a dead or dying tree. One ounce of forest soil may contain two miles of fungal threads.

Together, the plants and animals on the forest floor are interrelated in a complex **food web** with each species deriving its nourishment from one or more of its fellow inhabitants.

The forest floor is a remarkable habitat to study, to explore, and to visit. Sit quietly there sometime, watching and listening. Your most attentive self will catch only a fragment of all that is happening around you.

Suggested References:

Andrews, William, (ed.). *A Guide to the Study of Terrestrial Ecology.* Englewood Cliffs, NJ: Prentice-Hall, 1974.

Caras, Roger. *The Forest.* New York: Holt, Rinehart and Winston, 1979.

Farb, Peter. *The Forest.* New York: Time-Life Books, 1969.

Ketchum, Richard M. *The Secret Life of the Forest.* New York: American Heritage, 1970.

Mandahl-Barth, G. *Woodland Life.* New York: Blandford Press, 1966.

McCormick, Jack. *The Life of the Forest.* New York: McGraw-Hill, 1967.

Focus: *The forest floor serves as a habitat for millions of seen and unseen plants and animals. Together they form a complex food web and an efficient recycling system.*

ACTIVITIES	MATERIALS
Initial Question: What lives or might be found on the forest floor?	

MYSTERY BAGS

Objective: To introduce what is found on the forest floor through senses other than sight.

Put several different objects commonly found on the forest floor into separate bags, and pass them, one at a time, halfway around a circle of children. Each child feels the object and gives an adjective describing it. The other half of the circle tries to guess the bag's contents. The last child gets to reveal the object. Reverse the order so that everyone gets the chance to guess and to feel. Have the older children arrange the objects in the order of decomposition rates. This might initiate considerable discussion, as there will probably be more than one possible order.

- *cloth bags*
- *forest floor objects*
  wood
  moss
  leaves
  bark
  stick
  fungus
  bone
  cone

LIE DOWN AND LOOK

Objective: To experience through all the senses what life is like above and on the forest floor.

As you enter the woods, have the children lie down on their backs. Ask questions such as:

How far away are the tree tops?
Do you see shapes in the spaces between the leaves?
Are the leaves closest to you moving?
Are the leaves farthest up moving?
Is the ground under you soft or hard?

Have them turn over onto their stomachs.

What is covering the forest floor?
Dig a "nose hole" and sniff. Is the smell familiar?
Is it wetter or drier, warmer or colder under the leaf litter?
What's there?

Have them poke around with their fingers to see the decayed leaves, insects, seeds, roots, worms, spiders, etc.

ACTIVITIES	MATERIALS

FOREST FOOD WEB

Objective: To demonstrate the interconnectedness of life on the forest floor.

Divide into groups of no more than 20. Each child will represent a plant or animal that may be found in the woods (there can be duplicates). Explain that all living things in the forest are interrelated in a food web because of what they eat or whom they are eaten by. Plants are the most important part of the food web because only they can produce food for themselves, using sunlight to give them energy. Some animals are plant eaters, such as rabbits or mice. Other animals are meat eaters and eat the plant eaters, like owls or weasels. Hand out colored signs for the children to hang around their necks, each marked with an appropriate plant or animal:

Plants (green signs)

nut	bud
flower	seed
twig	leaf
berry	bark

Plant Eaters (blue signs)

mouse	bird
deer	insect
squirrel	rabbit
chipmunk	

Meat Eaters (red signs)

owl	fox
coyote	shrew
woodpecker	

Ask the children to stand in a circle with the 3 categories interspersed (i.e., don't have all the plants stand together). Hand each plant eater a string to connect with a plant to demonstrate who eats whom. When they have completed this, hand each meat eater a string to connect with a plant eater, again demonstrating who eats whom. (A child may be holding onto many strings at once.) To illustrate the complexity of the food web, use additional strings to make more connections between the children. Ask what happens when a forest fire destroys the plants (plants drop their strings so they are no longer connected to the plant eaters). The plant eaters starve (they drop their strings and are no longer connected to the meat eaters). The meat eaters then starve (they drop their strings) and the web is destroyed. What happens to all the plants and animals when they die? Their bodies are invaded by a group of plants and animals called **decomposers**, which help break down dead organisms, thus releasing stored nutrients back to the soil for reuse by growing plants.

Materials:
- *signs with yarn attached*
  1 for each child
- *pieces of string*
  about 10' long

ACTIVITIES	MATERIALS

DIGGING DEEPER INTO THE MATTER

Objective: To explore the layers of the leaf litter and to find what lives there; to see decomposition in action.

Depending on the age of the children, divide into small groups or pairs. Give each a loop of yarn. Have them place the yarn on the forest floor and very carefully begin taking off the layers within the loop. Have them write down, or record by sticking samples onto the cardboard, everything they find, layer by layer, down to the soil. Where is decomposition furthest along? Who lives in the leaf litter? Were there any white thread-like roots? Replace the leaf litter.

- *loops of yarn* 18 inches diameter; enough for each group
- *paper*
- *pencils*
- *writing surface*
- *8" x 11" piece of cardboard* with rows of sticky tape

FOREST FORAY

Objective: To notice different features of the forest floor.

Have each team, or pair, of children look for the following items listed on their Forest Foray cards.

- *Forest Foray cards*
- *thermometers*

- Things that feel soft, hard, crinkly, smooth, rough.
- Holes that might be homes for animals.
- The spot in the forest that gets the most sunlight, the least sunlight.
- The driest place and the wettest place.
- The coldest and the hottest spots you can find. Use thermometers.
- The oldest, the youngest thing.
- The most decomposed thing.
- Three pieces of evidence that insects have been around.
- Look for something that doesn't belong in the forest. Remove it if it's trash.

At the end of the search compare findings.

Note: You may want to organize this with separate cards for each category, having the children return for a new task card after each successful mission.

FOREST FANTASY TRAIL

Objective: To have fun imagining life as a tiny forest creature.

Have the children pair up and give them a Fantasy Trail packet. Ask them to make a fantasy trail by laying out the yarn on the forest floor, putting signs up at all interesting stops along the way. (A model trail may be set up prior to the workshop to give children a better idea of what you want them to do.) Encourage them to let their imaginations run wild. After trails are completed, have the children visit each other's trails and be guided along them by the creators.

- *Fantasy Trail packets* each containing: small pieces of paper toothpicks pencils yarn or string in 6 foot lengths

FOLLOW-UP ACTIVITIES

1. Mural
Have the children make a mural showing a forest floor and what lives on and beneath its surface.

2. Terrarium
Decide with the children what examples from the forest floor they would like to preserve in a terrarium. Leader should collect them and have the children arrange them in a glass container with pebbles for drainage on the bottom. Cover with see-through plastic. Moisten occasionally if necessary.

3. Fantasy Trail Story
Have the children write and illustrate a fantasy trail story.

Skills
Science Process: Observing, Inferring, Brainstorming, Communicating, Predicting, Comparing, Sorting and Classifying

Integrated Curriculum: Art, Drama, Writing, Language Arts

Suggested Reading for Children:

Atwood, Ann. *The Kingdom of the Forest.* New York: Charles Scribner's Sons, 1972. (y/o — nice photos, limited text)

Behnke, Frances L. *What We Find When We Look Under Rocks.* New York: McGraw-Hill, 1971. (y/o — good drawings, brief information)

Jaspersohn, William. *How the Forest Grew.* New York: Greenwillow Press, 1980. (y/o)

Patent, Dorothy H. *The World of Worms.* New York: Holiday House, 1978. (y/o — good diagrams, details)

Pringle, Laurence P. *Twist, Wiggle, and Squirm.* New York: Crowell Jr. Books, 1971. (y — general information)

Ryder, Joanne. *Snail in the Woods.* New York: Harper, 1979. (y)

Small Homes for Tiny Creatures

The goldenrod stem has a lump
The willow twig sprouted a bump
Some rumor a tumor
But I think I'd sooner
Believe it some kind of a mump!

What are those odd swellings on some plants, the lumps and bumps on certain leaves? Look closely, perhaps they are galls. A gall is an abnormal growth of plant tissue produced by a stimulus external to the plant itself. Stated more simply, some substance injected into a plant causes that part of the plant to swell or grow in a particular pattern. It may be on the leaf, stem, flowerheads, stalk, or root, but it can develop only while that part of the plant is growing, which explains why galls usually form in the spring.

Galls come in many shapes: round, conical, kidney, disc, or spindle-shaped. Their textures vary greatly, too, from almost fluffy to papery or woody, and from smooth to sticky, hairy, bumpy, scaly, or ridged.

The purpose of a gall is to provide a home for a tiny creature. And what an incredible home it is, with its solid outer walls and constant food supply. Insects and sometimes mites are the chief tenants of galls during the immature stages of their lives. Besides producing food and shelter, the gall keeps its occupants comparatively safe from parasites and predators, and it protects them from drying out.

Exactly what initiates the gall growth on the plant is not clear. It appears to be a chemical substance either injected by the mother insect at the time she lays her eggs or secreted in the saliva of the **larvae** as they bore into the plant for shelter or begin eating it for food. Sometimes the adult female seems to start the process and her offspring, carrying precisely the same chemical, continue to stimulate the growth of the gall.

How galls form and grow on a plant is intriguing. The initial stimulant causes starch to convert to sugar, resulting in an excess of food material, which stimulates the plant cells to enlarge and/or multiply and the gall to grow. Usually the presence of a gall does not harm the host plant. Although galls grow on a great variety of plants, oaks are the most popular, claiming 800 of the 2000 kinds of American galls, followed by willows, poplars, plants that belong to the rose family, such as blackberries and raspberries, and finally composite plants such as goldenrods and asters.

Each gall-making insect produces a specific kind of gall and usually it grows on just one species of plant. Often, especially in winter, you can identify a plant by recognizing the gall that grows on it. The goldenrod ball gall offers a good example. It is an easily recognizable ball-shaped swelling on the goldenrod's stem, forming only on the Canada goldenrod (Solidago canadensis). This particular gall is caused by a small, brown-winged fly, Eurosta solidaginis.

The life cycle of the Eurosta solidaginis is quite typical and shows clearly why the formation of a gall is vital to this insect's survival. The female fly lays her eggs on the surface of the growing goldenrod stem in the spring. Sometime in June the eggs hatch and each young larva that bores successfully through the stem's outer wall causes a ball-shaped gall to form around it. In the fall the larva makes a tunnel through to the outermost layer of plant tissue to provide the route for the

spring exodus as an adult, then retreats back to the center of the gall. Protected through the winter, it remains in its larval stage until it is time to transform in the spring to the **pupal** stage. When the pupal stage is complete in late spring, a balloon-like bladder forms on the front of the fly's head, which it inflates to push the end off the pupa case. It then crawls through the exit tunnel and batters through the final barrier of plant tissue by inflating and deflating the balloon, which is absorbed afterwards into the insect's head. The adult flies soon mate and the cycle begins again. Without the gall to protect the larva through the winter, it would perish and the species could not survive.

The interrelationship between animals and plants is evident throughout our environment, but nowhere is the dependency of animals on plants more dramatically illustrated than in galls.

Goldenrod Ball Gall

Suggested References:

Borror, Donald J., and Richard E. White. *A Field Guide to the Insects.* Boston, MA: Houghton Mifflin, 1970.

Brues, C. T. *Insects, Food and Ecology.* New York: Dover Publications, 1946.

Hutchins, Ross E. *Galls and Gall Insects.* New York: Dodd, Mead, 1969.

Focus: *Some species of insects create remarkable habitats for themselves by causing specific kinds of plants to form galls around them.*

ACTIVITIES	MATERIALS
Initial Question: What is a gall?	

VIEW A VARIETY OF GALLS

Objective: To learn what galls are and to see the differences among a variety of galls.

- *a variety of galls* preferably one for each child
- *hand lenses*

Give a gall to each child to examine with a hand lens. Notice color, shape, size, texture, where it grows on the plant, whether there are holes in it. Children introduce their galls either by telling something special about them or by asking a question. Try to include these points in the discussion:

1) Galls are temporary habitats for insects or other tiny creatures.

2) Galls form when the right kind of insect injects a chemical into its host plant, which causes the plant tissue to grow.

3) Gall-making insects must choose the correct species of plant or the gall will not form.

4) Each kind of gall insect causes its own specific type of gall to form.

TO EACH HIS OWN

Objective: To notice individual differences among look-alikes.

- *galls* all the same kind; enough for each child

All children are given the same kind of gall (goldenrod ball galls work well). Tell the children to examine their galls carefully so they can distinguish their own from other galls. Put all the galls together in a pile. Have the children find their own galls and explain distinguishing features. Have them guess what's inside.

GALL FANTASY

Objective: To understand the life cycle of a gall insect by experiencing the passage of time inside a gall.

- *Gall Fantasy*, p. 87
- *crackers* 1 for each child

Explain to the children that you will read them a story in which they are the characters. They should listen and follow the directions, silently. Give them each a cracker, which they may not eat until directed to.

GALL HUNT

Objective: To find as many galls as possible.

- *hand lenses*

In small groups, search outdoors for galls growing on flowers, bushes, or trees. Look on leaves, stems, ends of twigs. If there are many specimens of each kind, one of each could be picked for display or further study. Check for exit holes, or invasion holes by other insects; sometimes it's hard to tell the difference.

ACTIVITIES	MATERIALS

WHAT'S INSIDE

Objective: To see what an amazing habitat a gall is and what lives inside, and to learn the life cycle of one gall insect.

Each group of 5 or 6 should have a gall, a knife, and newspaper to work on. Look at the gall carefully. Is the exit hole visible? Cut the gall in half (an adult should do this for young children), and examine the halves to look for:

• insect — in its grub-like larval stage

• exit route — hold each half up to the light for easier inspection

• how much of the gall's interior has been eaten by the host larva and how much by other insect invaders

From the informational essay, describe the life cycle of the insect that makes the goldenrod ball gall.

Note: Children may express legitimate concern about destroying the insects and their homes. Discuss this. Possible answers include: 1) we have cut open a kind that had many specimens; most remain growing where they belong; 2) scientific knowledge is often gained by examining live specimens and our knowledge helps us understand and respect each creature's place in the natural world.

Materials:
• *goldenrod ball galls* (another kind if none available)
• *knives*
• *newspaper*
• *hand lenses*

GALL FANTASY

You are about to become tiny, defenseless creatures. Please, very quietly, get your jackets and find a place where you can be protected, but where you can easily hear my voice. Crouch, become as small as you can, put your jacket over your head and be very silent. Close your eyes.

It is fall now, the days are growing shorter and nights are cold. But you can't see the daylight nor feel the chill; you are snug in your gall home. You can eat, your food is all around you, warm and dry, you need only reach out to the nearest wall for food. *Eat*, rest, and *eat again*.

The leaves have fallen, beaten to the ground by gusty winds and pelting rains. You are safe and dry in your gall home. But you are alone and it is dark.

Autumn turns to winter. The snows have come, the ponds are iced, winter buries food for creatures like yourselves.

The sun is higher now, owls are nesting, streams are thawing, and you are growing bigger. Warmth, snow melting, sap running. You sleep your final sleep, deep inside your private gall. The time has come for you to change.

The days grow longer and warmer. Grass is green and flowers bloom. Your gall home is brown and dry. You feel an urge to stretch and move, stretch and move, and suddenly you are out of your gall, standing tall, soaking in the sunlight, drying your wings. You are an adult.

FOLLOW-UP ACTIVITIES

1. Keeping Galls
Encourage the children to store different kinds of galls in jars, covered with cheesecloth and with dampened cotton in them, to see what kind of insect emerges and when. Check similar galls in the wild and compare dates. Keep a record. Try to identify the galls and/or insects by using a guide.

2. I'm a Gall Insect
Have the children draw, or write a poem or short story about what it would be like to be a gall insect inside its home.

3. Paper Maché Galls
Make small or giant paper mache galls that the children can look into or actually climb into.

Skills
Science Process: Observing, Inferring, Communicating, Predicting, Comparing, Sorting and Classifying, Experimenting, Recording Data

Integrated Curriculum: Art, Drama, Reading, Writing, Language Arts, Math

Suggested Reading for Children:

Hutchins, Ross. *Galls and Gall Insects*. New York: Dodd, Mead, 1969. (o — informative, adult)

Nestor, William P. *Into Winter — Discovering A Season*. Boston, MA: Houghton Mifflin, 1982. (o — section on galls)

Many Ways to Cope With Winter

Animals that overwinter in cold climates have adapted to the rigorous conditions of snow, ice, and cold in one of three ways. 1) They migrate, sometimes hundreds of miles to a more plentiful food supply, a few hundred yards to a protected area such as the winter deer yards, or even a few inches to the underside of a rotting log. 2) They may **hibernate** or enter periods of **dormancy** through the coldest parts of the winter or 3) they may remain active, foraging and feeding as best they can.

Temperature is a key factor for overwintering animals. Until late December the earth continues to retain some of its summer heat, but even so the ground may freeze to a depth varying from a few inches to many feet. The lowest level of freezing is the **frost line**, below which many animals try to burrow to reduce the chances of freezing to death.

Snow helps to hold the earth's warmth by forming a protective insulating layer for the plants and animals underneath it. Absence of snow can cause severe damage and hardship. One study showed that the temperature of the soil two inches below the surface was 1.4°F where the ground was bare, and 30.2°F where soft snow covered the ground, both at the same air temperature. Even more dangerous to hibernators, especially insects, are intermittent warm and cold spells. Ideal conditions are steady cold with insulating snow cover.

Migration is not the survival device used by most mammals, but on a small scale, downward migration is how many insects and spiders, **reptiles** and **amphibians** arrive at their winter quarters. Overwintering insects and spiders who have summered in bushes and trees descend to weeds and grass roots. Ground-dwelling insects, snails, earthworms, and salamanders hide under leaf litter and in rotten logs; toads burrow into the soil below the frost line. Pond creatures creep down into the mud or swim to deeper water, which is usually about 39°F. Some amphibians such as leopard frogs and pickerel frogs return to the pond in winter. Many snakes migrate to their winter quarters, the same group usually on about the same date each year. The most obvious migrators, of course, are the birds who must move to insure having adequate food

supplies. Thus warblers and swallows go south to find active insects, water birds seek open water with available food, sparrows look for uncovered seeds.

Hibernation or dormancy is the alternative to migration for animals that cannot remain active in winter. Specific physical adaptations that include, for instance, a build-up of fat in **vertebrate** animals and a build-up of an anti-freeze type substance in many insects, enable animals to sleep relatively safely through all or much of the winter. True **hibernators** breathe slowly and unevenly, their heartbeats slow down, their temperatures drop way down, and they remain in this state throughout the winter months. Three true hibernating mammals are the woodchuck, little brown bat, and jumping mouse.

The bodily processes of **dormant animals** also slow way down and the animals become inactive and "sleep" for part of the winter, but their body temperatures remain higher than those of hibernators, and they may either venture forth during mild spells or wake and eat some of their stored food. The skunk, raccoon, and chipmunk are common dormant mammals; there continues to be differences of opinion as to whether the bear hibernates or is dormant.

Hibernation does not happen all of a sudden. Periods of drowsiness and wakefulness alternate until profound lethargy takes over. A study of woodchucks showed a variation of from three days to a month interval between full activity and deep sleep. Although hibernating animals merely look asleep, they are really in quite a different state. The body position of the majority of hibernating mammals is curled up with the hind legs covering the head so the eyes are hidden. They are motionless, often for days at a time, and breathe very slowly, as little as once per minute. Body temperatures fall; a woodchuck's hibernating temperature may be as low as 37.4°F, while his summer temperature is around 96.8°F. The heart beats slowly and irregularly during hibernation, for a woodchuck averaging four to five times per minute, as opposed to 160 times per minute when active. Awakening from hibernation seems to start with accelerated heartbeat followed by a rise in temperature. Finally, the animal opens its eyes, uncurls, stretches, and rises to its feet.

The third, and among mammals most common, way of coping with winter is to remain active. Many active overwintering animals go through physiological changes to prepare for winter. Fat accumulates and fur thickens on most mammals; a white-tailed deer's winter coat is actually composed of hollow hairs to trap extra body heat. Some animals' feet change in the winter to make walking on the snow easier; for example, scaly projections on the toes of grouse and extra fur on the feet of snowshoe hares. The greatest challenge is to find enough food to provide energy for hunting or foraging and for keeping warm. Some, like the mink, weasel, deer, and rabbit, must hunt their food daily, having no instinct to store food. Others, such as red squirrels and mice, rely on caches of hidden seeds and nuts.

A severe winter can create great hardship, but animals that spend it in an appropriate habitat have a good chance for survival. Those who do not almost certainly perish.

Suggested References:

Buck, Margaret W. *Where They Go in Winter*. New York: Abingdon Press, 1968.

Morgan, Ann H. *Field Guide to Animals in Winter*. New York: G.P. Putnam's Sons, 1939.

Stokes, Donald. *Guide to Nature in Winter*. Boston, MA: Little, Brown, 1976.

Focus: *Animals have differing habitat requirements during the winter depending upon their levels of activity and the availability of food.*

ACTIVITIES	MATERIALS
Initial Question: Why is winter hard for animals? What are some of the ways they deal with the hardships?	

WHERE DO THEY GO IN WINTER?

Objective: To introduce some habitats in which animals spend the winter.

Give a short presentation with slides or pictures to explain where different animals, including insects, reptiles and amphibians, birds, and mammals go in winter and why.

- *slides or pictures*

WINTER MURAL

Objective: To have the children figure out whether and where different animals could live on the winter mural.

Each child, in turn, chooses an animal card with words or pictures of the following: hawk, blue jay, woodpecker, mouse, squirrel, woodchuck, porcupine, beaver, bear, raccoon, skunk, weasel, fox, rabbit, deer, frog, salamander, toad, snake, turtle, butterfly, honeybee, mosquito. They should tape it to the winter mural in an appropriate habitat for that animal and explain why that place was chosen (availability of food and/or shelter).

- *winter mural* that includes pond, woods, field, trees with holes
- *animal cards* with words or pictures of hawk, blue jay, wood-pecker, mouse, squirrel, woodchuck, porcupine, beaver, bear, raccoon, skunk, weasel, fox, rabbit, deer, frog, sala-mander, toad, snake, turtle, butterfly, honey-bee, mosquito

ANIMAL SIGNS

Objective: To discover signs of animal activity outdoors.

Divide the children into groups. Give each an Animal Signs card that lists the following items to look for:

- Tracks of at least 4 different animals.
- Five potential food sources and who might eat them.
- Three signs of animals having eaten.
- Homes or shelters for 5 different animals.
- Stop, look, listen — what other signs of animal activity do you notice?
- Pick an animal — what makes today easy or difficult for your animal?

Return at a specified time to compare findings.

- *Animal Signs cards*

ANIMAL BINGO

Objective: To review facts about where animals spend the cold winter months.

Give each child a Bingo Card and cover-ups. Draw on your own knowledge or read facts from the Mammals in Winter Chart to describe each animal and its winter habitat until children guess and cover up correct pictures. Play continues until someone gets Bingo, or until all are covered.

- *Bingo Cards* with pictures of various animals
- *cover-up discs* or papers

MAMMALS IN WINTER CHART

Hibernates — prolonged deep sleep
Dormant — wakes and moves about occasionally

Species	Winter Habit	Winter Habitat	Winter Food Sources
Bat, little brown	Hibernates	In cave or mine	•
Bear, black	Dormant	Shelter between roots, under fallen trees, in caves	•
Beaver	Active	Pond, lodge door below ice	Bark & twigs, prefer poplar & birch
Bobcat	Active	Woods, brushy areas	Rodents
Chipmunk, eastern	Dormant	Below frostline in burrow	Cached seeds & nuts
Coyote	Active	Fields & woods	Small or medium-sized animals
Deer, white-tailed	Active	Sheltered woods, usually evergreen	Twigs, evergreens, buds, apples
Fisher	Active	Woods	Porcupines, hares, other small or medium-sized mammals
Fox, red	Active	Open, timbered & farmland	Mice, rabbits, insects, fruit, carrion
Hare, snowshoe	Active (white coat)	Brushy areas, woods	Buds, bark, own droppings
Mink	Active	Near water	Muskrats, small animals
Mole, eastern	Semi-active	Tunnels below frostline	Insects, spiders, slugs, seeds
Mole, star-nosed	Active	Marshes, stream edges	Snails, insects
Mouse, jumping	Hibernates	Below frostline	•
Mouse, meadow, or vole	Active	Tunnels under snow in fields	Seeds, roots, stems
Mouse, white-footed and deer	Active	Woods, and bordering fields, under snow	Seeds, nuts, bark, fungi, insects
Muskrat	Active	Cattail lodge in marsh	Roots, stems, clams, snails, fish, carrion
Otter, river	Active	Near water	Fish, amphibians, crustaceans
Porcupine	Active	Woods: dens in ledges; in, or under, trees	Bark & twigs, wood
Rabbit, cottontail	Active	Heavy brush patches	Bark, stems, twigs, sedges, own droppings
Raccoon	Dormant	Hollow trees, under rocks	Omnivorous, forages near streams
Shrew, short-tailed	Active	Under leaves and grasses	Insects, small animals, nuts, berries
Skunk, striped	Dormant	Fields, woods	Eggs, insects, roots, berries, small animals
Squirrel, eastern gray	Usually active	Eastern hardwood	Acorns, nuts, seeds
Squirrel, flying	Active	Hollow trees	Nuts, seeds, bulbs
Squirrel, red	Semi-active	Coniferous woods	Cone seeds, nuts, seeds
Weasel, short-tailed (ermine)	Active (white coat)	Varied: fields and woods	Small animals, insects, amphibians
Woodchuck	Hibernates	Below frostline in deep burrow	•

91

FOLLOW-UP ACTIVITIES

1. Weekly Record

Keep a record on the Winter Mural or on a calendar of which animals or animal tracks are noticed by the children each week. As winter progresses toward spring, are more animals seen?

2. My Favorite Animal

Children choose a favorite animal to research: how it spends the winter, what food it eats, how it keeps warm, where it lives, when it has babies. Have them draw its picture and write or give an oral report, or write the facts on a sheet of paper and make everyone guess what it is. (Animal's picture could be pasted under lift-up flap.)

3. Helping or Hurting Winter Habitats

Invite a forester, naturalist, or Fish and Wildlife official to talk about winter habitats. How can people help improve winter habitats for animals (e.g., brush piles and dead trees for shelter, tops and twigs from lumbered trees for food, large unbuilt-on tracts of land for habitats)?

Skills

Science Process: Observing, Inferring, Brainstorming, Communicating, Predicting, Comparing, Sorting and Classifying, Recording Data

Integrated Curriculum: Art, Social Studies, Reading, Writing, Language Arts

Suggested Reading for Children:

Bancroft, Henrietta, and Richard Van Gelder. *Animals in Winter.* New York: Crowell Scholastic, 1963. (y — different winter strategies)

Cosgrove, Margaret. *Wintertime for Animals.* New York: Dodd, Mead, 1975. (y/o)

Farber, Nora. *How the Hibernators Came to Bethlehem.* New York: Walker & Co., 1980. (y — also a filmstrip)

Fisher, Roland M. *Animals in Winter.* Washington, DC: National Geographic Society, 1982. (y — excellent photos)

Fox, Charles Phillip. *When Winter Comes.* Chicago, IL: Reilly & Lee, 1962. (Scott Foresman Reading Program) (y — basic)

Freedman, Russell. *When Winter Comes.* New York: E. P. Dutton, 1981. (y/o)

Markle, S. *Exploring Winter.* New York: Atheneum, 1984. (o — information and activities)

SNUG IN THE SNOW

Snow Is a Welcome Blanket for Many

Ashelter of frozen water vapor or snow may not seem like the coziest place to spend a cold winter day, but such shelter means survival for many plants and animals in the north. Snow serves as insulation much like insulation in a house or like a down vest. Air trapped in spaces between the snow granules keeps earth-warmed air in and cold air out.

When light, fluffy snow lands, the flakes face every which way, leaving space for large amounts of air. That's why powder snow insulates so well; the air spaces between the snowflakes actually trap the warm air radiating up from the earth. But snow changes as the crystals break down or bond together and the air spaces become smaller. Eventually all the snow grains are approximately the same size.

To the animals that must survive northern winters, the need for snow and differences in snow cover and snow types are a part of life. Snow creates a very stable environment beneath it (the **subnivean** layer), in which temperatures range from about 20°F to 30°F, whereas air temperatures can fluctuate from -25°F to 55°F.

Many small mammals spend the winter in the silent layer next to the ground where the snow changes gradually into a latticework of ice and air spaces. This environment of near darkness (one foot of snow is said to transmit about 8 percent of available light and two feet of snow only 1 percent) means survival for the small mammals, shrews, moles, voles, and mice that would freeze to death if exposed for too long. Their body surfaces are so great in proportion to their volume, that heat loss cannot be replaced quickly enough. As animals decrease in size, they are also less able to carry a thick enough coat to withstand continual exposure to cold.

The under-the-snow layer provides a good habitat for them. Many hide seeds and nuts for winter use. Weeds and grasses, flattened by the snow, add their seed heads to the larder. Bark of shrubs and small trees, plus surface roots, provide additional fare. However, there is considerable track evidence that many of these little animals spend time running across the top of the snow hunting for new food or taking the easiest route to a stored cache. Such exposure makes them vulnerable to predators. Even though much of this scurrying occurs at night, it is dangerous because many predators hunt at night.

Snow depth affects all northern creatures. Animals that live under the snow need at least a foot of snow to insure survival. Deepening snow raises the reach level of snowshoe hares and deer as they search for buds and twigs and bark. Red squirrels depend on tunnels in the snow for food storage and escape routes, and weasels, slimmer than you might think, follow their prey — squirrels, mice, voles — right into their tunnels. Grouse dive into deep snow for protection against the cold and predators. Snow on ponds helps keep water open under the ice, making it easier for beavers and muskrats to reach their food supplies.

Variations in the consistency of the snow can also mean life or death to those who live in it or walk on it. A crust, if hard enough, will support even a deer, whose tiny foot size means several pounds of pressure per square inch. But that same crust may trap a sleeping grouse or cause such a build-up of carbon dioxide in the lower layers that the small mammals succumb. Most of the small "mouse" holes you see in the open snow are actually air vents that allow the carbon dioxide, built up from decaying vegetation, to escape. Powder snow, although it has the best insulating properties and is light enough for heavier animals to walk through, causes problems for the lighter creatures, which flounder in it. On the other hand, these lighter animals, deer mice, meadow voles, and grouse, will be able to move about at will on top of deep, fairly dense or heavy snow, which in turn will prevent deer from moving about easily. Predators, too, such as fox, coyote, and even bobcat, will have trouble hunting in deep, dense snow.

The effect of snow on trees deserves mention too. Birds that do not migrate depend on the shelter of snow-laden evergreen trees for shelter during periods of great cold or wind or storm. Conifer boughs, heavy with snow, droop within reach of hungry deer and snowshoe hares, and many kinds of animals rest or take refuge in the comparatively shallow snow under such trees.

Snow, exquisitely beautiful, protective and destructive, covers nearly one quarter of the world's land surface each winter. Whatever your feeling as you watch snowflakes floating down and snow piling up, it should be remembered that many plants and animals would perish without a blanket of snow.

Suggested References:

Bell, Thelma Harrington. *Snow*. New York: Viking, 1954.

Kirk, Ruth. *Snow*. New York: William Morrow, 1978.

Webster, David. *Snow Stumpers*. New York: Natural History Press, 1968.

SNUG IN THE SNOW

Focus: *Snow serves as a vital winter habitat for many animals that depend upon it for shelter.*

ACTIVITIES	MATERIALS
Initial Question: How might snow help some animals in winter? ## PUPPET SHOW **Objective:** To show how snow protects small animals from severe cold weather and predators. Give the puppet show. Discuss the benefits of snow for the animals involved.	• *script, p. 96* • *puppets*
## SNOW CRITTER CONCENTRATION **Objective:** To identify some of the animals that spend time in or under the snow. Divide children into two groups. A child from one team starts by removing two discs from the snow mural, looking for matching animals. Then the other group takes a turn. When matching animals are found, leave off discs. Groups continue until all pictures are matched and uncovered. Discuss how the snow helps each of the animals.	• *snow mural* on cardboard with removable discs covering animal pictures (2 pictures of each animal: white-footed mouse, weasel, grouse, meadow vole, shrew, mole, red squirrel)
## 'S NO PROBLEM **Objective:** To think about ways snow helps some animals find food and shelter. Encourage the children to think of ways snow might help an animal find food or shelter. List them on a blackboard or newsprint. Divide into groups and give each an Animal Card with a name/picture on one side and food/shelter clues on the back. Possibilities include:	• *Animal Cards*

Snowshoe hare: whiteness helps conceal the hare; deep snow raises reach level for food

Ermine (weasel): whiteness helps conceal the weasel; can tunnel through it for food

White-footed mouse: shelter from the cold; place to hide seeds

Shrew: protection from cold

Mole: protection from cold; helps keep soil from freezing so food sources such as earthworms, insect larvae available

Red squirrel: shelter; place to store seeds; can tunnel under or through it

Ruffed grouse: dives in as protection from cold

Meadow vole: shelter from cold; can store seeds under it

Each group should act out its animal as well as how snow affects its life for the others to guess.

ACTIVITIES	MATERIALS

FROZEN JELLO

Objective: To show that snow acts as an insulator shielding animals from severe surface temperatures.

Stir, until dissolved, one tablespoon gelatin into 1 cup hot water, then fill film canisters half full. Divide children into small groups, and ask them to choose a shady exposed area for 1 canister, deep snow in which to bury the other canister. When sites are chosen, place surface canister *uncovered*, and under-snow canister with lid securely fastened. Mark the site of the buried canister. Close by, place one thermometer on top of the snow, and insert one under the snow near ground level. After a few minutes, someone should check the surface canisters for signs of jelling. When they begin to jell, children should return to dig up the buried container and compare the progress of the two. Which container jelled first? Why? Why might animals want to stay under the snow on a cold day? Check the thermometers. Is there a temperature difference? How much?

Note: One hopes the surface container will jell first; sometimes it doesn't. That too makes for good discussion. Admittedly, to leave the surface container exposed and to cover the buried one is cheating a little, but it speeds up the jelling of the first, and keeps snow out of the second.

Materials for Frozen Jello
- *thermos bottle*
- *steaming hot water*
- *gelatin*
- *film canisters*
  2 per group; half with covers
- *site markers*
  yarn or sticks

MOUSE HOUSE

Objective: To see firsthand whether there really are animals snug in the snow.

Each group from the previous activity should look for animal holes and/or tunnels in the snow. Then dig some tunnels and leave some seeds or nuts in them. The children can check during the next few days to see whether any have been eaten.

Materials for Mouse House
- *seeds or nuts*

DIORAMAS

Objective: To make creative snug-in-the snow habitats.

In small groups, construct a diorama depicting life under the snow. Lay a shoe box on its side and whiten the inside with chalk. Cut away the roof and replace it with a piece of styrofoam cut to size. Hold it in place with straight pins or toothpicks. Decorate the top with twigs, dried weeds, bits of evergreen. Make animals out of clay and playdough and place them where they belong, either under or above the snow.

Materials for Dioramas
- *shoe boxes*
  1 for each group
- *styrofoam pieces*
- *scissors*
- *chalk*
- *straight pins or tooth-picks*
- *twigs, dried weeds, evergreen sprigs*
- *clay*
- *white playdough*
  4 parts flour
  1 part salt
  enough water for pliable consistency

SNUG IN THE SNOW PUPPET SHOW

Characters: Marsha Mouse
Marvin Mouse (wearing easily removable ear muffs, scarf, and tail warmer)
Willie Weasel (in his white winter coat)

Stage: white cardboard with a tunnel cut from top edge slanting down toward the bottom, narrow strip of brown paper taped onto bottom with winter weeds stuck into it

Marsha Mouse: (on top of snow) Oh, I'm so excited. My favorite cousin Marvin Mouse is coming all the way up north from Florida to visit me. He was a little bit scared about coming north in the cold winter, but I told him it was lots of fun.

Marvin Mouse: (dressed warmly) Marsha, Marsha, is that you?

Marsha: Marvin! Is that you? What are you wearing?

Marvin: Well, I wasn't about to come and stay without my scarf, ear muffs, and tail warmer.

Marsha: But Marvin, you don't need any of those winter clothes. You'll be plenty warm without them.

Marvin: Oh no, I won't. I'm used to warm Florida. Besides, I bet you everyone out there in the audience wears warm clothes like this in the winter. Don't you children?

Marsha: Yes, but that's because they stay above the snow. I bet you no one in the audience buries themselves under the snow, do you children?

Marvin: Well, what does that have to do with anything?

Marsha: You'll see. Come with me. First take off all those clothes.
(Marvin shakes and his clothes fall off; both walk to hole and go under snow)

Marvin: Hey, it's warm down here. I'm not cold at all.

Marsha: Yes, not quite as warm as Florida, and you won't get a nice sun tan, but my little home in the snow does keep out a lot of cold.

Marvin: What was that grumble I just heard. Maybe it's a snow avalanche. Let's get out of here!

Marsha: That was no avalanche, it was just my stomach. I'm starving. Let's get something to eat.

Marvin: You mean we have to go back outside?

Marsha: No. There's all sorts of food to be found right here. If we just tunnel through the snow, we'll find delicious seeds to munch on.
(starts to eat the weed seeds)

Marvin: Yum, you're right. There's lots of good food under here.

Marsha: Quick, get back!

Marvin: Why, what's wrong?

Marsha: It's Willie Weasel. Stay back and stay quiet until he passes.
(Willie Weasel pokes his nose into tunnel, then walks by)

Marvin: What was he doing here?

Marsha: The same thing we are, looking for a place to stay warm and find food. The only difference is, *we're* his food!

Marvin: Oh my, that was a close call. I feel sick. It must be my nerves.

Marsha: No, you just need a nice breath of fresh air. Sometimes it feels very good to go up for air.
(poke heads outside of hole)

Marvin: (takes big breath) Ahhh, you're so right. That's just what I needed. Wow, I can't believe how cold it's gotten out here.

Marsha: Let's go back under. No matter how cold it gets out here, it stays pretty warm under the snow.
(go back under)

Marvin: Boy, this snow is great. It keeps you warm and you can tunnel through it to find food. I'm glad I came to visit. It's warmer under the snow than it is sometimes in Florida!

FOLLOW-UP ACTIVITIES

1. Compare Temperatures
On a cold day when there's at least a foot of snow, have the children measure and record the temperature on top of the snow and under the snow at ground level. Try it again on a warm day. How much difference is there?

2. Snow Vocabulary
Explain that peoples of the north use specific words to define different kinds of snow and places where snow is found. Have the children make up words to describe typical types of snow. Make a mini-dictionary with definitions and illustrations.

3. Snow Story
Ask the children to pretend they live under the snow and write a story about it. Is it dark or light? quiet or noisy? cozy or lonely?

Skills
Science Process: Observing, Inferring, Brainstorming, Communicating, Predicting, Comparing

Integrated Curriculum: Art, Drama, Social Studies, Reading, Writing, Language Arts, Math

Suggested Reading for Children:

Branley, F. M. *Snow is Falling*. New York: Thomas Y. Crowell, 1963. (y — general look at snow)

Lionni, Leo. *Frederick*. New York: Pantheon, 1969. (y — charming fiction about a mouse)

Nestor, William P. *Into Winter — Discovering a Season*. Boston, MA: Houghton-Mifflin, 1982. (o — lots of information)

Williams, Terry, and Ted Major. *Secret Language of Snow*. New York: (Sierra Club) Pantheon, 1984. (o — snow around the world)

Temporary Homes on the Forest Floor

The death and decay of a tree is a gradual process affected by seasons and weather and involving many plants and animals. During different stages of **decomposition**, the newly fallen tree and the rotting log it soon becomes serve as suitable habitats for various organisms, both plant and animal. The interrelationship among these organisms is well illustrated in a rotting log. In each stage of its decay, a rotting log hosts a multitude of plants and animals that either consume it or each other. In so doing, they alter the structure of the log and therefore gradually create a habitat no longer suitable for themselves, but increasingly appropriate for the next group of inhabitants.

The kinds of plants and animals that live on or in the rotting log vary in each successive stage, but the roles they play in relation to each other are constant. The **primary consumers**, whether plant or animal, obtain their nourishment from the log itself. The **secondary consumers** depend on the primary consumers as their food source. The third, and perhaps the most important group, are the **scavengers** and **decomposers**, which live on the dead remains of plants and animals and cause their physical and chemical breakdown. However, as is true in most systems devised to explain how things work, it is more complex than this brief description implies. Accordingly, many organisms in the rotting log have more than one role.

The first stage of decomposition begins while the tree is still standing. Insects invade the tree either by boring their way into it or by entering an opening in the protective bark, which has been created by disease, weather, fire, old age, or animal use. Beetles begin to burrow under the bark leaving their characteristic trails. Their tunnels allow moisture, air, and the **spores** of **fungi** to enter the tree. Tiny hair-like strands of the fungi penetrate the wood cells and live off of stored starches. Some fungi produce chemicals that actually dissolve the wood structure. This internal destruction is indicated on the outside by the appearance of fruiting structures on the bark. These visible fungi provide food for many bacteria, insect **larvae**, slugs, and snails. Beetles and large colonies of carpenter ants are also interested in the dying tree at this stage. Carpenter ants, which help attract woodpeckers, have special bacteria in their stomachs to help them digest wood.

All of this animal activity creates more openings for moisture and fungi to enter, weakening the tree until eventually it falls. Lying on the damp ground, the tree decays more rapidly because of its increased moisture content. Fungi and bacteria prefer moist areas for their work, while wood-boring insects and spiders inhabit the drier portions of the fallen tree. Most of the outer bark disintegrates rather quickly, and the outer wood becomes "punky," or soft and moist. Fungi continue to thrive and many other plants can now find root-holds and sustenance in the heavily decayed wood. Often the log becomes carpeted with lush mosses.

Salamanders and centipedes also find a rotting log to be a moist, protected habitat that offers both food and shelter. They may be inside the log or between the log and the damp ground on which it rests.

The intact structure of the log does not last forever. Gradually the outer shell collapses and becomes covered with other plant debris. Most of the wood-boring insects are forced to evacuate to younger rotting logs at this time, and decay is carried on by earthworms, microscopic organisms, and fungi.

Eventually, a point is reached when it is difficult to decide whether the mound is wood or soil. The newly formed soil provides the substances necessary for plant growth and many seedlings sprout on the site of the old log. The old tree is slowly being turned into a new tree, and the cycle is complete.

It takes approximately ten years for a dead tree to turn into soil. The succession of living things in decaying wood is usually different in different kinds of trees, and even the progression of organisms in the same kind of tree is not always the same. External conditions, including amount of moisture, the temperature, and climate help determine the way and rate at which a log decomposes and thus which plants and animals will live in it at any given stage.

SOME ANIMAL LIFE IN A ROTTING LOG

Primary Consumers

Fungi and Bacteria
Bark beetles
Click beetles
Wood borers
Engraver beetles
Carpenter ants
Termites

Secondary Consumers

Centipedes
Daddy longlegs
Wolf spiders
Mites
Ants (some species)
Salamanders
Woodpeckers

Scavengers

Millipedes
Pill bugs
Wood roaches
Snails
Earthworms
Mites
Slugs

Suggested References:

Jackson, James. *The Biography of a Tree.* Middle Village, NY: Jonathan David Publishers, 1978.

McCormick, Jack. *The Life of the Forest.* New York: McGraw-Hill, 1966.

Schwartz, George I., and Bernice S. Schwartz. *Life in a Log.* New York: Natural History Press, 1971.

Tresselt, Alvin. *The Dead Tree.* New York: Parent's Magazine Press, 1972.

Focus: *A rotting log serves as a habitat for many plants and animals, which vary according to the log's stages of decomposition.*

ACTIVITIES	MATERIALS
Initial Question: What might live in a rotting log?	

TREE-TO-TURF TIME MACHINE

Objective: To show the stages of a log's decomposition.

Divide the children into 3 groups: one to whistle like the wind, one to tap their fingers like the rain, and the third to chant the passing seasons "spring, summer, fall, winter." As a costumed professor, explain that you have invented a remarkable time machine that will show what happens to a tree when it dies. Open the flap of the Time Machine to reveal a recently cut piece of wood, then close it. Progress through the first 4 years, moving the seasons dial as Group 3 chants and the other groups make their sound effects. Then open the Time Machine (in which your hidden operator has switched logs) to see a log in initial stages of decay. Repeat this process for the passage of 4 more years, after which the secretly replaced log will look punky and soft, and then again for the last four years (total of twelve years), when the Time Machine log will be chunks of dirt. Afterwards, inspect and compare the 4 logs.

- *4 logs*
  in various stages of decay from freshly cut to nearly soil
- *Time Machine*
  large cardboard box painted with a seasons clock that has a movable dial, plus other numbers, gadgets, and dials; closable front and back flaps
- *costume for leader*

PUPPET SHOW

Objective: To introduce the concept that a rotting log can provide a home for many different animals.

Give the puppet show. Discuss what will happen to the log and which character will be able to live in it the longest.

- *script, p. 102*
- *puppets*

LOG LOOK

Objective: To explore a rotting log.

Have each group of children kneel around a rotting log with their eyes closed. Direct them to:

Listen — as they tap the log, does it sound hollow or solid, wet or dry?

Smell — does it smell wet or dry? like anything they've smelled before?

Feel — does it feel hard or soft, wet or dry, rough or smooth?

Have the children predict in which parts of the log they will find the most creatures. Now explore the log with eyes open. Gradually pull it apart. Use hand lenses to investigate what's inside the log, under it, on top of it. Return the investigated log and its inhabitants to the place where it was found.

Note: Using field guides, older children may wish to identify what they found.

- *hand lenses*
- *rotting logs*

ACTIVITIES	MATERIALS

SOIL SOUP

Objective: To concoct a recipe that will create the best soil soup out of a rotting log.

Divide the children into small groups. Tell them they are going to be cooks and make soil soup. Give each group a large can wrapped in brown construction paper to resemble a rotting log. As cooks, they will have to decide which ingredients will be needed to make soil soup. Offer a list of possible ingredients if you wish, such as:

shade
rain
salamanders
ice
ferns
moss
ants
beetles
centipedes
woodpeckers
worms
daddy longlegs
pill bugs
slugs
spiders
mushrooms
insect eggs
snakes
sun
millipedes
snails

- *empty cans wrapped to look like logs*
- *paper and pencils*
- *scraps of paper and cloth*

As each ingredient is chosen, add its name or a picture of it to the soup container. After all soups are complete, ask each group what ingredients they used and why. Older children can also be asked to write up their recipes. For example: Take 1 rotting log. Add 3 salamanders and 2 handfuls of moss. Let it sit for 4 months. . .

SHARING CIRCLE

Objective: To give the children a chance to summarize and share feelings about a rotting log.

Sit in a large circle. Go around the circle and ask each child to complete either of these two statements. "The thing I liked best about the rotting log was . . ." or "The thing I liked least about the rotting log was . . ."

ROTTING LOGS PUPPET SHOW

Characters: Rocky Raccoon
Benji Bear
Charlotte Spider
Wendy Worm

Props: A real or constructed rotting log
A piece of paper with "directions" on it taped to a stick

Rocky Raccoon: Benji Bear, I've been looking for you. As king of the forest you must have a list of all the individual homes around here.

Benji Bear: I sure do. Are you in need of a home, Rocky Raccoon?

Rocky: Yes I am. Nothing too fancy, no moss-to-moss carpeting or anything, just a fairly dry place with a roomy hole for me to stay in.

Benji: I know just the home for you Rocky. It has a soft, comfortable floor and thick, well-insulated walls. I'm sure you'll find it a perfect, snug home for the winter. Just follow these simple directions and you'll have no trouble finding it.
(hands him a piece of paper)

Rocky: Thanks a lot, Benji.
(walks off; Charlotte Spider appears)

Charlotte Spider: Hey Benji, I'm in need of a home too. Do you have anything for me?

Benji: What kind of place are you looking for Charlotte Spider?

Charlotte: The older the better, with a lot of little cracks and crevices for me to crawl under and through. I need a safe place for my sac of eggs and a spot where I will be protected and warm enough to spend the winter.

Benji: I've got the perfect place for you, Charlotte. This home will help protect you from predators and be a great place for you to find food. These directions will show you how to get there.
(hands her same paper and Charlotte walks off; Wendy Worm appears)

Wendy Worm: Oh Benji, can you help me? I'm having a terrible time finding a home.

Benji: Sure, Wendy Worm. What kind of home do you want?

Wendy: Us worms go for damp soil. It offers all the comforts and conveniences of ground life. I'd like a soft place with lots of rotting things so I can find good food.

Benji: Well, it just so happens I know of a place with nice, rich, damp soil. Here are the directions to get there.
(hands her same paper)

Wendy: Thank you Benji. I knew I could count on you.
(log comes up; Rocky and Wendy each approach it from opposite sides)

Rocky: This rotting log over here must be my new home.

Wendy: Your home! Benji Bear told me it would be my new home.

Charlotte: (creeping up over the log) Hey you guys, quit the joking. This is my new home.

Rocky and Wendy: Your home!

Rocky: We can't all live in the same place. I'm a raccoon and I need solid walls and nice dry leaves.

Charlotte: I'm a spider, and I like small spaces to hide in and places to catch my food.

Wendy: And I'm a worm. I'm a prisoner inside solid walls, and dry leaves are rough on my skin. I like dirt, myself, where I can move around easily.

Charlotte: I don't know. What do you think, audience? *Could* we all use the same rotting log for our homes? (wait for answer)

Rocky: There's a nice big hollow space at this end for me.

Charlotte: The middle of the log has great places for me to crawl around in and plenty of juicy insects to eat.

Wendy: Well, I can live over at this end where the rotting wood has almost turned to soil.

Rocky: So, I guess we all *can* live together. (yawns) I better go test my new bed. (leaves)

Charlotte: This rotting log provides a nice home for each of us. I think I'll hide behind here and wait for dinner. (leaves)

Wendy: So it doesn't matter that I'm a worm, and he's a raccoon and she's a spider. Life in this log is good for all of us. I better go burrow in that damp soil; this dry air is too much for me. Bye, bye everyone. (leaves)

FOLLOW-UP ACTIVITIES

1. Pill Bugs
Help the children put about 6 pill bugs in a large jar darkened with black construction paper held on with rubber bands. Add several slices of apple and raw potato, which provide food and moisture. Ask the children to watch and record their activities at different times of the day. Do they seem to prefer light or dark? How much do they eat? Release the pill bugs back to their home within a week.

2. Log Tag
Designate a fairly small area for the game. Choose one person to be "it." That person tries to tag people who can only save themselves by crouching before being tagged and naming a plant or animal that lives on or in a rotting log. As long as the same person is "it" there can be no naming repeats. If a person can't think of an organism to name and is tagged, that person becomes "it" and all plants and animals can be used again.

3. Word Games
Make up a crossword puzzle or a hidden words game using rotting log plants and animals.

Skills
Science Process: Observing, Inferring, Brainstorming, Communicating, Predicting, Comparing, Experimenting, Recording Data

Integrated Curriculum: Art, Drama, Reading, Writing, Language Arts, Math

Suggested Reading For Children:

Behnke, Frances L. *What We Find When We Look Under Rocks*. New York: McGraw-Hill, 1971. (y/o — good drawings, brief information)

Cobb, Vicki. *Lots of Rot*. New York: J. B. Lippincott, 1981. (y)

Newton, James R. *Forest Log*. New York: Crowell Jr. Books, 1980. (y — nice pictures)

Tresselt, Alvin R. *The Dead Tree*. New York: Parent's Magazine Press, 1972. (y)

The Challenge of a Moving, Watery World

Streams are among the oldest bodies of water on earth. They form when volumes of water, unabsorbed by the soil, are pulled by gravity across the surface of the earth. As the water moves, it carves a course for itself, following the path of least resistance. Streams that continue to flow during dry periods are sustained by ground water surfacing through springs. Other streams are dependent on heavy rains and run-off and dry up in periods of low rainfall. Sometimes streams change course, sometimes they are empty, but they rarely disappear entirely.

Plants and animals that inhabit streams must overcome potentially difficult situations. Algae (the chief **producer**, or plant food source, of the stream) and moss can grow in the current, but most rooted plants must become established in the backwaters. For animals, moving around in the current is difficult at best. With one wrong step a fragile insect may get dislodged and battered against rocks and sticks. The normal functions of life — eating, breathing, moving or holding fast, laying and hatching eggs — are all more difficult in the stream.

The current is, however, an advantage. As water flows over a rough bottom it becomes a giant mixer, saturating the water with air. It also picks up soil run-off and nutrients from decomposing plant and animal matter along the way. Being an efficient solvent, moving water can thus create a dilute soup of vital, dissolved nutrients. Some have called stream water "liquid soil."

Heavily shaded banks and cold springs help to keep the stream water cool. This is crucial since the amount of oxygen and other gases that water can hold is inversely related to its temperature. A cooler stream can hold more dissolved oxygen, which is often the limiting element in aquatic life. Trout are normally stream-dwelling fish because they need highly oxygenated water.

Mayfly

Animal life is abundant in the stream. From crayfish to fish, salamander to snail, there are a great variety of creatures, each living in the part of the stream best suited to its needs and abilities. But of all the stream creatures, the insects are probably the easiest to find and observe, marvelous examples of diversity within a habitat.

Stream insects possess amazing survival adaptations for their flowing, wet world. In the still pools at the water's edge, an insect is often found flitting along the surface, its shadow frequently more noticeable than the creature itself. This is the water strider, whose hair-fringed legs skate along on the surface as it prowls for unlucky insects that have fallen in.

Not all stream insects, however, can be seen from the banks. Truly aquatic insects spend entire periods of their lives submerged and must be sought amid the rocks, gravel, and plants found under the water. Since most of these creatures are nocturnal, they remain well hidden during the day.

As you lift your first rock, some tiny (one-quarter inch) black **larvae** may be seen swaying in the current. Black fly or buffalo gnat larvae are unmistakable with their rumps anchored firmly in place. Sieve-like hairs project from the side of their heads to strain algae, tiny animals, and plant debris from the water. If dislodged, these larvae will creep spider-like back up the current on a silken thread.

Under the rocks you are likely to find common stonefly and mayfly **nymphs**. Flattened and with strong hooks on their feet, they dwell within the narrow space between the bottom of the rock and the stream bed where the current is very weak. Mayflies have gills on their abdomens and usually three feathery-looking tail-like appendages. Stoneflies have gills that look like fuzzy tufts at the base of each leg and only two tail-like appendages. Most mayflies and some stoneflies are **herbivorous**, although some of the larger stoneflies prey on insects.

The gravels of the streambed provide yet another type of habitat, where crane fly larvae may be found in abundance. Cream-colored and maggot-like in appearance, a crane fly larva is one and one-half to two inches long and bears some appendages on its head that look like the fleshy feelers on a star-nosed mole. Adult crane flies resemble giant mosquitoes, but they do not bite.

As you continue to turn over rocks, sift gravel, and explore the stream, you may discover a tube-shaped caddis home of sand grains or leaf pieces. Caddis larvae construct their homes by weaving an intricate tube of silk threads that is closed at one end. Depending on the species, the silk tube is covered with either sand grains, leaf pieces, or small sticks, often in a neat, spiral pattern. These elaborate cases supply protection and ballast. Caddis larvae are mostly herbivorous, eating moss, algae, and dead leaves.

A stream is a constantly changing and sometimes perilous habitat. It is also a complete habitat for many, concentrating the essentials for life within its waters.

Suggested References:

Andrews, William (ed.). *A Guide to the Study of Freshwater Ecology.* Englewood Cliffs, NJ: Prentice-Hall, 1972.

Caduto, Michael J. *Pond and Brook: A Guide to Nature Study in Freshwater Environments.* Englewood Cliffs, NJ: Prentice-Hall, 1985.

Coker, Robert E. *Streams, Lakes, Ponds.* New York: Harper and Row, 1968.

Klots, Elsie B. *The New Fieldbook of Freshwater Life.* New York: G. P. Putnam's Sons, 1966.

Reid, George K., and Herbert S. Zim. *Pond Life.* New York: Golden Press, 1967.

Usinger, Robert L. *The Life of Rivers and Streams.* New York: McGraw-Hill, 1967.

Focus: *A single stream can contain amazingly different habitats that host a variety of plants and animals.*

ACTIVITIES	MATERIALS
Initial Question: What would it be like to live in a stream?	
## DREAM A STREAM	
Objective: To show how varied a stream can be.	• *paper* • *pencils* • *roll of paper* • *crayons*
All children should sit in a circle, close their eyes, and imagine themselves at a stream. What does it look like? sound like? Each child should tell or write down an adjective to describe the imagined stream. Sort the children into groups according to types of stream adjectives, such as fast-flowing, slow-moving, etc. Review the different types of streams represented. Roll out a long sheet of paper and have each group illustrate its stream on a section of it, forming one long stream with varying sections. (Save the completed stream for follow-up activity.)	
## PUPPET SHOW	
Objective: To introduce some common stream insects and their adaptations to stream life.	• *script, p. 109* • *puppets*
Give the puppet show. Discuss the adaptations mentioned in the show and why, living in a stream habitat, these adaptations were necessary. Show pictures of other stream animals and point out their special adaptations.	
## STREAM SAM AND SALLY	
Objective: To think about some adaptations that aquatic insects need for living in fast-moving water.	• *colored paper* • *scissors* • *tape* • *yarn or string* • *pipe cleaners* • *balloons* • *straws* • *crayons* • *egg cartons* • *cardboard tubes from toilet paper or paper towels*
Divide the children into small groups. Tell them they will be turning one of their group members into a stream critter. Using the materials supplied, they will make and attach body parts to that person so the newly created critter can do all of the following while submerged on the stream bottom: • Catch food and eat it • Breathe • Move around on the bottom • Lay eggs • Keep from getting washed away • See Have them name their critter. A spokesperson from each group will then explain how their critter can perform each of the appointed tasks while living on the stream bottom.	

ACTIVITIES	MATERIALS

STUDY A STREAM

Objective: To explore a stream and its life.

Divide the children into small groups and give each group a Stream Studies sheet to complete during their explorations. Put needed equipment in a central spot. Send half of the groups to a slow part of the stream and half to a fast-moving section. When Stream Study sheets are complete, compare results:

- What is the bottom like where the water is moving fast? slow?
- Where were the most animals found?
- How are animals different in fast and slow sections of the stream?

Look at collected animals and then release them in the part of the stream where they were found.

Note: A field guide will help older children and leaders identify some of the findings.

Materials:
- *Stream Studies sheets, p. 108*
- *cardboard clipboards*
- *pencils*
- *community dishpan*
- *pieces of string measuring 10' long*
- *hand lenses*
- *plastic containers*
- *nets*
- *thermometers*
- *microscope if available*

FAST FLOATERS

Objective: To have fun in the stream.

Fill a bag with natural floatable objects of different sizes and shapes. Divide into groups and have each group pick out one object. After every group has given its fast floater a name, the floating race will begin. Start at a common point and have spotters stand at the finish line to see which crosses first. After the race discuss why the winner probably won: shape, size, course in stream, obstructions.

Materials:
- *bag of floatable objects*

STREAM STUDIES

Physical Factors *(need thermometer, watch, ruler)*

1. What is the bottom of the stream like?

_____ rocks and gravel _____ sand _____ mud and silt _____ bedrock

2. How quickly is the water moving? To determine this, drop a floatable object onto the water and time how long it takes for it to be transported 10 feet. (Use the formula below to gauge the water's speed.)

velocity = $\dfrac{10 \text{ feet}}{x \text{ seconds}}$ = _____ feet/second

3. What is the approximate depth of the stream? (Mark water level on a stick, then measure with a tape or ruler.) _____

4. How cold is the water? (Use a thermometer.) _____

Plants

1. Are plants growing on the edge of the stream? Which of the following?

_____ trees _____ bushes _____ ferns _____ grass _____ flowers

_____ other

2. Are plants growing in the stream?

3. Are plants growing on rocks in the stream? Feel some rocks for slippery algae. Look for moss.

4. Is there evidence of dead or decayed plants on the bottom? leaf litter? twigs or branches? muck?

Animals *(need hand lenses, nets, plastic containers)*

1. Are there animals on top of the water? How do they move?

2. Do you see animals swimming in the water? fish? insects? other?

3. Are any tiny animals clinging to the tops of rocks?

4. Take a rock out of the stream. Are there animals on its underside? Look at them closely with a hand lens. Do they scurry away?

5. Collect an interesting specimen and put it in the community dishpan.

STREAMS PUPPET SHOW

Characters:	Willy Water Bug
	Gregor Grasshopper
	Mable Mayfly Nymph
	Lucy Black Fly Larva
Props:	coat hanger
	toilet plunger
	"magnifying glass" — a 12" circle of cardboard with 11" circle cut out of center, attached to a handle.

Willy Water Bug: Oh, the start of another day swimming about in this little pond. Life is so boring in this pond, no excitement at all.

Gregor Grasshopper: Hi, Willy Water Bug.

Willy: Hello, Gregor Grasshopper.

Gregor: I heard you complaining. Why don't you come out and hop in the fields with me. Then you won't be bored.

Willy: I can't be hopping in the fields. I'm a water bug. I have to live in the water.

Gregor: Well, you could still live other places besides this boring little pond. Why don't you go live in a stream. That would be exciting, with all that rushing, bubbling water. Don't you think so, audience?

Willy: Hey, that's a great idea. Do you know where there's a stream around here?

Gregor: I sure do. In fact, if you crawl on my back I'll hop you over to one.
(Willy gets on and they cross the stage.)

Gregor: Here's the stream. Jump right in.

Willy: Thanks for the ride, Gregor. (jumps off Gregor's back and Gregor leaves.) Yikes! This water is moving pretty fast. I can't swim in here. Help! Help! (Mable Mayfly Nymph appears)

Mable Mayfly Nymph: Oh my, it looks like he's in trouble. I better save him.
(pulls Willy out of stream.)

Willy: Thanks for saving me. Who are you?

Mable: I'm a mayfly nymph. My name is Mable.

Willy: Boy, Mable. I don't know how you stay in that water. It moves so fast.

Mable: That doesn't bother me. I have something very special on my feet that helps me hold on to rocks and other things in the stream.

Willy: I don't see anything so special on your feet. Do you audience?

Mable: Oh, you have to look very closely. You need a magnifying glass or hand lens.

Willy: Does anyone here have a magnifying glass or lens? (someone from audience with the magnifying glass comes up) Hold it right in front of Mable's feet so we can all see. (Mable goes down; hooked end of coat hanger appears behind 'glass') Boy, you do have special feet. You've got hooks on your feet to hold onto the rocks. That's why Mable's feet are so special. Thanks for the use of the magnifying glass.
(person with glass sits down again)

Mable: Well, back to the stream for me. Bye, bye.

Lucy Black Fly Larva: (from below) You don't need hooks. We go in the stream and we don't have hooks.

Willy: Who said that? I heard you, but I don't see you.

Lucy: I'm on this rock in the stream. Pull me out if you'd like to talk.

Willy: (reaches down for Lucy) My, you are on a rock. (Lucy appears) If you don't have hooks, how do you stay on that rock?

Lucy: I have something else very special at the end of my body.

Willy: Oh yeah? What?

Lucy: Well, get that magnifying glass and take a look.

Willy: (to person in audience with glass) Could you come up here again? Thank you. (when glass gets to stage, Lucy goes down and toilet plunger comes up) Wow, that is different from a hook! If I had that at the end of my body, I bet I'd stick to rocks too. Don't you think so audience? Thanks for the magnifying glass. (glass and plunger exit) Well, what do you think audience? I don't have anything special to help me hold on to things. Do you think I can live in a stream? Should I go back to the pond? Could you help me call Gregor? I can't walk back from here, and I'm too tired to fly.

Willy: (with audience) Gregor. Gregor. (Gregor comes back)

Gregor: What's wrong Willy? Don't you like living in a stream?

Willy: Well, the audience and I decided that I'm not really equipped to live in a stream, right audience?

Gregor: O.K. Climb on my back and I'll hop you home.

Willy: Thanks Gregor, and thanks for your advice audience. I'm sure I'll be happier and safer in the pond. Bye, bye.

FOLLOW-UP ACTIVITIES

1. Stream Mural
Have the children recall the stream animals that were found. The children can each draw and cut out an animal and, when everyone is done, place them in the appropriate part of the stream drawing.

2. History of a Local Stream
Have the children interview local residents or read in old newspapers about the history of a local stream (uses, floods, bridges, pollution) and write an article for the newspaper. If the stream is currently polluted, what can be done to clean it up?

3. Diary of a Stream
Visit a stream regularly with the children, and have them keep a journal of what they see.

Skills
Science Process: Observing, Inferring, Brainstorming, Communicating, Predicting, Comparing, Sorting and Classifying, Measuring, Recording Data

Integrated Curriculum: Art, Drama, Social Studies, Reading, Writing, Language Arts, Math

Suggested Reading For Children:

Bartlett, Margaret F. *The Clean Brook*. New York: Crowell, 1960. (y)

Buck, Margaret Waring. *In Ponds and Streams*. Nashville, TN: Abingdon Press, 1955. (o — identification help)

Headstrom, Richard. *Adventure With Freshwater Animals*. New York: J. B. Lippincott, 1964. (o — suggestions for observing and experimenting)

Life in Still Waters

A pond might be described as a shallow body of standing water in which enough sunlight reaches the bottom to allow rooted plants to grow from shore to shore. Another definition suggests relatively uniform water temperatures throughout, and a third describes a pond as small enough so that the wind does not have much impact on any of its shores.

Although a pond may have distinct and different habitats within it, all ponds share some common characteristics. Most important, of course, is that a pond contains water. As a life-giving substance, this water includes dissolved oxygen and other gases, plus nutrients that have flowed into or decomposed in it. The ability to adapt to this unique environment — to breathe, to move about, and to find nourishment — is what determines who lives in a pond.

Temperature also helps to determine what pond life can survive because it influences the rates of growth and **decomposition** as well as the amount of oxygen in the water (warmer water normally contains less oxygen). Annual changes in temperature are especially significant. Because water is heaviest at 39°F, surface water sinks when autumn temperatures cool it to 39°F and sinks again when spring temperatures warm it to 39°F. These fall and spring overturns are vital to insure the mixing and dispersal of oxygen and nutrients throughout the pond at least twice a year.

To appreciate the diversity in a pond, it is helpful to divide it into four distinct habitats: open water, the water's edge, the surface film, and the bottom. Open water is the area in the center of the pond where rooted plants do not extend to the surface of the water. Life consists of large, free-swimming animals, such as fish and turtles, and small microscopic plants and animals that drift suspended in the water.

The water's edge is where the land meets the water. Rooted plants of great variety are found growing here. Frogs, fish, insects, worms, snails, and a variety of microscopic animals find shelter among the plants.

The surface film is the habitat of many of the creatures that get their oxygen directly from the air, such as water striders, which walk on top of the film provided by the water's **surface tension**, and the mosquito **larvae**, which hang on the underside of it.

The pond bottom is the area of decomposition where bacteria help to recycle nutrients by attacking dead organisms that sink to the bottom. Many insects, especially those in their larval form, hide from predators here. Worms, crayfish, clams, and **nymphs** of mayflies, dragonflies, and damselflies burrow into the bottom mud.

There are many kinds of green plants in a pond that are not immediately evident. Fresh water algae are the most important, serving as food for snails, polliwogs, water fleas, and mosquito larvae. There are also **submergent**

plants whose leaves and flowers do not grow above the surface of the water, invisible to the shore-bound pond observer. They are often referred to as pondweeds. Many pondweeds also have floating leaves, such as water lilies. Then there are the **emergent** plants, which are easier to notice because their stems, leaves, and flowers rise out of the water. Plant life in a pond is as varied and fascinating as animal life, but children can rarely be diverted from their encounters with frogs, newts, and insects long enough to study it.

There are a number of **predators** in a pond. In both the larval and adult forms the dragonfly is predatory, as are the water strider, whirligig beetle, water boatman, and predaceous diving beetle, whose larvae are aptly named water tigers. Some of their favorite foods might include frog eggs, tadpoles, and insects. The red-spotted newt, as well as many species of frogs, turtles, and snakes, are all animals that eat other animals in the pond.

Pond-dwelling creatures have amazing adaptations to underwater life. Air-breathing adaptations take many forms. Gills serve to obtain air from the water. Fish gills are familiar, but dragonfly nymphs also have gills, along their rectal lining. While the damselfly's gills protrude like three feathers from the ends of its body, the stonefly's are tucked at the base of each leg. The whirligig beetle carries a bubble of air under its abdomen when it submerges, using this bubble as an oxygen tank. Some beetle larvae bore into plant stems to get their oxygen. Mosquitoes, in their pre-adult stage, and water scorpions breathe through tubes that penetrate the water's surface. Most salamanders use air that diffuses through their skin.

There are many methods for moving through the water. Turtles and beavers use webbed hind feet for paddling, and fish swim with swift, undulating movements. Some insects, like the predaceous diving beetles, have oar-like feet for paddling along. Most exotic are the dragonfly nymphs that draw water into their rectal gill chambers and then shoot it forcefully out of the anal pore, a kind of jet propulsion.

The pond is a special place, with suitable habitats for many kinds of plants and animals. A pond is also a beautiful place to sit in silence, to listen and to watch.

Suggested References:

Amos, William H. *The Life of the Pond.* New York: McGraw-Hill, 1967.

Andrews, William (ed.). *A Guide to the Study of Freshwater Ecology.* Englewood Cliffs, NJ: Prentice-Hall, 1972.

Caduto, Michael J. *Pond and Brook: A Guide to Nature Study in Freshwater Environments.* Englewood Cliffs, NJ: Prentice-Hall, 1985.

Coker, Robert E. *Stream, Lakes, Ponds.* New York: Harper and Row, 1968.

Grave, Eric V. *Discover the Invisible: A Naturalist's Guide to Using the Microscope.* Englewood Cliffs, NJ: Prentice-Hall, 1984.

Read, George K., and Herbert S. Zim. *Pond Life.* New York: Golden Press, 1967.

Focus: *The pond is composed of different habitats, each of which hosts a number of creatures especially adapted to live there.*

ACTIVITIES	MATERIALS
Initial Question: What problems would you have living in a pond?	

LIFE IN A POND PUPPET SHOW

Objective: To introduce the idea that pond creatures must have special adaptations to survive in the pond.

Perform, or have children perform, the puppet show. Discuss the information conveyed.

Materials:
- *script, p.115*
- *puppets*

PICTURE A POND WITH YOUR EARS

Objective: To become aware of the variety of sounds around a pond.

Upon arrival at the pond, all should sit quietly together, close their eyes, and concentrate on listening. Hold up one finger for each different sound heard. When most children have five fingers up, tell them to open their eyes. Discuss the sounds, identify them if you wish, and why they were or were not typical pond sounds. Which sound did they like the most? the least?

HABITATS OF THE POND

Objective: To identify some habitats found within a pond.

Ask the children to look at the pond and think about different habitats in the pond and the special features of each. Discuss briefly the differences among the surface film, the open water, the water's edge, and the bottom.

POKING AROUND IN THE POND

Objective: To have a good time observing and collecting some pond creatures.

Start out by carefully explaining your "oks" and "not-oks" at the pond. Give one dishpan to each group of children and instruct them to fill it with pond water. Then, within your preset limits, they should find, observe, and possibly collect pond animals from each of the 4 habitats and put them in the dishpan. Watch to see if the collected creatures stay on the surface, swim through the water, or walk along the bottom. Using a *Pond Life* guide, you and the children could try to identify what was collected. Older children could pair up, choose a specimen, place it in a small water-filled container and research its identity on their own.

Materials:
- *plastic dishpans* light colored
- *strainers*
- *nets*
- *hand lenses*
- *small plastic containers* (e.g., cottage cheese containers)
- *copies of Pond Life* from the Golden Nature Guide Series

POND PANTOMIME

Objective: To learn through close observation, and to translate that observation into personal experience.

The children should look closely at their specimens to see what parts of the animals' bodies are moving and why? to propel themselves? to eat? to breathe? Then each child chooses an animal and imitates its motions. The others guess what it is by name or by pointing to the correct one in the dishpan. Which pond habitat does each pantomimed animal spend most of its time in, and why? End the activity with a special release ceremony so all animals are returned safely to the water.

SHARING CIRCLE

Objective: To summarize and personalize each child's pond experience.

Sit together in a circle. Each child should complete the sentence: "I would (or would not) like to live in a pond because . . ."

- *collected animals*

LIFE IN A POND PUPPET SHOW

Characters: Mother
Polly
Dream Fairy
Willy Water Strider
Bengie the Whirligig Beetle
Dana Damselfly Nymph
Pond Polly (with all her pond
    adaptations)

Mother: Polly, where are you going?

Polly: Out to the pond, of course. I need a quick swim before bedtime.

Mother: But Polly, you just came in from your after dinner swim. In fact, you've been doing nothing but swimming in the pond all day. I think you've had enough.

Polly: But, Mom . . .

Mother: No 'buts,' 'how comes,' or 'that's not fair!' It's your bedtime anyhow so hop to it.
(mother leaves)

Polly: Hop to it. I wish I were a frog so I could hop to the pond. Or maybe I'd like to be one of those little bugs that swim about the pond all day. I'd be anything if I could spend my whole life in the pond. Well, I may as well get to sleep. The sooner I fall asleep, the sooner I'll be able to wake up and go to the pond.
(falls asleep; Dream Fairy enters)

Dream Fairy: As Expert on Dreams, I think it'd be good
To make sure you know all that you should.
For life in a pond is not all it may seem
As you will find out in this very next dream.
(Dream Fairy leaves; dream begins)

Polly: Oh, I'm so happy. My mother said I could live in the pond forever. I don't have to even bother packing a suitcase. I'll just go in my bathing suit.
(Willy Water Strider appears)

Willy Water Strider: Wait a minute Polly. I think you need more than a bathing suit.

Polly: Who are you?

Willy: I'm Willy the Water Strider.

Polly: Oh, of course. I've seen you skimming around right on top of the water. Maybe one day I'll get around in the water as well as you. I guess it just takes lots of practice.

Willy: It takes more than practice and more than just a bathing suit. We water insects are well equipped for life in a pond.

Polly: Well, what do I need to be well equipped?

Willy: The first thing you've got to change is that figure of yours.

Polly: My figure! Mother says I'm skinny now, but I'll fill out later.

Willy: Yes, but you won't fill out in the right places. You've got to have a shape like mine and all the other swimmers of the pond.

Polly: You mean shaped like a boat?

Willy: Well, we call it streamlined, but yes, it is rather like a boat. Helps us move through the water quickly. Of course, our legs are another big help.

Polly: You do have an awful lot of them. And they're nice and long, like paddles.

Willy: Actually, we only use four of them for moving. We push with the middle two and steer with the last two.

Polly: Well, I could push with my hands and steer with my feet.

Willy: But then what would you use to capture your food with? That's what we use our two front legs for.

Polly: Well, I could get my dad's two canoe paddles and tie them to my waist so I . . .

Willy: Wait a minute, I'm not finished. There's still other things that contribute to my success. Look very closely at my legs and body. What do you see?

Polly: Why, you're all covered with little hairs. They must get in your way. Should I shave them off for you?

Willy: No! Why those hairs are the secret to my success, and many other water bugs as well. They stop us from getting too wet and heavy. Why, if it weren't for them, we'd sink. They also help us capture bubbles of air so we can breathe under water.

Polly: Breathe under water! I never even thought of that. I suppose I could get a snorkel.

Willy: Before you get anything, Polly, maybe you should meet some of the other water bugs and see what kind of equipment they have.

Polly: But what more could I need? You've told me . . .
(Willy disappears; Bengie the Whirligig Beetle pops up)

Polly: Ahh, who are you?

Bengie the Whirligig Beetle: Bengie the Beetle — the Whirligig Beetle that is.

Polly: Oh, you're one of those little bugs that go whirling about the pond like bumper cars — only you never bump into one another.

Bengie: That's because of these two antennae on our heads. They feel all the tiny waves in the water so we know where we can and cannot go.

Polly: I guess you need antennae because your eyes are so weird. No offense, but it looks like they're split in half.

Bengie: They are, but for good reason. We can look up from the water with one half of the eye and down into the water with the other half.

Polly: Wow, even Willy couldn't do that. Do you have a hairy body like Willy?

Bengie: Oh yes. Capture an air bubble and under I go.
(Bengie disappears)

Polly: Oh, this is very depressing. I don't have anything I need.
(Dana the Damselfly Nymph appears)

Dana Damselfly Nymph: Cheer up. You don't need hairs to capture air bubbles to breathe under water.

Polly: Now, who are you? This dream is getting awfully crowded.

Dana: I'm Dana Damselfly Nymph.

Polly: Well, if you're a fly, what do you know about breathing under water. And what's a nymph anyway?

Dana: Well, before I turn into a dainty damselfly flittering *above* the pond, I live *in* the pond, breathing *under* the water. And while I live underwater, I'm called a nymph.

Polly: And don't you have tiny hairs to capture air bubbles?

Dana: I do not.

Polly: Then I *could* do it without hairs.

Dana: Sure you could. As long as you have gills you can . . .

Polly: Wait a minute. Did you say gills?

Dana: Yes, what do you think these tails at the end of my body are for — wagging?

Polly: I thought they were just tails.

Dana: These tails have gills.

Polly: You mean like fish gills?

Dana: Kind of like fish gills. I couldn't breathe under water without them. Speaking of under water, I better get back there.
(Dana disappears)

Polly: Boy, things sure come and go quickly around . . .
(Willy appears)

Willy: Well, Polly, have you figured out everything you need to live in the pond?

Polly: I don't know. There's so much to remember.

Willy: I thought you'd say that, so I made a little model for you. Once you look like this, then you can live in the pond.
(Willy disappears; Pond Polly appears)

Polly: Ahhh (Polly faints, then wakes up) What a nightmare I just had. I've had bad dreams before with monsters, but never one where I was the monster. At least it taught me something. Swimming in a pond is one thing, but living there, forget it! Bye, bye everyone.

FOLLOW-UP ACTIVITIES

1. A Pond Aquarium

Set up a pond aquarium with plants, animals, and water from a nearby pond. Make sure the water is kept cool and food is replenished or return the animals to the pond within three days. Watch to see what eats what and which are most active. Keep a record.

2. Pond Mural

Have the children make a pond mural with animals drawn in the appropriate pond habitats.

3. A Summer Day

Suggest that the children pretend they are pond creatures and have them write about a summer day.

4. A Closer Look

Use microscopes to see plankton, the smallest organisms in the pond.

Skills

Science Process: Observing, Inferring, Brainstorming, Communicating, Comparing, Sorting and Classifying, Experimenting, Recording Data

Integrated Curriculum: Art, Drama, Reading, Writing, Language Arts

Suggested Reading For Children:

Buck, Margaret Waring. *In Ponds and Streams.* Nashville, TN: Abingdon Press, 1955. (o — identification help)

Carrick, Carol and Donald Carrick. *The Pond.* New York: MacMillan, 1970. (y — story format)

Gorvett, Jean. *Life in Ponds.* New York: American Heritage Press, 1970. (o)

Hoffman, Melita. *A Trip to the Pond: An Adventure in Nature.* Garden City, NY: Doubleday, 1966. (o — what lives in ponds)

Pringle, Laurence P. *Waterplants.* New York: Crowell, 1975. (o)

Schwartz, George I. *Life in a Drop of Water.* Garden City, NY: Natural History Press, 1970. (y/o)

Waters, John F. *Neighborhood Puddle.* New York: Frederick Warne, 1971. (o — detailed)

CHAPTER III — CYCLES

When studying the natural world, it soon becomes apparent that life has few clear-cut beginnings and endings, but rather passes through stages that are part of a continuing cycle. A leaf bud contains the beginning of new life, but it is also the final product of a summer's growth. A flower dies, leaving seeds to carry on.

The cycles of all living organisms reflect the seasonal cycles of their surroundings. The stages of their lives are often timed to coincide appropriately with the weather; a resting stage during harsh seasons, an active stage at times when there's enough food and warmth to survive. Many moths and butterflies survive the winter in the egg stage, the tiny caterpillars programmed to emerge when tender new leaves unfurl. The caterpillars and their food are synchronized to assure adequate nourishment for the insect's important growth stage.

The Cycles concept concentrates on the seasonal and life cycles of trees, insects, flowers, and birds; a pair of workshops on each of these topics emphasizes the message of ongoing change.

Surviving the Seasons in Stages

Insects are perhaps the most successful form of animal life on this planet. Related to spiders and lobsters, they are **arthropods** with external skeletons and jointed legs, but belong to a separate class, Insecta.

There are many reasons why insects have endured and survived through 300 million years of climatic and habitat changes. Their small size, the ability of most to fly, the wide variety of foods they can eat, and the rapidity with which new generations are produced all have contributed to their continued existence. But there is one especially effective strategy that insects have developed to a high degree of perfection: **metamorphosis**. Metamorphosis describes the transformation process by which an insect proceeds from the egg stage to that of mature adult. There are two forms of metamorphosis: incomplete and complete.

Incomplete metamorphosis consists of three stages: egg, **nymph**, and adult. The newly hatched insect, or nymph, usually resembles the adult, but it is smaller, and among winged insects, the nymphs are wingless. As it grows it molts, usually several times, shedding the exterior skeleton after having grown a new, larger one underneath it. Many nymphs hatch from eggs deposited in the water and spend their whole nymphal stage feeding beneath the surface and breathing with gills. Dragonflies and damselflies are examples of this. Nymphs of many aquatic species, when ready to emerge as adults, crawl out of the water, split their skins for the last time, and start breathing in the air as winged adults. Insects having this type of life cycle (egg, nymph, adult) include dragonflies, damselflies, bugs, mayflies, grasshoppers, and cicadas.

About 87 percent of all the known insect species go through **complete metamorphosis**, including moths, butterflies, bees, wasps, ants, beetles, and flies. This life cycle consists of four stages: egg, **larva**, **pupa**, and adult. The egg hatches into a larva, which does not resemble the adult. It often lives in a different habitat from its adult stage and usually has chewing mouthparts even though as an adult it may not. In addition, it lacks its parents' compound eyes. Larvae have been given several names: fly — maggot; beetle — grub; butterfly and moth —

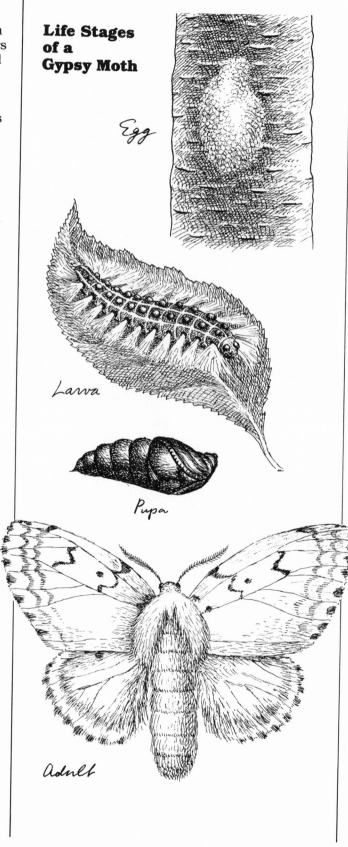

Life Stages of a Gypsy Moth

Egg

Larva

Pupa

Adult

caterpillar. During this stage the insect feeds. It is only during this stage that actual growth occurs. As it increases in size, the number of cells in the body does not increase, they merely become larger. Thus the larva grows, molts several times, and having completed its growth, stops feeding. At this point it enters a resting state called the pupa. It may spin a silken covering, such as the cocoon of a moth, to house itself, or, as in the **chrysalis** of a butterfly that has shed its outer caterpillar coat, the pupa may be protected by nothing but a thin membrane. When this transformation occurs, the larval cells begin to die and clusters of adult cells, inactive up to this point, are stimulated by hormones into growth. During the pupal stage the larval tissues are torn down and slowly rebuilt into organs more suited to adult life. Essentially the body is reorganized: wings develop, reproductive organs are formed, mouthparts change, and most of the muscular system is transformed. The adult then emerges from the pupal case ready to reproduce.

Metamorphosis greatly contributes to insect survival because it allows flexibility to deal with temperature extremes, variable food supplies, droughts, and other harsh conditions. Eggs are often encased in hard coats that can withstand extreme cold or dryness, and emergence is usually delayed until the proper conditions are available. The larval stage of any given insect is timed and located to coincide with the appropriate food supply. Colorado potato beetle larvae hatch out when and where the succulent potato leaves are ready to eat, monarch caterpillars emerge a few days after their eggs are laid onto tasty milkweed leaves. For many insects, it is in the pupal stage that they are best able to survive extreme conditions, so many insects overwinter in a pupa or chrysalis. Finally, the adult stage of insects has but one mission, to make sure eggs are laid for the next generation so the species will survive. Some adults, such as stoneflies and mayflies, live a very short time and do not even have eating mouthparts. They mate, lay eggs, and die. Conversely, in many species of beetles, the adult life is longer than the larval stage, and the adult consumes more food than the larva.

Insect life cycles are adapted to take advantage of this earth's resources and habitats, while expending a minimum of energy to do so. Metamorphosis is one of the reasons why they are so successful.

Suggested References:

Barron, D. J., and R. E. White. *A Field Guide to the Insects of America North of Mexico.* Boston, MA: Houghton Mifflin, 1970.

Farb, Peter. *The Insects.* New York: Time-Life Books, 1968.

Hutchins, Ross E. *Insects.* Englewood Cliffs, NJ: Prentice-Hall, 1966.

Kohl, Judith. *A View from the Oak: The Private Worlds of Other Creatures.* San Francisco: Sierra Club, 1977.

Stokes, Donald W. *A Guide to Observing Insect Lives.* Boston, MA: Little, Brown, 1983.

Teal, Edwin Way. *The Strange Lives of Familiar Insects.* New York: Dodd, Mead and Co., 1962.

INSECT LIFE CYCLES

Focus: *Insects go through different stages as they grow from egg to adult. The stages of their life cycles are timed to fit in with seasonal cycles.*

ACTIVITIES	MATERIALS
Initial Question: What do you know about the stages of insects as they grow up?	

PUPPET SHOW

Objective: To introduce complete and incomplete metamorphosis.

Give the puppet show. Discuss and compare how the grasshopper and the butterfly grew to be adults. Using a chart showing the various stages, discuss complete and incomplete metamorphosis. Point out that the "eating stage" of the insect coincides with the availability of food, usually in warm weather.

Materials:
- *script, p. 124*
- *puppets*
- *chart* showing stages of complete and incomplete metamorphosis

METAMORPHOSIS PUZZLE

Objective: To emphasize the two main life cycles followed by insects.

Give each child an insect puzzle piece that portrays one stage in the life cycle of some insect. Ask the children to look for others whose puzzle pieces fit with theirs. When they've completed the puzzle, review incomplete and complete metamorphosis. To make it more challenging for older children, make puzzles of different kinds of insects in their various life stages.

Materials:
- *insect puzzle pieces* 3-piece incomplete metamorphosis puzzles and 4-piece complete metamorphosis puzzles, enough for one puzzle piece per child

DATE A MATE

Objective: To show how efficiently some insects, such as moths and butterflies, find their mates through a highly developed sense of smell.

Note: Explain that when insects reach their adult stage, their most important mission is to lay eggs so there will be a new generation. Being small, and often with very few weeks as adults, they must find their mates quickly. Some use their sense of smell.

Everyone forms a circle. Choose up to half the group (should be an even number) to go inside the circle. The outsiders form the boundary. The insiders are male and female moths. Blindfold half the insiders and give each a scented object. These are the males who will identify their partners through their sense of smell. Give each remaining insider a duplicate scented object. These are the females who will be found by their scents. The "females" position themselves in *one* place within the circle. The blindfolded "males" try to find the "female" who has the same scented object as they. When successful, the pair joins the outer circle. At the end, discuss other means insects use to recognize mates (sound, like crickets; light signals, like fireflies).

Materials:
- *blindfolds*
- *scented objects* 2 of each kind

ACTIVITIES	MATERIALS

INSECT HUNT

Objective: To get a firsthand look at insects in the different stages of their life cycles.

- pencils
- Insect Stages Search cards

Divide into small groups and give each a pencil and an Insect Stages Search card with the following directions on it:

- Look for adult: butterflies/moths; grasshoppers; crickets; bees; ants; flies; beetles; etc.
- Look for cocoons or pupa cases
- Look for nymphs: grasshoppers without wings; small earwigs; wingless leaf hoppers; dragonfly nymphs in the water; others
- Look for larval stages: fuzzy caterpillars; inchworms; caterpillars with interesting patterns or colors; camouflaged larvae; leaves eaten by larvae
- Look for eggs (often on underside of green leaves) or insects laying eggs

The groups should visit at least three different areas (e.g., playground, field, under trees, hedgerow, building ledges) to conduct their search. Check off findings. Older children should record some specific details: where found, special characteristics, what it was doing. Possibly use a Field Guide to identify a few.

ZAP

Objective: To review the stages in complete metamorphosis.

- Disc with complete metamorphosis insect stages drawn on it, and spinner attached at the center of it

(Grades K-2) The children should be in a group about 10 feet away from the leader. Leader spins to select an insect stage. Children pantomime that stage, moving toward, leader if it's a moving stage. When the leader says Zap, the children should stop (if they are moving) and call out what the next stage would be. Repeat the game a few times.

(Grades 3-6) The children should be in a group about 15 feet away from the leader. The leader spins to select an insect stage. The children quickly pantomime that stage, remaining in place if it's an immobile stage, moving toward the leader if it's a mobile stage. After a few seconds, the leader says Zap, and the children pantomime the next stage of metamorphosis, remaining in place if immobile stage, moving toward leader if mobile stage. Repeat the game until most children reach the leader.

SHARING CIRCLE

Objective: To consider the differences among the various stages in an insect's life cycle.

Sitting in a circle, have each person take a turn completing the following sentence. "If I were an insect, I would like to be a _____ (egg, larva, pupa, nymph, adult) because . . ."

INSECT LIFE CYCLES PUPPET SHOW

Characters:
Grasshopper Egg
Grasshopper Nymph
Grasshopper Adult
Butterfly Egg
Butterfly Caterpillar
Pupa Case, attached to a plant
Butterfly Adult
Insect Fairy

Grasshopper Egg: Hey, you up there. Hey, little egg. I see you. Can't hide from me. What's it like being a leaf egg?

Butterfly Egg: I'm no leaf egg. I'm a butterfly egg. I was just placed on this leaf by my mother butterfly. Who are you, anyway?

Grasshopper Egg: I'm a grasshopper egg. Pretty soon I'll be hopping circles around you.

Butterfly Egg: Is that so? While you're hopping in circles, I'll be flying through the air over fields and ponds.

Grasshopper Egg: You flying? I can't believe that. No way is there room for wings inside your egg.

Butterfly Egg: You'll see. I'll be flying . . .

Grasshopper Egg: Oh my, oh my goodness. I think I'm about to be born as a grasshopper. Oh, oh. (egg goes down; grasshopper nymph appears) See that? I am a grasshopper. I told you I'd be hopping circles around you.

Butterfly Egg: Not for long. I think my time has come too. I think I'm about to become a butterfly! Oh, oh (egg goes down; caterpillar appears) See that, I am a . . . Oh no, I'm not a butterfly.

Grasshopper Nymph: Ah ha ha ha! Why you're a caterpillar. Where'd you get the idea that you'd be a butterfly? You better get used to crawling, rather than dream about flying. (leaves)

Caterpillar: Oh, (crying) I'm so upset. I know I was supposed to be a butterfly, I just know it. (Fairy enters)

Insect Fairy: Stop crying little caterpillar. You're just going to get that leaf all soggy and not at all good for eating.

Caterpillar: Who are you?

Fairy: I'm the Insect Fairy. I look after all the insects of the earth. Please stop crying or everyone will think I'm not doing my job.

Caterpillar: Well, you're not doing your job. I was supposed to be a butterfly and look at me. I'm nothing but a caterpillar.

Fairy: Stop worrying. You'll turn into a butterfly and be able to fly, but you need to have patience, and you need to eat a lot. You know, your mother laid the egg you were in on just the right kind of plant for you to eat. So start chewing!

Caterpillar: Patience! Why do I have to wait so long? That grasshopper went straight from an egg to a full grown grasshopper.

Fairy: First of all, you're different from a grasshopper, and second of all, she's not a full grown grasshopper.

Caterpillar: What do you mean? I saw her go hopping. . .

Fairy: I know she looks like a full grown grasshopper, but if you had looked a little more closely instead of wetting your eyes with tears you'd have seen she doesn't have wings.

Caterpillar: What! No wings?

Fairy: That's right. Full grown adult grasshoppers all have wings. That little grasshopper is just a nymph. She looks like an adult, but has not yet grown her wings.

Caterpillar: What did you call her, a nymph? Ha, ha, that's a good one. I'd rather be a caterpillar than a nymph any day.

Fairy: Well, one day you'll be a butterfly. So no more tears. (leaves)

Caterpillar: Boy, I wish that grasshopper would come back here. She thinks she's so grown up and adult. Wait 'til I tell her she's nothing but a nymph! (Nymph appears)

Grasshopper Nymph: Hi, little caterpillar. Still waiting to turn into a big butterfly?

Caterpillar: As a matter of fact, I am waiting to turn into an adult. If you took time to look at yourself, you'd notice *you are too.*

Grasshopper Nymph: What do you mean *I am too?* I already am an adult grasshopper, aren't I audience? (pause for response)

Caterpillar: No. Adult grasshoppers have wings. You haven't grown your wings yet, so you're just a nymph. Nothing but a little grasshopper nymph. But I can't stand around talking, I have to keep eating. Bye. (caterpillar leaves)

Grass-hopper Nymph:	She's right. I don't have any wings yet. I'm not a full grown grasshopper. I am just a nymph. I guess I better be on my way too. It'll be a while before I'm big enough to get my wings. (grasshopper nymph leaves; grasshopper with wings appears; plant with pupa case hanging from it appears also)
Grass-hopper Adult:	I've been feeding here for almost a month, and I keep looking for that caterpillar, but I can't find her anywhere. Do any of you see her? (Butterfly appears)
Butterfly:	Here I am, here I am.
Grass-hopper:	Where did you come from?
Butterfly:	I came out of this pupa case that's hanging from the leaf.
Grass-hopper:	But when I saw you last, you were a caterpillar.
Butterfly:	Well, when I grew to be big enough and old enough, I split my caterpillar skin and this pupa case was underneath it. The whole time you were looking for me, I was right there inside the case changing from a caterpillar to a butterfly. Just before you got here this morning, I came out as a full grown butterfly.
Grass-hopper:	So you were right. I'm sorry I didn't believe you.
Butterfly:	And I'm sorry I called you a silly nymph. I see you already have your wings.
Grass-hopper:	Oh yes. It took a few more skin sheddings and then I found I had a full set of wings.
Butterfly:	You know Grasshopper, I think it's amazing that we're both grown-ups now, we both can fly, but we grew up in such different ways. I changed completely and you just kept changing a little at a time.
Grass-hopper:	Yup, you're right. And I guess we both better think about finding a good place to lay eggs before winter. Maybe next summer our kids will have the same argument we had. That would be funny. See you around.
Butterfly:	I'll be off too. Got to find the right kind of plant to lay my eggs on, just like my mother did. Bye.

FOLLOW-UP ACTIVITIES

1. Monarch Butterflies
Have the children research the life cycles of monarch butterflies and find out where they spend the winter. How far do they fly?

2. Cocoon Watch
Keep a cocoon in a large jar with moistened cloth in the bottom of it and air holes in the lid. Put the jar in a cool, dimly lit place. Watch to see what emerges.

Note: The insect will probably emerge too early in the season to survive by itself outdoors. Discuss this before deciding to keep one.

3. Creative Writing
Invite the children to write a story about what it would be like to go through metamorphosis.

Skills

Science Process: Observing, Inferring, Brainstorming, Communicating, Comparing, Sorting and Classifying, Experimenting, Recording Data

Integrated Curriculum: Drama, Social Studies, Reading, Writing, Language Arts, Math

Suggested Reading For Children:

Armour, Richard. *Insects All Around Us.* New York: McGraw-Hill, 1981. (y/o — informative poems about 10 insects)

Green, Ivah, and George A. Smith. *Hatch and Grow; Life Stories of Familiar Insects in Close-up Photos.* New York: Abelard-Schuman, 1967. (o — good reference)

Johnson, Sylvia A. *Ladybugs.* Minneapolis, MN: Lerner Publications, 1983. (o — excellent photos)

————. *Mantises.* Minneapolis, MN: Lerner Publications, 1984. (o — excellent photos and information)

Mari, Iela, and Enzo Mari. *The Apple and the Moth.* New York: Pantheon, 1970. (y — picture book, moth life cycle)

McClung, Robert. *Green Darner: The Story of a Dragonfly.* New York: Morrow, 1956. (y)

Oxford Scientific Films. *The Butterfly Cycle.* New York: Putnam, 1977.

————. *Mosquitoes.* New York: G.P. Putnam's Sons, 1982. (y/o — excellent photos of mosquito life cycle)

Samis, Kathy. *The Beginning Knowledge Book of Butterflies.* New York: MacMillan, 1965. (y — life cycle pictures)

Selsam, Millicent E. *The Harlequin Moth: Its Life History.* New York: Morrow, 1975. (o — great metamorphosis photos)

Seymour, Peter. *Insects: A Close Up Look.* New York: MacMillan, 1984. (y/o — pop-up book)

Tarrant, Graham. *Butterflies.* New York: Putnam, 1983. (y — pop-up book)

The Sum of Many Parts

"A tree is a woody plant with a trunk." Such a simple definition hardly gives credit to this complex and beautiful creation. Suppose you read in the newspaper that in this energy conscious period someone had invented a machine that was run by sun energy, had an automatic thermostat and humidifier, manufactured its own food out of water and carbon dioxide, was powerful enough to split a rock or support tons of weight, produced oxygen, water, food, and fuel and, rather than pollute the air, actually cleansed and beautified its surroundings. Incredible? Yet this too is an accurate description of a tree.

The parts of a tree are familiar to most of us, but their functions are worth mentioning. The trunk's main function is to support the branches and twigs, which in turn expose the crown of leaves to the sunlight. The trunk also contains the conductive cells that transport water and minerals from the roots upward, and food from the leaves downward. The upward pull of water has been estimated as 100 times more efficient than the best suction pump ever made.

These water and food channels are called the **xylem** and the **phloem** respectively. Both are added to each year by a tiny ring of growth cells just inside the bark called the **cambium** layer. The phloem cells form on the outer edge of the cambium layer, close to where leaf stems can pass on the sugars manufactured by the leaves. The xylem cells form on the inside of the cambium layer and are what we commonly call wood; new active cells are referred to as sapwood, old cells nearer the center of the tree become the heartwood. The age rings one counts in tree stumps are the xylem growth layers of the cambium. The lighter colored ring shows the fast spring growth that consists of large, thinner-walled cells and the neighboring darker ring shows the smaller, thicker-walled cells of summer when growth is slower. The width of the annual rings in a stump tell the history of good times and bad times: the wider the ring, the greater the growth that year.

The roots of a tree are perhaps its most aggressive, persistent part. Roots can split rocks, or inch their way along cliffs to find life-giving soil. It has been calculated that a growing root three inches wide and four feet long can lift fifty tons. The function of roots is to anchor and support the tree and to absorb water and minerals from surrounding soil. Most **conifers**, or evergreen trees, have a shallow, fibrous root system parallel to the surface of the ground. Many **deciduous** trees (those that lose their

Phloem

Cambium
(invisible to the naked eye)

Xylem

leaves at the end of the growing season), in addition to a spreading root system, have a long, perpendicular taproot. Notice which trees topple first in gale winds. They are the ones with shallow root systems. The actual absorption of water and minerals is accomplished by miles of tiny root hairs, which keep growing anew just behind the tip of the constantly elongating root.

Most picturesque, perhaps, are the leaves or needles of a tree. They manufacture food for the entire tree, converting water and carbon dioxide to sugars and starches in the presence of chlorophyll and sunlight. This process is called **photosynthesis**, vital to the tree itself, and important to all of life as a source of oxygen and water. (See information for Variations On a Leaf, p. 174). Oxygen is released as a by-product of photosynthesis, and more than 99 percent of the water drawn up into the tree is **transpired** out through the leaves. A giant oak may transpire 300 gallons of water per day, and one source claims that a full grown birch could give off 900 gallons of water on a hot summer day.

Leaves are also adapted to protect the tree against dryness and extreme cold. The greatest danger to trees in winter is drying out — ground water is congealed into frost and not readily available through root hairs to the tree. If deciduous leaves continued to transpire in winter, the tree would quickly dehydrate. Deciduous trees prevent this water loss by forming a waterproof, corky layer where each leaf is attached to the twig. When the leaf falls off, this **abscission layer** serves as a waterproof, disease-resistant patch. Deciduous trees in the north must therefore accomplish most of their growth and seed production within the few warm months. Conifer needles, on the other hand, can remain attached year-round as they have less surface area through which to lose moisture and are covered with a waxy substance that greatly

retards moisture loss. Also, they are filled with a resinous substance that resists freezing and the subsequent breakdown of cells.

Tree shapes are an excellent means of identification, but they are also an adaptive answer to certain of the tree's needs. Most important is that the maximum amount of leaf surface be exposed to direct sunlight so photosynthesis can take place. A tree that is closed in on one side by other trees will have the longest branches and a greater number of leaves on the open sunlit side. A tree growing in a field will reach out in all directions. Plantation pine trees planted in close rows will have dead or dying branches for most of the length of their trunks because the lower branches and needles receive little sunlight. Paper birch trees survive almost to the edge of the Arctic tundra because of their supple trunks and light crowns of foliage, which can bend and whip in high winds without breaking.

A tree is a magnificent combination of productive efficiency and beauty. A better understanding of how they function can only increase our respect and awe, and our appreciation for their existence.

Suggested References:

Brockman, Frank C. *Trees of North America*. New York: Golden Press, 1968.

Harlow, William M. *Trees of the Eastern and Central U.S. and Canada*. New York: Dover Publications, 1957.

Hutchins, Ross E. *This Is A Tree*. New York: Dodd, Mead, 1964.

Jackson, James. *The Biography of a Tree*. Middle Village, NY: Jonathan David Publishers, 1979.

Raven, Evert and Curtis, *Biology of Plants* (3rd ed.). New York: Worth Publishers, 1981.

Focus: *A tree is the sum of many parts, each designed to perform a necessary function within the tree's life and within its seasonal cycles.*

ACTIVITIES

MATERIALS

Initial Question: How do trees change from season to season?

THE SUM OF MANY PARTS

Objective: To illustrate how different parts of a tree function.

Introduce a young sapling, pass around previously collected parts of a tree, or use pictures to discuss characteristics and functions of the parts of a tree.

- *parts of a tree*
  leaf, twig, bark, log showing annual rings, a root, or
- *pictures of tree parts*

DRESS A TREE

Objective: To review the parts of a tree and their roles.

Place a 2" diameter vertical stick in front of the children. Explain that this represents a skeleton tree that needs dressing. Give each child a card with a tree part written on it: roots, bark, twig, leaf, bud, flower, fruit, or nut (or for younger children, a picture of a tree part). The children should make their assigned tree parts and, when called upon, take them to the tree skeleton and help dress the tree. As they place their part on the tree, they should tell what function it serves.

- *cards — each with a tree part written on it*
- *skeleton tree (a 2 inch diameter stick)*
- *construction paper*
- *cloth scraps*
- *pipe cleaners*
- *styrofoam scraps*
- *cardboard*
- *scissors, glue, tape*
- *yarn or string scraps*

REACH OUT AND TOUCH

Objective: To get to know a tree using senses other than eyesight.

The group should split into pairs and gather at Point X. Each pair receives a blindfold. The sighted partner carefully leads the blindfolded partner to a tree and asks the blindfolded partner some questions to help guide the exploration. Can you reach around the tree? feel any branches? describe the texture of the bark? find the roots? touch a leaf? Both return, blindfold still on, to Point X. Remove the blindfold and have the partner that was blindfolded find the touched tree. Switch roles — sighted person becomes blindfolded — and repeat the activity.

- *blindfolds*

ACTIVITIES	MATERIALS

MEET A TREE QUESTIONNAIRE

Objective: To familiarize children with a particular tree.

Divide the children into small groups and give each a Meet a Tree questionnaire:

- In what sort of habitat or surroundings is your tree growing?
- Stand back from your tree. What is its shape?
- Does your tree have seeds, nuts, fruits, cones?
- Look at the bark. Notice color, texture, injuries. Make a bark rubbing.
- Can you find a leaf on or under the tree? Make a rubbing of it or tape one to your questionnaire.
- What kinds of plants are growing under or on your tree (lichens, mosses, fungi, vines, other)?
- Look for signs of animals, insects, and birds on your tree. Any holes leading under the tree? in the tree itself?
- Estimate the tree's height by having someone of known height stand next to the tree and estimate how many times that person's height the tree is. Estimate the circumference around the trunk.
- Is your tree healthy? How do you know?

Send them off to choose a tree and answer the questions. Compare findings when all have finished. Each child should ask the tree a question. Record the questions for use in follow-up activity.

Note: Simplify the questionnaire for younger children. Consider sending a leader with each group.

Materials:
- *clipboards or cardboard*
- *pencils*
- *crayon*
- *paper* for bark rubbing
- *questionnaire*

TREE POEM

Objective: To see a tree from different perspectives and record its image in a poem.

Divide the children into small groups. Designate one person in each group to be the secretary with paper and pencil. The group may use its adopted tree or may choose a new tree. At the tree each person should be placed at a different distance from the tree (20 feet away, 5 feet away, under it looking up, nose to the bark, arms around it). After a moment's study, each person should give 3 words to describe the tree from his or her perspective, and the secretary should write them down. The group then creates a poem about its tree, using all the adjectives. Groups share poems, either introducing the tree or making the other groups find it from the description.

Materials:
- *clipboards or cardboard*
- *paper*
- *pencils*

FOLLOW-UP ACTIVITIES

1. Tree Questions
Help the children try to find out answers to their questions. Answers could uncover some interesting local history or lead to identification skills.

2. Stay in Touch
Encourage the children to visit their tree in different seasons and to notice how it changes.

3. Bring Back the Trees
Initiate a project to plant some trees where they might give shelter to people or animals, and care for them.

4. What a Tree Might See
Have the children pretend to be trees. They should write a journal describing the goings-on they might see in, under, or around them during the four seasons of the year. Draw pictures to illustrate.

Skills

Science Process: Observing, Inferring, Brainstorming, Communicating, Comparing, Sorting and Classifying, Measuring, Recording Data

Integrated Curriculum: Art, Social Studies, Reading, Writing, Language Arts, Math

Suggested Reading For Children:

Brandt, Keith. *Discovering Trees*. Mahwah, NJ: Troll Associates, 1982. (y — cycles, nice illustrations)

Garelick, May. *The Tremendous Tree Book*. New York: Four Winds Press, 1979. (y — colorful, basic)

Gibbons, Gail. *The Seasons of Arnold's Apple Tree*. San Diego, CA: Harcourt Brace Jovanovich, 1984. (y — story and pictures)

Mabey, Richard. *Oak and Company*. New York: Greenwillow Books, 1983. (y/o — nice illustrations)

Selsam, Millicent E. *Maple Tree*. New York: Morrow, 1968. (y/o — photographs)

Where Do the Birds Go and Why?

Konkaree! Konkaree! A red-winged blackbird announces his return in early spring. In August hundreds of swallows line up on telephone wires, the signal that soon they will all be gone. Since people first began watching birds they have wondered about their disappearance in the fall and their return in the spring.

How and why did migration originate? There are many theories about this. Most agree that the glacial periods affected migratory habits and routes, but exactly when, and precisely what combination of environmental, climatic, or ecological factors initially motivated migration, remains a mystery.

One theory, advanced by many, proposes that the ancestors of migratory birds lived and nested on what is now their wintering range. When the climate and environment became suitable further north, they gradually moved northward to nest, where there was less competition for space and food, returning to their southern ancestral homes for the winter. Another theory places migratory birds as erstwhile permanent residents of northern territories, driven periodically southward by wintry climates; those that did not learn to migrate perished.

Apart from the early reasons for migration, why do many species of birds migrate today? Some migrate only short distances, but a majority fly thousands of miles each year. In fact, more than one third of all the world's bird species migrate with the seasons. It is from the northern half of the world that most migratory birds come. Winter in these regions is an extremely challenging season in that 1) the food supply is reduced or altered, 2) the length of day and thus time in which to hunt for food is shortened, and 3) the amount of energy needed for a bird to keep warm is increased. Some birds can survive these pressures and remain in the same environment year round with adequate food supplies, but most cannot and must change either their behavior or location.

Among the many mysteries of migration is the question of how birds know when to set forth on their migratory routes. It is known that birds undergo internal physical changes just before and just after the nesting season, and it is during these periods of change that most birds migrate. Experiments show that these changes are triggered in migratory birds by an innate hormonal clock. Another factor in the timing of these changes is light, the lengthening days of

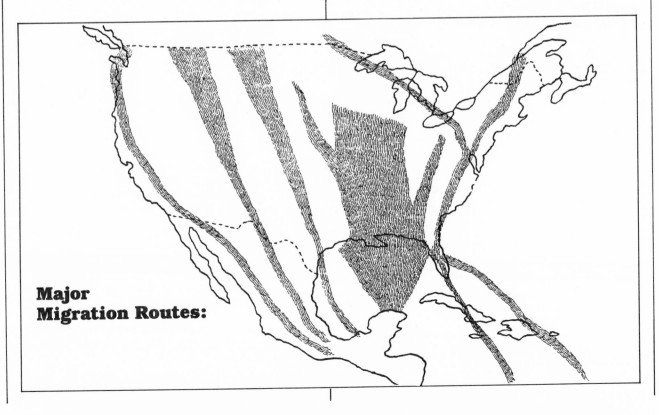

Major Migration Routes:

spring and the shortening days of autumn. Weather also affects take-off time. A cold spring can delay migration. However, when the bird's inner clock says to go, and the weather is fit for flying, the bird leaves for its distant destination.

How can birds traveling long distances, often in the dark, keep on a regular course and, in some cases, find their way back to exactly the same breeding or wintering grounds used in previous years? What about the immature birds, often travelling alone, on their first trip?

It is thought that land birds that migrate by day tend to use their eyes to guide them, recognizing such check points as river valleys, coastlines, and ridges. Studies have shown that some day-flying birds may use the position of the sun, in addition to landmarks, to help them navigate. Some internal sense enables them to orient themselves by the position of the sun. When the angle of the sun changes, the bird takes account of the change and is able to adjust its course. Similarly, experiments with night migrants show that they navigate by the stars.

Small land birds, which do most of their long-distance flying at night, generally fly with the airflow. They travel northward in the spring on warm air masses coming up from the south, southward in the fall on cool winds flowing down from the north.

Some of the journeys documented by bird banding are extraordinary, such as the Arctic tern, banded on the Arctic coast of Russia, that flew more than 14,000 miles to spend the winter off Australia. Certain routes are used by so many birds in fall and spring that they have been called flyways. There are five such routes that follow prominent geographical features running north-south on the North American continent: Atlantic, Mississippi, Central, Mountain, and Pacific.

Migration poses great risks, and hundreds of millions of migrating birds never reach their destination. It is said that over half of first year birds perish before they complete their first round trip of migration. Although birds can sense the changing of the seasons, they do not have a built-in weather-forecasting system as some people believe, but seem to be triggered by the barometric pressure and other meteorological conditions prevailing at the start of their journey. Strong winds frequently carry them so far off course that they are unable or too weak to find their way. Fog seems to confuse their sense of direction; on misty nights light attracts them so that they often crash into lighthouses or high, lighted buildings. Light beams over airports often are very confusing; at Robbins Air Force Base in Georgia, 50,000 birds were killed in a single night.

There remain unanswered questions about bird migration. Some of the answers may come from more observation in the field, new banding data, and other research experiments. Some questions may never be answered, but to those attuned to watching birds come and go with the seasons, migration touches an inner responsive chord.

Suggested References:

Fisher, Allan C. Jr. "Mysteries of Bird Migration." *National Geographic.* (August 1979).

Griffin, Donald R. *Bird Migration.* New York: Doubleday, 1964.

Mead, Chris. *Bird Migration.* New York: Facts on File, 1983.

Pasquier, Roger F. *Watching Birds.* Boston, MA: Houghton Mifflin, 1977.

Welty, Joel Carl. *The Life of Birds.* Philadelphia, PA: W. B. Saunders, 1962.

Focus: *Many birds find it necessary to migrate at the end of the summer in order to find enough food. When they leave and where they go varies according to what they eat.*

ACTIVITIES	MATERIALS
Initial Question: Why do birds migrate?	

MIGRATION PUPPET SHOW

Objective: To introduce the concept of migration, the reasons behind it, and the risks it involves.

Perform, or have the children perform, the puppet show. Discuss the problems that caused Rhonda and Willy to decide to leave and the difficulties they ran into along the way.

* *script,* p. 135
* *puppets*

WHY MIGRATE?

Objective: To illustrate that a bird's food requirements determine whether or not it must migrate.

Have each child pretend to be a bird. Pass out "You eat" cards. Some possible foods are:

mosquitoes, worms, berries, fish in small ponds, squirrels, caterpillars, frogs, nectar, ants, fish in streams, seeds, mice, snakes, rabbits, grasshoppers, insects under bark

Each child says what it eats, whether or not its food is available in winter, and whether or not it will migrate.

* *cards* with "You eat . . ." written on them or with a picture of a food

CONCENTRATION

Objective: To give graphic examples of the summer and winter locations of some migrating birds.

On a map of the western hemisphere, tape covered pictures of a few species of migrating birds onto the northern part of the U.S. Tape the second set onto southern sections where they might be found during the winter. Emphasize your section of the country. The children are divided into teams, and members of each team take turns trying to find matching pictures.

* *2 sets of pictures* each with 5-10 species of migrating birds
* *map of western hemisphere*

Summer — across much of the country.

Common Winter Grounds:

robin — southern U.S.
yellow warbler — Central America
bobolink — southern South America
barn swallow — northern South America
red-winged blackbird — southern U.S.
common yellow-throat — Mexico, Central America, West Indies
kingbird, western — Mexico and Central America
　　eastern — South America

Check a guide to birds for more information.

Note: Older children might compute round-trip distances.

ACTIVITIES	MATERIALS

MIGRATION OBSTACLE COURSE

Objective: To point out the many hazards of migration and the fact that many birds do not survive the trip.

(Outdoors) Three quarters of the children will be migrating birds while the other one quarter will be obstacles. Within set boundries, mark a south section and a north section at the opposite end. Obstacles place themselves within the boundaries. They must keep their left foot planted in one spot while they try to tag the migrators. Have migrating birds attempt to fly south without being tagged by an obstacle. If tagged, the bird "dies," stopping in place or falling dramatically to the ground, until all birds have either safely migrated or been waylaid by obstacles.

• *obstacle signs* depicting fog, high wind, towers, lack of food, cold rain, with string for hanging around neck

WHO'S HERE NOW?

Objective: To notice which birds are present.

Divide into small groups and give each a Who's Here Now? card with the following questions on it:

• *Who's Here Now? cards* 1 for each group

• Do you see many different kinds or many of the same kind of bird?

• Are they making any sounds? singing any songs?

• Where are they?

• What are they doing?

• Do you think the birds live here year round or do they migrate?

Tour the nearby outdoors to listen and look for birds. Have the children write down their answers to the questions. Periodically tour the same area and compare findings.

NIGHT FLIGHT

Objective: To give the children an opportunity to role-play night migration flight.

Set up a course of stars, with each star in a prominent place giving directions to the next star and finally to wintering grounds. Lead a short discussion on the manner in which both day- and night-migrating birds find their way to wintering grounds. Explain that the children will role-play a flock of songbirds flying at night. Designate one child as the lead flyer and blindfold the rest of the group. Everyone holds onto a rope. (Wing-flapping should be encouraged!) Lead flyer finds and leads group to first star, then goes to end of line. Second child becomes lead flyer and leads group to second star. Children take turns until they arrive at the winter feeding grounds, where blindfolds are removed, and food is available.

• *cardboard signs* posted; possible sign directions: Bright Star turn left River valley turn right Magnetic Pull turn right Wintering Grounds — food for all (cookies or popcorn)

SHARING CIRCLE

Objective: To wrap up and personalize an understanding of migration.

Form a sharing circle and have each child state either, "If I were a bird, I would like to migrate because . . ." or, "If I were a bird, I would not like to migrate because . . ."

FLYING FEATHERS PUPPET SHOW

Characters: Rhonda Robin
Willy Wood Thrush

Props: Sign saying — 9:00 PM Monday
Black strip of cardboard with yellow "light" on top

Rhonda Robin: Boy-oh-boy, am I excited!

Willy Wood Thrush: Hi, Rhonda Robin. What are you so excited about?

Rhonda: Why, hello, Willy Wood Thrush. I'm packing my bags for a long trip. I'm getting ready to migrate, not just a hop and a jump to the nearest worm, but a trip of many hundreds of miles. It's the most exciting thing I've ever thought of doing in my whole life. Want to come along?

Willy: Even though your whole life has lasted only four months, Rhonda, I have to agree with you that it does sound exciting.

Rhonda: Think of the views, the meals out, the friends we'll meet. And I hear we end up in a nice sunny spot where there are hundreds of worms and bugs in every acre.

Willy: Wow! It sounds too good to be true. Your timing couldn't be better, Rhonda. It's starting to get quite cold here in the north, and I find I have to eat more and more bugs just to keep warm.

Rhonda: Yes, and on top of that, have you noticed how short the days are getting, how early it gets dark? There's hardly enough time to find our food in the daylight.

Willy: Before you know it, Jack Frost will have made the ground as hard as rock, and we won't be able to reach the worms no matter *how* much daylight we have.

Rhonda: That's right. So the sooner we head south, the better. You better stuff yourself the next few days, Willy, because flying takes heaps of energy.

Willy: O.K. When shall we leave?

Rhonda: How about next Monday at 9 o'clock.

Willy: Sounds good. I'll try to be up by then.

Rhonda: Up by then? I mean 9 o'clock *at night*.

Willy: At night?

Rhonda: Of course at night. Then we can stop and rest during the day, and we'll be able to see to find our food.

Willy: Oh, ok, I guess that makes sense. Bye for now.
(both leave; sign comes up saying 9:00 p.m. Monday; both appear)

Rhonda: All set, Willy?

Willy: Oh, yes, Rhonda. It may take a little work for me to get off the ground as I have been eating ever since I saw you, but I am ready.

Rhonda: Then, let's go.
(birds fly)

Willy: Hey, this is fun, Rhonda. But slow down, if I lose sight of you, I'm lost for good.

Rhonda: Don't worry, Willy, just follow the stars. They're like a lit-up road map.

Willy: Uh oh. Here comes one and we're mighty close!
(put up and take down a black strip of cardboard with yellow "light" on top)

Rhonda: Yikes! That's what I call a narrow escape.

Willy: What happened, Rhonda?

Rhonda: I thought that was a star, and it turned out to be a high tower with a light on top of it. Glad we saw it in time.

Willy: Me, too. Boy, this takes a lot of work. Are you having to beat your wings fast, Rhonda?

Rhonda: Yes, I sure am. I think we've headed into a storm. (wind noises) These winds are terribly strong, and I think we've been blown a little off course. I'm glad daylight's coming so we can stop and rest awhile, eat and get our bearings.

Willy: Me, too! Let's head down to that big field with some shrubs near it. Maybe we can find a few bugs on them.

Rhonda: Yes, and there ought to be some fat, juicy earthworms under the grass.
(land on ground)

Rhonda: Pheew! It's nice to finally have my feet on the ground.

Willy: And it sure feels good to stop and rest. This trip isn't exactly all you cracked it up to be, Rhonda.

Rhonda: What do you mean, Willy?

Willy: Well, to begin with, you said the view would be terrific. The only view I got was of a huge tower from about two inches away. How can you have a view when it's almost pitch black out?

Rhonda:	Well, uhh . . .
Willy:	Yeh, and meals out sounded like a real treat, but when you have to find your own meals and you're in a strange place, it's not all that easy *or* that much fun.
Rhonda:	That's true.
Willy:	Besides, we haven't had time to make *any* friends. If you ask me, migration is for the birds.
Rhonda:	Well, you have to admit it's nice and warm and sunny here in the south, and it looks like we won't have any trouble finding breakfast.
Willy:	Yes, you're right about that. It's so nice that I think I'll spend the rest of the winter here. Want to join me?
Rhonda:	Now that you mention it, it sounds like a great idea. I thought I'd like to travel and see the sights, but I can easily wait for that until next spring when we fly back north. I've had enough adventure for one fall! Bye, bye, everyone. Have a good winter.

FOLLOW-UP ACTIVITIES

1. My Favorite Bird
Have each child select a favorite bird, draw and color it, and write a story about its adventures, whether as a migrating bird or a permanent resident.

2. Hawk Watch
If there are hawk watches nearby, have the children join one. Study the silhouettes of different species of hawks first.

3. Feed a Feathered Friend
Invite an Extension Service agent or Fish and Wildlife officer to explain to the children what shrubs, bushes, and plants provide good food for migratory or overwintering birds. The children could raise money, buy, and plant some in the spring.

Skills

Science Process: Observing, Inferring, Brainstorming, Communicating, Comparing, Sorting and Classifying, Recording Data

Integrated Curriculum: Art, Drama, Music, Social Studies, Writing, Language, Arts, Math

Suggested Reading for Children:

Arnold, Caroline. *Animals That Migrate.* Minneapolis, MN: Carolrhoda Books, 1982. (y/o — chapter on arctic terns)

Freschet, Bernice. *The Flight of the Snow Goose.* New York: Crown, 1970. (y/o — poetic, informative story)

Kaufman, John. *Wings, Sun, and Stars: The Story of Bird Migration.* New York: Morrow, 1969. (o — lots of text)

_____. *Robins Fly North, Robins Fly South.* New York: Crowell Jr. Books, 1970. (y/o — excellent information)

INSECTS IN WINTER

Where Have All the Insects Gone?

Out of sight, out of mind. That is how many of us deal with the apparent absence of insects during the winter. Where are they? In order for any species to survive, at least some of its members must make it through the winter.

Insects have a remarkably simple solution to the problems of surviving frigid winters. They cease activity if they cannot maintain adequate temperatures, and they seek shelter. Rest is a biological necessity for all forms of life, and insects have managed to time one resting phase of their lives to coincide with the worst weather. During this time their activities cease and/or their development may be arrested until favorable environmental conditions cause resumption of their life cycles.

The timing of an insect's winter "pause" must also be synchronized with appropriate life cycle stages. By the onset of cold weather the insect should have reached the life stage best suited to withstand cold, drought (water is mostly in a frozen state in winter and therefore inaccessible), and lack of food. The timetable for each species of insect has succeeded in doing just that.

It would seem there might be one single optimum winter life stage for all insects, but nature is more energy efficient than to have all species of insects competing for food at the same time. Staggered timing of the life cycles among insect species insures that the food needed by the insects will be available when they reach their eating stages of life.

Those insects that develop through **complete metamorphosis** live through four life stages; egg, **larva**, **pupa**, and adult. One might guess that either the egg stage or the pupal stage would be most suited to winter, each being an immobile stage when there is a protective covering to withstand the cold. In fact this is true, but there are also some insect species that overwinter as larvae, and others that overwinter as adults.

Examples of insects that spend the winter in each of the four life stages are numerous; the following will help illustrate the phenomenon. The family of Lasiocampid moths, known to most of us as tent caterpillars, overwinter in the egg stage. The shiny, hard, three-quarter inch, capsule-shaped egg masses can be found in winter encircling twigs of apple and cherry trees. The woolly bear caterpillar is the most familiar example of an overwintering larva. The caterpillar stops eating in the late summer, before its food supply has dwindled, and finds a sheltered spot under leaves and grasses. In the spring it forms a cocoon and emerges as an Isabella moth. The cecropia moth survives the cold season in its pupal stage, a papery pod-shaped cocoon attached to the plant on which the caterpillar has fed. Of the insect species that overwinter as adults, most are in a torpid state, sheltered in crevices or under cover. Honeybees remain fairly active, eating stored honey and beating their wings to create warmth in the hive. Other adult insects may appear on warmer days when their bodies heat up enough to move around. Mourning cloak and red admiral butterflies are often seen during warm spells in late winter. Maple sugaring is apt to attract hungry adult insects, especially moths and butterflies.

Insect species that have an **incomplete metamorphosis**, with the three stages of egg, **nymph**, and adult, most often overwinter in the egg stage. Picture a sunny field in September alive with jumping, rasping grasshoppers and crickets. Most of them die, leaving eggs deposited in the ground to hatch next spring.

Insects that spend part or all of their lives in the water, and are thus protected from below freezing temperatures, may overwinter successfully in their nymph or their larval stages. Stonefly nymphs, hellgrammites, caddis fly larvae, dragonfly nymphs, and young backswimmers or water boatmen, are some of the insects you might see swimming or crawling under the ice of a pond or stream.

The ability of some insects to withstand very cold temperatures is quite remarkable. Each species of insect has its own tolerance for heat and for cold, and those that live where the weather often exceeds those extremes are programmed to enter into a resting phase. But how do insects, not so programmed, react to chilly temperatures? Cold eventually produces stiffness and a lowered metabolic rate in all insects. When the cold becomes too severe, the cell structure becomes altered, and cell walls may burst under the expansion of body fluids caused by freezing.

To partially modify these potentially disastrous effects, many insects lose a high proportion of water from their bodies and the cellular fluid becomes a highly concentrated, sugary substance that acts as an antifreeze. Most important, however, is being adequately sheltered. Some insects overwinter in shelters of their own making, like galls or the cocoons of certain moths. Others must either snuggle into cracks and crevices in trees, rocks, or buildings, hide in or under plants, grasses, or fallen leaves, or descend into the ground. Snow cover and steady temperatures also help insects survive the winter; few can withstand wildly fluctuating temperatures where they repeatedly thaw and freeze.

Insects have remarkable ways of coping with winter. When spring and summer come, one sees how successful their methods have been.

Suggested References:

Buck, Margaret Waring. *Where They Go In Winter*. New York: Abingdon Press, 1968.

Farb, Peter. *The Insects*. New York: Time-Life Books, 1968.

Russell, Helen Ross. *The Winter Search Party*. New York: Thomas Nelson, 1971.

Stokes, Donald W. *A Guide to Nature in Winter*. Boston, MA: Little, Brown, 1976.

Focus: *Insects can survive the winter because each species overwinters in the particular life stage and shelter that assures it the best protection.*

ACTIVITIES	MATERIALS
Initial Question: Where do insects go in the winter?	

PUPPET SHOW

Objective: To understand where and in what stages some insects spend the winter.

Give the puppet show. At the end, review the stages of complete and incomplete metamorphosis. (See information for Insect Life Cycles, p.120)

* *script, p.142*
* *puppets*

WHERE HAVE ALL THE INSECTS GONE?

Objective: To give children some basic information on the life stages and winter whereabouts of a few common insects.

Post a winter mural depicting field, woods, pond, and building. Give each small group of children a folded card. The outer flap has a name or picture of a familiar insect. Inside is the name or picture showing the stage in which the insect overwinters. Leader should call out the insect name and those children with that insect come up to the mural and tell the class in what stage they overwinter. Leader asks the children if they know where the insect belongs, then reads the appropriate rhyme to confirm or to explain where the insect overwinters. Each group places its insect in an appropriate spot on the mural.

* *mural*
* *folded cards* with a picture of an insect on front and correct life stage inside
* *masking tape*
* *rhymes*

Name	Stage	Where
Lady bug	Adult	Lady bugs, lady bugs, where have you gone? To hide under the leaves near last summer's corn.
Honeybee	Adult	Honeybees you can no longer make honey. You're in the warm hive and sneak out when it's sunny (and warm).
Monarch Butterfly	Adult	Monarch butterflies we know where you go. You fly thousands of miles to Mexico.
Housefly	Adult	Houseflies, you hide in cracks out of sight. But when there's warm sun, you crawl into its light.
Woolly bear	Larva (of Isabella Moth)	Woolly bears under leaves you're sound asleep But I've seen you on snow, how slowly you creep.
Dragonfly	Nymph	Dragonfly nymph you live in the pond. It's the mud at the bottom of which you are fond.
Firefly	Larva	Fireflies you rest as "worms" in the ground. Come spring, you'll glow when you crawl around.
Praying Mantis	Egg	Praying Mantis you live in a hard brown case. As eggs on a branch in some sheltered place.
Grasshopper	Egg	Grasshopper eggs you were laid under grass To be snug under snow until winter is past.

ACTIVITIES	MATERIALS

SHUFFLE FOR SHELTER

Objective: To emphasize how important it is for insects to find adequate shelter for winter.

- *chairs*
- *habitat labels*
- *woodpecker picture*
- *music*

Discuss the hardships (cold, lack of water, lack of food) insects face in winter and why good shelter is important for their protection. Label chairs with different shelters and cover labels with lift-up flaps. One chair should have a picture of a woodpecker under its lift-up flap. The children are told they are insects and, when the music stops, they must find a suitable habitat (empty chair). Once seated in a chair, lift up the label to make sure it is a safe habitat. Any insect who has no chair or finds the woodpecker is eliminated. Remove two chairs, change the woodpecker picture to another chair and repeat.

Note: At the end, discuss what insect might live in each of the habitats.

WINTER HIDEAWAYS

Objective: To find insects in their various winter stages in their winter homes.

- *maps* showing building(s) and grounds

Either have predrawn maps or have the children draw maps of the nearby area. Divide the children into teams, each team with a map. Explore school grounds and building for overwintering insects, marking discoveries on the map. Back inside, combine all discoveries on one master map.

SHARING CIRCLE

Objective: To review and personalize the study of insects in winter.

Have the children complete the following sentence, "If I were an insect I would spend the winter . . .(where)"

INSECTS IN WINTER

How and Where Some Insects Overwinter

Insect	Species	Overwintering Stage	Special Preparation	Active or Inactive	Where
Ants	Carpenter	Adult	Produce glycerol	Inactive	In trees or logs
Aphids	Most	Egg	None	Inactive	In bark crevices or base of twigs
Bumblebees	●	Queen	Prefertilized eggs inside queen	Inactive	Underground, under leaves or logs
Butterflies	Monarch	Adult	Migrate	Semi-active	Mexico or California
	Mourning Cloak	Adult	Lose body moisture	Inactive	Under bark
	Painted Lady	Adult	Lose body moisture	Inactive	Under bark
	Swallowtails	Pupa	Form crysalis	Inactive	Attached to stems or on the ground
Crickets	Most	Egg	●	Inactive	In the ground
Dragonflies	Some	Egg	●	Inactive	On the bottom of a pond
	Some	Nymph	●	Semi-active	On the bottom of a pond
	Some	Adult	Migrate	Active	Unknown
Fireflies	Most	Larva ("worms")		Inactive	Underground
Flies	Cluster (wings overlap)	Adult	●	Inactive except when warm	In crevices of buildings or cracks in hollow trees
	House (wings diagonal to side)	Adult	●	Inactive except when warm	In crevices of buildings or cracks in hollow trees
Grasshoppers	Most	Egg	●	Inactive	In the ground
Japanese Beetles		Larva (grubs)		Inactive	In the ground
Honeybees	●	Adult	Store food	Semi-active	Hive in a tree or manmade box
Lady bug	All	Adult	Cluster together	Inactive	Under leaves and grasses
Mantises	Many	Egg	Brown, hardened-foam egg case	Inactive	On bushes
Mosquitos	Most	Adult females	●	Inactive	Sheltered place
Moths	Gypsy	Egg			On tree trunks
	Isabella	Larva (Woolly Bear)	●	Usually inactive	Under leaves and grasses
	Cecropia	Pupa	Spins a cocoon	Inactive	On branches
	Maple Sugar	Adult	Loses moisture	Inactive	Under bark
Stoneflies	Many	Nymph to Adult	●	Active	Stream to land

INSECTS IN WINTER PUPPET SHOW

Characters (and Props):
Dad
Boy
Boy in miniature
Woolly Bear Caterpillar
Cecropia Moth Cocoon ("Ceci")
(Tent Caterpillar egg case on twig)
Lady Bug

Boy: Dad, where have all the insects gone?

Dad: Well, I don't know. I suppose they flew away.

Boy: Where did they fly to?

Dad: I don't know. I read somewhere that monarch butterflies go to Mexico for the winter. And speaking of going somewhere, it's time for you to go to bed. Tomorrow we'll find out where the insects went.

Boy: (yawning) Aw, gee whiz. Ok dad, I am sleepy.
(both leave)

Boy: (smaller version of boy appears) Where am I? Everything looks so big. What is that? It looks like a rolled up rug with feet, and it's coming towards me.
(Woolly Bear appears)

Woolly Bear: Hello, young man. Did I hear you ask where the insects were?

Boy: Um, er, yes, but what, or should I say who, are you?

Woolly Bear: I am Isabella.

Boy: Isabella? You look like a woolly bear. But you're awfully big.

Woolly Bear: On the contrary, my friend. *You* are awfully small. But it's just as well, because if you'll get on my back, I can take you around to visit some insects. Then you'll know where they go in winter.

Boy: Thank you, Woolly Bear. I've never ridden bear back. (gets on her back) You're pretty scratchy. Couldn't you get a haircut?

Woolly Bear: My hair, as you call it, is what keeps me warm in the winter. That's why you find me curled up in woodpiles, or even, occasionally, walking across the snow.

Boy: Why did you say your name was Isabella when we all know your name is Woolly Bear?

Woolly Bear: I am a woolly bear caterpillar now, but I won't always be. Do you know about the life stages of an insect?

Boy: Yup, I learned them; egg, larva, pupa, adult for some kinds; egg, nymph, adult for other kinds.

Woolly Bear: My, my, little boy. You are up on your insects. Let's see if the audience knows what stage *I'm* in. Audience, what do *you* think? (pause) Yes, the larval stage. After I pupate in the spring, I will become an Isabella moth, so my name will be Isabella. Oh, here's a relative I'd like you to meet. Hi, Ceci.

Boy: What do you mean, hi Ceci. That's an old dead leaf.

Woolly Bear: That's what you're supposed to think, camouflage you know. Hi, Ceci. (Cecropia cocoon appears)

Ceci: (talk with hand over mouth to muffle sound) Hi.

Woolly Bear: What did you say?

Ceci: (muffled) I said hi. Stop bothering me, I'm resting.

Woolly Bear: I wanted you to meet my new young friend. He wonders where all the insects have gone.

Ceci: (still muffled) Well this one has gone to sleep. If you have trouble hearing me, it's no wonder. I'm wrapped up inside two layers, the one you're looking at and a smaller case inside that one. Keeps me warm and dry.

Boy: I know what stage he's in. It's, it's, it's . . . help me audience, I forgot the name. (hopefully they say pupa) Oh yes, the pupal stage.

Woolly Bear: That's right, Ceci will become a Cecropia moth. Well goodbye Ceci. Guess the next time we meet, we'll both be moths. Have a good winter.
(pupa goes down; tent caterpillar case comes up)

Boy: Hey Woolly, what's that big barrel around that branch?

Woolly Bear: That's no barrel. Some cousins of mine live there. Maybe the audience can guess what stage they're in. What do you think boys and girls? (pause — egg stage) You got it! They won't hatch until the new leaves grow on that twig next spring.

Boy: Hatch? Sounds like baby birds.

Woolly Bear: Well, same idea. Baby birds hatch at the time of year when there's food for them. And baby insects hatch when they too can find food.

Boy: What will they hatch into?

Woolly Bear: Caterpillars. They're called tent caterpillars because they make themselves a silk tent to live in when they're not off eating.

Boy: I thought spiders spun silk.

Woolly Bear:	They do, but they're not the only ones. Tent caterpillars also leave trails of silk behind them when they travel to new branches so they can find their way home. (twig goes down)
Boy:	That's neat. Then they never get lost. Where are we going now?
Woolly Bear:	I'm looking for a certain big pile of leaves near this cornfield.
Boy:	Is that it over there, right next to that big old tree?
Woolly Bear:	Yes. You have sharp eyes my friend. We'll go make a call.
Boy:	Everytime we talk to someone it's either inside, on, or under a bunch of leaves, or a twig. No wonder I never saw insects in winter, except sometimes I've seen you, Woolly.
Woolly Bear:	Hello, hello in there. Anyone awake on this gorgeous sunny day? (Lady Bug appears)
Lady Bug:	Well, bless my soul. It is nice out, but it's hardly time for us to wake up. What time is it anyway?
Woolly Bear:	It's wintertime lady. I'm sorry to interrupt your long winter nap, but I wanted to introduce my friend here to an insect in its adult stage. He wondered where insects went in winter.
Lady Bug:	We lady bugs go to sleep. It's very cozy all bunched up together under a nice big pile of leaves. Makes good insulation, especially if there's snow on top of them. No point staying awake when there's nothing to eat. It's not like I can fly to the nearest Dunkin Donuts you know.
Boy:	Excuse me lady. What *do* you eat?
Lady Bug:	Little insects called aphids. Delicious, sweet, yet full of protein. You ought to try them sometime. (yawn) I'm getting tired, got to save my strength until aphid season. Think I'll go back to sleep. Bye. (leaves)
Boy:	Sleep! That's it! I'm asleep and this is a dream. I can't wait to wake up and tell my dad what I've found out. Thanks Woolly. I think I'll get off you now and go home. You have a good winter, and if I see you next spring, I'll call you Isabella. Ok? Bye.
Woolly:	Bye.

FOLLOW-UP ACTIVITIES

1. Bingo
Make up a bingo game using the nine insects from "Where Have All the Insects Gone." Add others from the chart if you want to make it harder.

2. Closer Look
Bring in a hornet's nest from last summer or other specimens for the children to examine.

3. Creative Writing
Have the children write a story pretending to be a certain kind of insect going through the winter and waking up the next spring.

Skills
Science Process: Observing, Inferring, Brainstorming, Communicating, Predicting, Comparing, Recording Data

Integrated Curriculum: Drama, Reading, Writing, Language Arts

Suggested Reading for Children:

Buck, Margaret Waring. *Where They Go In Winter.* New York: Abingdon Press, 1968.

Nestor, William P. *Into Winter — Discovering a Season.* Boston, MA: Houghton Mifflin, 1982.

Selsam, Millicent E. *Where Do They Go? Insects in Winter.* New York: Four Winds Press, 1982.

Rugged Remnants of Summer Flowers

Wildflowers are a cherished part of many landscapes, from those that bloom in early summer in the desert or on the forest floor, to those that fill the fields in summer and fall. In winter the blossoms are dead, but many remain standing, reminders of seasons past and holding promise for the future. These winter weeds can be a beautiful interruption to the smooth, white fields of snowy landscapes or add exquisite detail to otherwise bland winter scenes. With their delicate patterns and subtle shades of browns and grays, they are rugged, resilient plants that stand up to the winter winds and storms until they are buried by the snow or disintegrate with the freeze, melt, freeze cycle of northern winters. Their presence provides pleasure for those who notice them, seeds for the birds that find them, homes for wintering insects, and food and building materials for small mammals.

Lasting into or through the winter is important to the life cycles of these hardy plants because it gives them extra time to disperse their seeds. Plants with stiff, but not easily broken, stalks may catapult their seeds when the stalks whip about in strong winds or are brushed against by animals. Sturdy stalks, like milkweed, hold their seed pods well into winter so that every last seed has the chance to be torn out and carried off by the wind. Hitchhiker seeds, like burdock, need the extra months to catch a ride on unwary passersby.

Winter weeds exhibit the hardiness characteristic of plants that typically grow where they are not wanted. Many grow where other plants could not survive, where the soil is poor and/or the climate is harsh. In so doing, these plants often hold the soil and prevent erosion. How many flowering plants can grow on sun-baked gravel banks of roadsides or on hot rocky ledges? Mullein can, for one. So-called weeds grow primarily on land disturbed by natural or human interference, and they succeed because they are such aggressive colonizers. Most pro-

duce thousands of seeds that travel great distances by wind or are carried by animals. Their seeds are often the first to arrive in a newly disturbed area, and, with their needs very simple in terms of nutrition and climate, the weed-colonizers are quick to settle in.

Once their seeds have sprouted, weeds have remarkable physical adaptations that help them survive. These may include hairy or fuzzy outer layers of stems and leaves to reduce moisture loss, fibrous, almost woody, stems, and long strong taproots or tenacious root systems from which new shoots can grow each year. Hardy adaptations such as these help to explain how so many weeds stand up to the rigors of winter, and why they are such effective send-off platforms for their   seeds.

Most winter weeds are **herbaceous** plants, which means the living parts of the plant above the ground die by the end of each growing season. Herbaceous plants have three possible life cycles. Annual plants die above and below the ground after just one growing season. These are thus adapted to grow quickly and are usually the first plants to succeed in a newly exposed area (for example, beggar ticks, pigweed, and ragweed). Effective seed dispersal is especially vital to ensure continuation of annual plants. Biennial plants have a two-year life cycle with the first year producing a flattened circle of leaves near the ground and the second year sending up a flowering shoot. Biennials follow close behind annuals in colonizing (for example, black-eyed Susans, Queen Anne's lace, and evening primrose). Finally, perennial plants send up new shoots in the spring from surviving underground parts. Goldenrod and chicory can thus be found growing in the same fields and along the same roads for many years.

Most of the plants we consider weeds are not native; the seeds were brought by European settlers, either on purpose or hidden in belongings and supplies by accident. The damp, moist forests of New England would not have been hospitable to the seed newcomers, but as soon as the settlers began to clear the land, the sun-filled fields and waste places provided perfect habitat with little competition from native shade-loving plants. Once established in the east, the seeds of these plants soon found their way west.

Winter weeds can be appreciated for their beauty and their benefit to wildlife, or for the story they tell about the land on which they grow. They also deserve admiration for standing tall, in rugged defiance of winter, to insure their seeds' dispersal.

Suggested References:

Brown, Lauren. *Weeds in Winter.* New York: W. W. Norton, 1976.

Common Weeds of the U.S. Dover, NY: Agricultural Research Service of the U.S. Department of Agriculture, 1971.

Smith, Helen V. *Winter Wildflowers.* Ann Arber, MI: Michigan Botanical Club, Special Publication No. 2. (Write M.B.C., c/o Herbarium, University of Michigan, Ann Arbor, MI 48104.)

Stokes, D. *A Guide to Nature in Winter.* Boston, MA: Little, Brown, 1976.

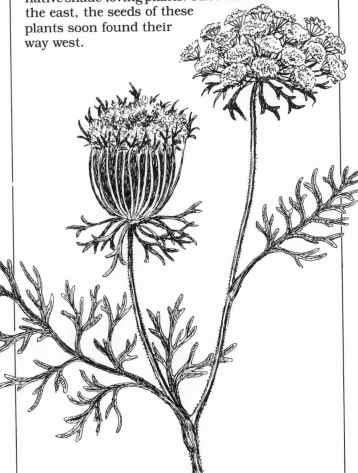

WINTER WEEDS

Focus: *Winter weeds are stalwart remnants of last summer's flowers, carrying the seeds for future plants and beautifying the winter landscape.*

ACTIVITIES	MATERIALS
Initial Question: Why might some flower stalks, even though the flowers are dead, continue standing through the winter?	

LOOK ALIKES

Objective: To encourage close observation of winter weeds.

Each person is given a winter weed and asked to examine it until ready to distinguish it from the others. Gather the weeds and spread them out in a central place (if more than 15 children, perhaps divide into two groups). Everyone must then choose his or her own weed and describe its unique features. Conclude by asking the children why those plants remain sturdy after the summer. (To hold the seeds for more efficient dispersal.) Look closely at the seeds. How are they held by the plant? How big and how numerous are they? What does a seed look like under a hand lens? How might the seeds finally get away?

Materials:
- *winter weeds* of the same kind, with seeds still on or in them
- *hand lenses*

CARD PARTNERS

Objective: To introduce the children to some of the common winter weeds in their area.

Give each child a card. Tell them to look at the weed on it closely to notice one special feature. Then walk around to find a partner who has the same kind of winter weed. When all have partnered-up, each pair introduces their weed and tell what's special about it. The leader may add information and name if appropriate. Pairs of older children might look theirs up to identify it. Show pictures of the blooming flowers and ask which card partners belong with each picture.

Materials:
- *winter weeds or their seed heads* mounted on cards (labelled if you wish) 2, or multiples of 2, of each kind; enough cards for all children

WEED POEMS

Objective: To use winter weeds as a catalyst for a group creative-writing exercise.

Divide into at least three groups. Each group takes a different winter weed, secretly, to a private corner. Each member of the group takes a different position relative to the weed, and then gives one or two adjectives describing the weed. Each group composes a poem from the adjectives. Groups reassemble and winter weeds are centrally displayed. Leader reads each poem, and everyone guesses which weed it describes. To make it harder, add an extra weed.

Materials:
- *variety of winter weeds*
- *paper bags* or other hiding devices
- *clay* to use as a base for weed to stand in
- *pencils*
- *paper*

ACTIVITIES	MATERIALS

WINTER WEED WALK

Objective: To notice the variety of winter weeds and some of their special characteristics.

Divide the children into groups. Give each a hand lens and a Winter Weed Walk card with the following instructions:

- Find a winter weed:

  with a seed head that looks like an umbrella;
  that has seeds in a circular pattern;
  with seeds that stick to your clothes;
  with a stalk that looks rough and tough;
  with a stalk that looks fragile.

- Match these colors to winter weeds (use brown, tan, gold, gray color chips from paint sample cards).

- Find three different weeds that have a lot of seeds in them. Can you guess why the seeds are still there? How do you think the seeds will finally escape?

- Notice a weed that is all by itself.

- Find the biggest patch of one kind of winter weed. Count the number of plants.

Ask them to find the objects listed and to examine some of their discoveries with hand lenses.

- *Winter Weed Walk cards*
- *hand lenses*

SNOW BOUQUETS

Objective: To emphasize the variety and beauty of winter weeds and to give the children an opportunity to create a miniature winter scene.

Drape a white cloth over books to look like a snow-covered landscape. Give each child a golfball-sized chunk of white play-dough, and pass out collected winter weeds from which they may choose a specified number. Each child should make a winter bouquet and place it on the landscape.

- *playdough — mix to clay consistency: 4 parts flour to 1 part salt water (add in small amounts)*
- *collection of winter weeds*
- *clippers or scissors*
- *white or unbleached cloth*

FOLLOW-UP ACTIVITIES

1. Winter Seeds
With the children, gather some seeds from local weeds. Plant the seeds to see if they will germinate. Explain that some seeds need winter's cold exposure in order to grow in the spring. Record what happens and when.

2. Life as a Winter Weed
Have the children write a story about life as a winter weed, including the coming of fall and the arrival of spring.

3. Mystery Weeds
Place a marker among some unidentified winter weeds outdoors. Check in the spring or summer to see what flowers are growing there.

Skills
Science Process: Observing, Inferring, Brainstorming, Communicating, Comparing, Sorting and Classifying, Experimenting, Recording Data

Integrated Curriculum: Art, Reading, Writing, Language Arts, Math

Suggested Reading for Children:

Dowden, Anne Ophelia. *Wild Green Things in the City.* New York: Crowell, 1972. (o — nice illustrations)

Signs of Four Seasons

When trees lose their leaves many people feel they also lose their identity, but a bare tree has its own stark beauty when its branching pattern and individual twigs become visible. Careful examination of its winter twigs reveals many distinguishing features about each kind of tree. The wide variety of shapes, colors, textures, and patterns are exciting to see and to learn about.

Twigs give a miniature account of the tree's past, present, and future. At the tip of the twig, or close to it, there should be a bud. Buds, formed the previous summer, are miniature branchlets containing next spring's leaves and flowers. These are protected by bud scales, the arrangement of which is characteristic for each tree species. Bud scales are really modified leaves serving to protect the delicate growing point within from drying out or from injury. Willows characteristically have only one bud scale which unzips and comes off like a hood in spring. Maples have several overlapping scales while oaks have many scales arranged in five rows.

Buds at the tip of the branch are called **terminal buds**. They mark the end of one season's growth and contain the embryonic stages of the next season's growth. Last year's bud scales are also evident. Look for a narrow band of fine markings around the twig; the distance between the new terminal bud and last year's bud scale rings show how much the twig grew in one year.

Oaks have a cluster of terminal buds. Aspens have a single terminal bud. Some trees, like staghorn sumac and elms, have pseudoterminal buds. These are actually the final lateral or side buds formed on the twigs during the growing season and are thus not centered at the end, but pointed slightly to one side.

Buds on the side of the twig are called **lateral buds** and may contain flowers or leaves. When two sizes of lateral buds occur on one twig, the larger usually contains flowers and the smaller leaves. The location of these buds in an **opposite**, **alternate**, or **whorled** pattern is useful in identifying specific trees. Opposite buds, for example, will open to become twigs, growing opposite each other. These patterns are reflected in the branching pattern of the entire tree. Only a few trees have opposite branching; an easy way to remember them is to think of the acronym MADCAP HORSE. The letters stand for different families: M — maple; A — ash; D — dogwood; CAP — Caprifoliaceae (the family of plants including honeysuckle, elderberries, and viburnums); and HORSE — horse chestnut tree.

Before leaves are shed each autumn a corky layer develops across the leaf stem where it joins the twig. Called the **abscission layer**, it gradually cuts off the supply of water and food. When the leaf drops off only a scar is left behind on the twig. The shape of the leaf scar reflects the shape of the end of the leaf **petiole** or stem. In most trees it is an oval, a crescent, or a triangle, but in a few trees such as sycamore and staghorn sumac it is almost circular, enclosing a lateral bud. The veins that serve to conduct food and water between the leaf and the twig also leave scars (within the leaf scars). Referred to as bundle scars they vary in numbers and patterns specific to different types of trees. In examining twigs carefully, one can find very interesting leaf scars; the butternut scar resembles a monkey face, with the bundle scars forming the monkey's eyes and mouth.

Lenticels are the corky vents through which gases are exchanged between the tree tissues and the outside air. The size, color, and density of these marks vary: on white birches lenticels appear as dark horizontal lines, on cherry trees the horizontal lenticels are light colored and smaller than those of the birches, and on maple and alder twigs they are light colored dots. Color is another characteristic of different twigs. Some are red (dogwoods and striped maple), others are golden yellow (weeping willows), and others vary from soft greys and browns to deep purples and bronze greens.

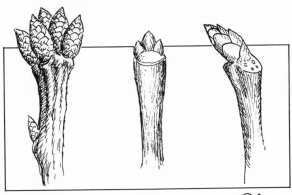

Oak   *Aspen*   *Elm*

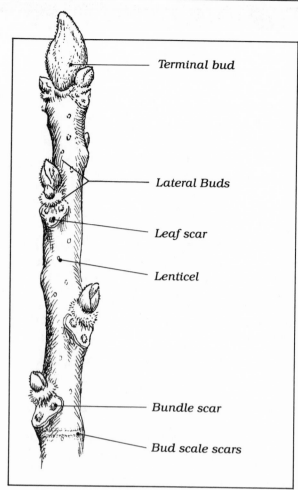

Terminal bud

Lateral Buds

Leaf scar

Lenticel

Bundle scar

Bud scale scars

Butternut

Twigs have one distinguishing feature that can only be seen by cutting through the twig itself. The very center, called the pith, is soft, food storage tissue. It varies in color, shape, and structure. Years ago the large central pith used to be pushed out of the twigs of some trees, such as elderberry and staghorn sumac, to make spouts for sugaring or whistles.

Sometimes the odor of a bruised twig is a noseworthy feature. Spicebush, sassafras, and tulip tree twigs have an extremely spicy odor. Both black birch and yellow birch smell and taste like wintergreen. Cherry twigs have a strong, bitter, almond-like odor and taste.

Winter trees may appear as lifeless skeletons against a sombre landscape, but careful examination of their twigs reveals the prophecy of spring and the history of seasons gone by.

Suggested References:

Core and Ammons. *Woody Plants in Winter.* Pacific Grove, CA: Boxwood Press, 1973.

Harlow, William M. *Fruit Key and Twig Key to Trees and Shrubs.* New York: Dover, 1946.

Rockcastle, Verne. *Winter Twigs.* Cornell Science Leaflet, Vol. 58, No. 2. Ithaca, NY: Cornell Science Leaflets, Cornell University 14853. (25¢/copy)

Symonds, George W. D. *The Tree Identification Book.* New York: William Morrow, 1958.

Stokes, Donald W. *A Guide to Nature in Winter.* Boston, MA: Little, Brown, 1976.

Focus: *The winter twigs of each kind of tree are unique, but some of the features common to all show evidence of seasons past, and promise for the coming spring.*

ACTIVITIES	MATERIALS
Initial Question: How are twigs important to a tree?	

TWIN TWIGS

Objective: To become familiar with general differences in appearance among several kinds of twigs.

Divide into groups of 5. One person from each group should select a "secret" twig from the duplicate pile, face away from the group and describe the twig. The rest of the group, with examples of the different twigs spread before them, chooses the correct twig from the description. Check to make sure the two twigs are twin twigs. Repeat to match other twigs.

• *matching sets of twigs* 4 or 5 different kinds, 1 set for each group and an additional set for the duplicate pile

COMPLETE A TWIG

Objective: To introduce the parts of a twig and their functions.

Give each pair of children a twig to examine carefully. Two parallel lines representing a skeletal twig should be drawn on the blackboard and the leader should complete the twig from the children's directions, or the children could take turns filling in the details, based on their observations. Include terminal bud, lateral bud, leaf scar, bundle scar, bud scale rings, and lenticels. Children may draw their own complete twigs.

• *twigs* enough for each pair to have one
• *hand lenses*
• *blackboard and chalk* or
• *felt board* and cut out twig parts

TWIG HUNT

Objective: To match some common twigs to the correct species of trees.

Divide into small groups. Each group should be given a set of twigs from the various kinds of trees found growing nearby. Have the children look carefully at each twig to see special features so they will know what to look for outdoors. Point out that those with opposite buds will have opposite twigs on the trees, alternate buds will have alternate twigs. Outdoors, find the trees to match the twigs, and if possible, collect a seed or a leaf from those trees.

Note: In early spring children might tie a string to one twig and check it weekly to watch its buds open.

• *sets of twigs from trees* found on school grounds

ACTIVITIES	MATERIALS

BE A TREE

Objective: To give the children a chance to experience the life cycle of a tree and to reinforce how leaves make their food.

Tell the children to pretend to be trees. They should stand a little more than arm's length apart, listen to the story, and pantomime it. (Leader demonstrates while reading the script.) At the start of the story, their arms should be spread like branches, their fingers should be closed in fists like unopened buds, and their toes, like roots, should press down-ward. After the story, review the seasonal cycles of the tree. Ask the children which time of the year they think is most difficult for the tree.

- *script, p.153*

SPRING TWIGS

Objective: To encourage the children to think about what winter twigs will look like in the spring.

Show the children some pictures of bare winter trees and flowering/leafing spring trees. Have each child draw a picture of a tree in winter with its winter twigs. Then imagine how that tree will look in the spring when its buds have opened into leaves and flowers. Draw a spring tree. Older children could refer to tree books to help make their pictures more accurate.

- *pictures of winter and spring trees*
- *paper*
- *crayons*

BE A TREE

You are small trees standing in a big field. It is the end of winter and your roots are stiff, frozen in the ground. Your branches are bare. Last year's leaves fell off months ago and next year's leaves are tight buds, hiding from the cold. The sky is gray. The last snowstorm of the year starts to swirl around you, your branches move stiffly in the wind, your trunk sways back and forth.

Finally spring comes and the ground thaws, allowing water to reach your roots. Feel the cold water trickle between your roots. Your branches and twigs become thirsty, they need water so that the tight buds can grow into leaves. Pull the water up through your roots. Stretch tall so that the water can work its way up into your trunk and out to your branches. As more and more water rises and finds its way to the tips of your twigs, the once tight buds now begin to swell. Suddenly they break open, and the leaves burst out (fingers uncurl and hands spread open). One by one, the leaves unfold and reach toward the sky.

It is growing time for trees. You are hungry and your leaves are working hard to make food for you. Spread your leaves wide to catch the sun. Feel the warmth soaking in. You need water from your roots — reach for more water; sunlight from the sky — reach for more sunlight.

Summer passes and you have grown taller and wider. Stretch your roots, your trunk, your branches. As the weather grows colder, your leaves stop making food. Suddenly one fall day, the winds blow hard and the rains pelt down. Feel the cold and the wind. Sway and move your branches. Now that your leaves have weakened, they fall off and blow away, leaving tight buds behind (fists clenched again). Those buds are next spring's leaves.

FOLLOW-UP ACTIVITIES

1. Open Up
Force twigs by placing them in water for several days. The buds will open if they have been subjected to the proper temperatures outdoors. Ask the children to watch carefully and record to see when and how the leaves emerge.

2. Twig Display
Have the children make a twig board with common twigs tied on to a board or cardboard and labelled. Add a tree picture beside each twig.

3. Dissect a Bud
Divide into small groups. Each group should have a bud to dissect. Either carefully cut down the center and look at the parts, or remove the scales and notice the layers. Discuss when the bud was formed and what it will become.

4. Keying Twigs
Use a twig key to identify some common twigs. (A good key is *Winter Tree Finder* by May Theilgard Watts and Tom Watts, published by Nature Study Guild, Box 972, Berkeley, CA. 94701)

Skills
Science Process: Observing, Inferring, Brainstorming, Communicating, Predicting, Comparing, Sorting and Classifying, Experimenting, Recording Data

Integrated Curriculum: Art, Drama, Reading, Writing, Language Arts, Math

Suggested Reading for Children:

Graham, Ada. *Let's Discover Winter Woods*. New York: Golden Press, 1974. (y/o)

Russell, Helen Ross. *The True Book of Buds: Surprise Packages*. Chicago, IL: Children's Press, 1970. (y — story, twig investigations)

Selsam, Millicent E. *Maple Tree*. New York: Morrow, 1968. (y/o — photographs)

Musical Messages

The sound of birds singing has inspired composers and poets for centuries. It has also been a joyful affirmation that winter is past and spring is here. Rachel Carson's choice of title for her book, *Silent Spring*, was extremely effective as it raised the dreaded prospect of an eventual spring without birds, without song.

Why do birds sing? And why especially in the spring? Song plays an important role in the annual cycles of many birds as it signals the courtship proceedings and defines the territorial holdings vital to producing and successfully rearing their young. When one considers the small size of birds, the distances that may separate them, and the many obstacles that act as visual barriers, like leaves and trees, it is no wonder that songs, or calls, are the most effective ways to communicate.

Songbirds form the group of birds known as passerines, or perching birds. The name passerine comes from the Latin "passer" which means sparrow. Being small, and often having to migrate hundreds or thousands of miles annually, their life spans are relatively short. It would be unusual for both partners to live through many seasons, thus songbirds do not mate for life, but rather find a mate each season. It could well be the same mate which instinctively flew back to the same territory and responded to the previous year's mate, but it is thought that the pairbond does not last beyond caring for the young in most species. The song is thus very important to reproductive success as it quickly and effectively announces the presence of a particular species of bird, its desire to mate, and the territory which that particular bird has staked out.

It is important to emphasize that each species of bird has its own specific song, although there are, occasionally, regional dialects. This species-specific song is what enables potential mates to recognize, respond to, and find each other, and also what causes a flight or possibly a fight response in a bird that intrudes into the territory of a like bird. Within the song pattern of a given species there are, however, individual characteristics that enable birds to distinguish their mate's songs. Sophisticated recordings and visual renditions of songs in sonograms have allowed researchers to study the subtle differences inaudible to the human ear.

Male birds are usually the songsters because it is they who most often establish the territory and attract a female into it, and then defend it. There are a few common exceptions in which females occasionally sing as well, such as the bluebird, the northern oriole, the cardinal, and the white-throated sparrow.

Birds do not have vocal chords, but rather produce their songs by controlling the frequency of vibrations made by the membranes in the syrinx, or voice box. Air, when released from the lungs under a certain amount of pressure, causes these membranes to vibrate. The number of syringeal muscles in a given species of bird determines its ability to vary the vibrations. Crows and mockingbirds, which produce a great variety of sounds, have eight pairs of muscles, while pigeons, with their simple cooing, have only one pair.

Some birds are born with the ability to sing their species' song; others have to hear it and practice. Young birds begin singing anywhere from eight days to thirteen weeks after hatching. Their early songs are called subsongs and consist of notes or phrases from what should become the primary song. If reared among members of its own species, the young bird usually has perfected its song by the spring after its year of birth.

The time of year when birds sing is related to their reproductive cycle, which in turn is timed to coincide with the maximum food supply for the offspring, usually spring and

summer. It is thought that the length of day, that is, increasing daylight in late winter and early spring, stimulates the production of hormones that result in breeding behavior and readiness. The ability and desire to sing is part of that process. When they cease to sing varies; some as soon as mating has occurred, others not until all care of the young is completed.

The daily song cycle also varies. Most birds sing early in the morning with the amount of light again triggering the impulse. Members of the thrush family are often the first heard at dawn, followed by insect eaters which can find their flying food outlined against the early morning sky. Many seed eaters and hole nesters seem to wait for better light. In the heat of the day most birds are quiet, although one account decribed a red-eyed vireo that sang its song 22,000 times in the course of ten hours. Towards evening, many birds resume their singing.

Songs serve well to attract mates and to mark territories, but there are other messages that need to be communicated: aggression, alarm, location of food. Most of these are conveyed by brief, relatively simple call notes, such as the blue jay's warning scream.

The study of bird songs can last a lifetime. First, one becomes aware of differences among the sounds. Then gradually certain songs are associated with specific birds until eventually it is ears even more than eyes that tell the experienced birder what birds are in the area. To learn about birds and their songs is to give new dimension to the world around you.

Suggested References:

Jellis, R. *Bird Sounds and Their Meaning*. Ithaca, NY: Cornell University Press, 1984.

Pasquier, Roger. *Watching Birds*. Boston, MA: Houghton Mifflin, 1977.

Peterson, Roger Tory. *The Birds*. New York: Time-Life Books, 1963.

Terres, John K. *The Audubon Society Encyclopedia of North American Birds*. New York: Alfred A. Knopf, 1980.

Welty, Joel Carl. *The Life of Birds*. Philadelphia, PA: W. B. Sanders, 1962.

The Wonder of Birds. Washington, DC: National Geographic Society, 1983.

"An Evening in Sapsucker Woods" (record). Ithaca, NY: Cornell Laboratory of Ornithology.

Kellogg, Dr. Peter A., and Dr. Arthur A. Allen. "A Field Guide to Bird Songs" (record). Boston, MA: Houghton Mifflin.

Focus: *Most songbirds sing special songs in the spring to attract mates and to establish and defend territories; other calls may communicate messages such as danger or food sources.*

ACTIVITIES	MATERIALS
Initial Question: Why do birds sing? ## PUPPET SHOW **Objective:** To show some reasons why birds sing. Give the puppet show. Discuss the advantages to each kind of bird having its own distinct song. Review Mr. Bird's reasons for singing.	• *script, p.158* • *puppets*
## CLOCK CHORUS **Objective:** To show that each species of bird has its own song and its own favorite time to sing. Lead a brief discussion on the general times of day when birds sing. Give each child a bird tag with one of the following possibilities written on it: Robin: "cheerio cheery me cheery me" (4 am) Ovenbird: "teacher-teacher-teacher" (4 am) White-throated sparrow: "poor Sam Peabody-Peabody-Peabody" (4 am) Eastern meadowlark: "sweet spring is here" (5 am) Eastern wood pewee: "pee-a-wee" (5 am) Redwinged blackbird: "konk-la-ree" (5 am) Yellowthroat: "witchity-witchity-witchity" (6 am) Blackcapped chickadee: "chick-a-dee-dee-dee" or "fee-bee" (6 am) Red-eyed vireo: "going up — coming down" (6 am) Yellow warbler: "sweet sweet sweet I'm so sweet" (6 am) Chestnut-sided warbler: "pleased-pleased-pleased to meet you" (6 am) Goldfinch: "potato chip — potato chip" (7 am) Phoebe: "fiby-fiby" (7 am) White-breasted nuthatch: "yank-yank" (7 am) Ask all to check their tags for the name of the bird, what its song sounds like, and when it starts singing. Children put on the tags, then practice the songs. Leader moves the hands of the clock from midnight to noon. As the appropriate time arrives, the respective birds should begin singing. By 7 a.m. *all* birds should be singing, and around noon all should quiet down. If desired, the clock can progress until evening when songs are often sung again.	• *clock with movable hands* • *bird tags* — 2 of each kind cut in bird shape • *string attached to tags for wearing around necks*

ACTIVITIES	MATERIALS

WHICH BIRD SINGS WHICH SONG?

Objective: To introduce the children to a few common bird songs and to help them hear differences among them.

Play one bird song at a time to the children. Have them repeat the song in words, then listen to the bird song again. Show them a picture of the bird. Do this for 3 to 5 bird songs, depending on the age of the children. Play through all the songs again and see if they can remember which bird sings which song.

- tape of 3 to 5 bird songs common to your area
- bird pictures

MAP AND TREK

Objective: To see and hear how individual birds stake out territories with their singing. To notice habitat preferences of different birds.

Note: Best done early in the day.

Have the children draw, or leader prepare in advance, map sketches of the area showing main features: building, trees, swings, etc. In small groups of 5 or 6 children, take maps and walk around the immediate area until a bird song is heard. Stop and mark the spot on the map with a symbol. At the bottom of the map, mark down the symbol and what pattern of song it indicates. Continue walking around the area until another bird song is heard. If the pattern of the song is the same, indicate its location on the map with the previous symbol. If the song pattern is new, put a different symbol at this location, and explain it also at the bottom of the map. Although names of the birds will inevitably be asked, emphasize the uniqueness of each species' song, referring to them by their song's pattern, rather than their common name, until all are familiar with the song. Get together with other groups and compare where different songs were heard.

- school ground maps
- pencils
- binoculars if available

MATING MATCH

Objective: To become aware of how male birds attract mates with their songs.

Divide the children into two equal groups. Pass out two like sets of bird tags from Clock Chorus activity, one set per group, one tag per child. Explain that one group represents male birds who should sing their assigned songs at a given signal. The other group represents female birds, who will be blindfolded and who will have to find their mates by following the sound of their assigned song. (Females must check the back of their tags before being blindfolded.) At Go, the singing starts and the search is on. Remove blindfolds and stand aside as partners are found.

- blindfolds
- bird tags

BIRD SONGS PUPPET SHOW

Characters: Rocky Raccoon
                  Mr. Bird - brightly colored
                  Ms. Bird - same shape, duller coloration

Prop: Sign saying: Next day 5:00 AM

Mr. Bird: Twee Tweedle Dee, Titter Tatter Teer
                  Twee Tweedle Dee, Titter Tatter Teer

Rocky Raccoon: (waking up) Uh, Mr. Bird, Mr. Bird. You have been singing that same song with those same words over and over and over again since 5:00 this morning. No offense, but it's *driving me crazy!* If you insist upon singing for so long, can't you at least change the song?

Mr. Bird: Change the song! I can't just change my song. It'd be like asking you to start barking like a dog.

Rocky: What do you mean? I hear lots of different bird songs.

Mr. Bird: Yes, but they're coming from lots of different birds. Each different kind of bird has a different special song of its own and mine is Twee Tweedle Dee, Titter Tatter Teer, Twee Tweedle Dee . . .

Rocky: Yes, yes I know what your song is. Ok, I accept the fact that you only sing one song. But *why* do you have to *keep singing* it?

Mr. Bird: Because I'm looking for a mate, a partner, a Mrs. Bird . . .

Rocky: Oh brother, I should have known, the same old story.

Mr. Bird: That's what my song means:
                  Twee Tweedle Dee
                  Come see me
                  Titter Tatter Teer
                  I'd like you here
                  (flies off singing)

Rocky: Twee Tweedle Dee, Come see me. I think this bird is going to drive me crazy. I think it's *driven* me crazy. I'm starting to talk to myself. Well, I think the only way I'll get that bird to stop singing is to find him a mate. Here goes: Twee Tweedle Dee, Come see me. Titter Tatter Teer, I'd like you here. Come on audience, I could use some help. Twee Tweedle Dee, Come see me. (Ms. Bird appears)

Ms. Bird: Why I could have sworn I heard a Twee Tweedle Dee, Titter Tatter Teer coming from here. But I don't see any bird like me around. (starts to leave)

Rocky: Don't leave yet, Ms. Bird. If you go right by that tree over there, I'm sure you'll find yourself a handsome mate.

Ms. Bird: Thanks for the advice, Rocky. (leaves)

Rocky: Oh, I think this is going to work. Maybe I'll be able to sleep late now. (Mr. and Ms. Bird seen flying around together) It looks good. It looks very good! Thank you so much for the help audience. No more 5:00 mornings for me. (lies down, snores a little; sign saying Next Day 5 AM appears)

Mr. Bird: Twee Tweedle Dee, Titter Tatter Teer. (repeat)

Rocky: (waking up) I don't believe it. He's still singing at 5:00 in the morning. Mr. Bird. What is going on? I found you a mate.

Mr. Bird: Yes, but my song is not only to find me a mate.

Rocky: But you told me it meant Twee Tweedle Dee, Come see me. Titter, Tatter Teer, I'd like you here. Isn't that right audience? (pause)

Mr. Bird: Yes, but it also means:
                  Twee Tweedle Dee
                  Stay away from me
                  Titter Tatter Teer
                  Don't come near

Rocky: One song means two different things?

Mr. Bird: You said it. To a Ms. Bird it means one thing and to a Mr. Bird it means something else.

Rocky: But why are you trying to keep birds away?

Mr. Bird: Because this is *my* territory, *my* home. Mrs. Bird and I are going to build a nest and raise young here. My song will keep other birds like me away.

Rocky: Have you ever considered No Trespassing signs?

Mr. Bird: I'd rather sing.

Rocky: So when spring is over and Mrs. Bird and you have built your nest, raised your young, and we're well into summer, *then* will you be quiet?

Mr. Bird: Well, not completely quiet. I won't be singing my Twee Tweedle Dee so much, but I'll still be making my short calls to warn others of danger and tell them where there's food.

Rocky: As long as there won't be *quite* so much Twee Tweedle Deeing.

Mr. Bird: Speaking of which, I better get singing. Twee Tweedle Dee, Titter, Tatter, Teer. Bye, bye everyone. Twee Tweedle Dee . . .

FOLLOW-UP ACTIVITIES

1. Still Singing?
Encourage the children to return with their song maps (from Map and Trek activity) to the map and trek area on another day and see if the same songs can be heard in the same places. What does this say about bird nesting territories?

2. More About Me
Have the children look up the species of bird each portrayed in the Clock Chorus. Draw their individual bird, color it, and place it in its appropriate habitat, either on a group mural or by adding habitat details to their drawings.

3. Bird Walks
Using field guides and binoculars, take the children on birdwalks and learn to identify a few common birds. Mention the effects people can have or do have on the nesting habitats of the birds you find and of other common species (e.g. meadowlarks and bobolinks prefer to nest in unmown fields, barn and cliff swallows take advantage of buildings).

Skills
Science Process: Observing, Inferring, Brainstorming, Communicating, Comparing, Sorting and Classifying, Recording Data

Integrated Curriculum: Art, Drama, Music, Social Studies, Reading, Language Arts, Math

Suggested Reading for Children:

Ford, Barbara. *How Birds Learn to Sing*. New York: J. Messner, 1975. (o — very detailed)

Gans, Roma. *Bird Talk*. New York: Crowell Jr. Books, 1971. (y)

Flowers as Parents in the Plant World

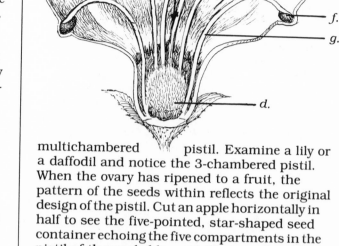

From the wilted handful of dandelions presented by a young child to its mother, to the glorious bouquet of red roses given to someone special, flowers have long been considered as one of nature's most perfect gifts. It's hard to believe, when looking at the soft pink blossoms of an apple tree or smelling the heavy sweetness of Easter lilies, that these beautiful flowers exist for one purpose only: to produce seeds. How they are shaped, their color, size, and smell all contribute to success in this vital mission.

The structure of a typical flower includes all the parts necessary for producing seeds, although there are many variations. In the center is the **pistil** (a), the seed producing organ. (The song "Pistol Packin' Mama" helps some remember its gender.) At its tip is the **stigma** (b) which is sticky or feathery to trap the **pollen** which lands there. It is held aloft by a stalk called the **style** (c). At the base of the pistil is the ovary (d) where the **ovules** with their egg cells await fertilization.

The male parts of the flower, which produce the pollen needed for fertilization, are called the **stamens** (e). As the pollen must travel to the stigma of another flower, the stamens are placed where they will be the most exposed to whatever agent will carry the pollen, whether wind or insect. The pollen is formed in the **anther** (f) at the top of the stamen. When it is ready for dispersal, the anthers split open and curl back to release it. Under a hand lens many anthers look like canoes or hot dog rolls. The anther is held aloft by the **filament** (g).

The petals are usually the most conspicuous part of the flower, and purposely so, for they serve as a banner to attract insects and also as a landing platform. Many petals even have lines on them to guide the insects to the nectar, encouraging them to brush against the pistil and stamens as they go. Wind-pollinated flowers, like those of an elm tree, have very unobtrusive petals or none at all. Beneath the petals are green leaf-like structures called sepals, which once enclosed and protected the bud.

A typical flower has all the parts thus far described. However, the arrangement of the parts varies considerably with a gradual streamlining of design having occurred among flower families over the millions of years flowering plants have existed. The early types of flowers, similar to buttercups, had numerous pistils and many stamens. Since then many kinds of flowers have reduced the number of their flower parts by joining the pistils together into a single multichambered pistil. Examine a lily or a daffodil and notice the 3-chambered pistil. When the ovary has ripened to a fruit, the pattern of the seeds within reflects the original design of the pistil. Cut an apple horizontally in half to see the five-pointed, star-shaped seed container echoing the five compartments in the pistil of the apple blossom. The number of stamens has also been reduced with more efficient placement within the flower.

In some flowering plants male and female parts are contained in separate flowers on different plants: sassafras, staghorn sumac, and holly bushes. Occasionally, in such plants as the beech tree, male and female flowers grow separately but on the same plant.

Whether wind-borne or insect-ferried, the pollen grain, once deposited on the stigma of the same kind of flower from which it came, sends forth a microscopic pollen tube to penetrate the ovary wall. Some of these tubes connect with the ovules providing passage for the male cells, which then fertilize the eggs. Once that has occurred, ovules grow into seeds and the ovary wall becomes the encasing fruit around the seeds. Picture a tomato or a milkweed pod, both ripened ovaries containing seeds.

To look closely at a flower is to find perfection in miniature. To consider its transformation into seeds and fruit is to be confronted by a miracle.

Suggested References:

Dowden, Anne Ophelia T. *Look at a Flower.* New York: Thomas Y. Crowell, 1963.

Meeuse, B. J. D. *The Story of Pollination.* New York: Ronald Press, 1961.

Newcomb, Lawrence. *Newcomb's Wildflower Guide.* Boston, MA: Little, Brown, 1977.

Peterson, R. T., and M. McKenny. *A Field Guide to Wildflowers of Northeastern and North-central North America,* Boston, MA: Houghton Mifflin, 1968.

Focus: *Wildflowers, while beautiful to look at, are designed to produce seeds. Their structure, color, and perfume all contribute to this purpose.*

ACTIVITIES	MATERIALS
Initial Question: Why do plants have flowers?	

POLLINATION PUPPET SHOW

Objective: To explain the basic method of pollination.

Give the puppet show. Discuss the roles played by the flower, Peter Pollen, Esther Egg, and the bee. What if the bee had not come along?

- *script, p. 163*
- *puppets*
- *2 big handmade flowers*

FLOWER PARTS

Objective: To allow the children to discover the basic structures of a flower and become acquainted with their functions.

- *flower puzzle pieces*

From the puppet show, review the important parts of a flower. Divide the children into groups and give each a set of flower-part puzzle pieces. Ask them to put the pieces together in a way that makes sense to them. After each group is finished, join everyone together to discuss different ways the puzzles were arranged noting that there are also many variations in design among real flowers. Briefly summarize the functions of the various parts.

Labels: Anther, Pollen grain, Stigma, Pollen tube, Style, Filament, Stamen, Ovule, Ovary, Petal, Sepal

ACTIVITIES	MATERIALS

DISSECT A FLOWER

Objective: To observe closely the different parts of a flower.

Give each group a flower to open up and examine, preferably with hand lenses. Ask them to try and identify the parts discussed in the puzzle. Cut the flower in half, lengthwise, and look for eggs/seeds in the ovary.

- *one flower per group* daffodil, tulip, or gladiola are easy to examine
- *hand lenses*

FLOWER HUNT

Objective: To observe the variety of flowers in the area and to notice differences among them.

Give each group a Flower Hunt card with the following instructions on it:

- Find a flower with a) petals bigger than a baby fingernail, b) 3 petals, c) more than 3 petals.
- Find a plant with a) many flowers on one stalk, b) a single flower on one stalk.
- Find a a) white flower, b) red flower, c) yellow flower.
- Find a flower that a) smells sweet, b) has no smell.
- Find a flower that a) lies on the ground, b) grows on a tree.
- Find a flower where the pistils and the stamens are a) easy to see, b) hard to find.
- Find a flower with a) one insect on it. Can you see pollen on the insect? b) With more than one insect on it. What are they doing?
- Choose a favorite flower. Draw a picture of it.

Tell the children to record their findings on the card while exploring the area for flowers. After a set time, all groups should come together and share the information about one of their flowers.

- *Flower Hunt cards*

MAKE A FLOWER

Objective: To give the children an opportunity to creatively express what they have learned about the form and function of a flower.

Briefly review what parts a flower needs in order to make seeds. Each child should make a flower and, depending on age level, explain what each part is and its use. The flower can be made as 1) a picture, 2) a paper flower, or 3) a three-dimensional flower, according to available materials. (If time is limited, use for a follow-up activity.)

- *Option 1* — paper and crayons
- *Option 2* — colored construction paper, glue, possibly paper plates
- *Option 3* — above, plus clay, straws, pipe cleaners, bits of styrofoam

POLLINATION PUPPET SHOW

Characters: Suzy
Father
Peter Pollen Grain and Paul Pollen Grain — dime-sized discs attached to pipecleaners, resting on stamens of one flower
Esther Egg — in pistil of the other flower
Bee

Props: Two flowers

Suzy: Dad, are we going to plant the seeds in our flower garden today?

Father: Oh, yes, I just bought a bunch of seeds in the store.

Suzy: Well, where did the store get the seeds from?

Father: Where do you think? The seed company.

Suzy: Where do the seed companies get them from?

Father: I suppose they get them straight from the flowers.

Suzy: Where do the flowers get the seeds from?

Father: The flowers make the seeds. You know about all that, don't you Suzy?

Suzy: Know all about what?

Father: Oh boy. Well, I guess I'll let the flowers speak for themselves. Let's go find some flowers.
(Father leaves; two flowers appear, one with pollen grains sitting on top of protruding stamens, the other with an egg in the center of the pistil)

Flower #1:

Peter: You know, it's pretty boring being a pollen grain. I mean, all we do is sit here on the end of this stem that sticks up out of this flower.

Paul: Peter, I've told you a million times. We're not sitting on the end of a stem. The stem is what the flower's sitting on. We're on top of the *stamen*.

Peter: Ok, the *stamen*, the *stamen*. What's the difference. It's still boring.

Paul: Well, it won't be boring for long. I've been told we're in for some great adventure.

Peter: An adventure? What kind of adventure?

Paul: I'm not sure exactly, but I think we're in for a little field trip.

Peter: You mean I won't be sitting on top of this stamen all my life?

Paul: Oh no, that I can promise you.

Flower #2:

Esther Egg: Oh gosh, I'm so lonely. Here I sit day in and day out at the bottom of this dark flower pistil. Of all the wonderful parts of a flower, I had to be the little egg that sits by itself at the bottom of the pistil. I have a feeling that some day, someone will come down here and visit me. But meanwhile, I'm so lonely. Most people don't even know there is an egg in a flower. What a lonely life I live.

Flower #1:

Peter: Oh no, what's that loud buzzing. (buzzing noises; bee flies around)

Paul: It's a bee. She's come to get the sweet nectar from the flower.
(bee flies to Peter)

Peter: Well, she's coming awful close to getting me. Yikes! (bee picks up Peter and flies around with him; flowers leave) Oh no, what's to become of me? I'm getting air sick. Uh oh, we're going in for a landing. (bee and Peter leave; Peter talks from backstage) Boy, that was a rough one. Now what's happening? I'm travelling down a long dark tube inside this flower. (Flower #2 reappears with Peter beside Esther)

Esther: Who are you?

Peter: I'm Peter Pollen Grain. Who are you?

Esther: I'm Esther Egg. I think I've been waiting for you a long time!
(Flower #2 leaves; Father and Suzy appear)

Father: So Peter Pollen Grain joins Esther Egg and together they become the most important part of the whole flower.

Suzy: What part is that, Father?

Father: Anyone in the audience know? (pause) The seed!

Suzy: The seed, of course. And that seed can start a whole new beautiful flower. Speaking of that, come on Dad, let's go plant our flower garden. Bye, bye everyone.

FOLLOW-UP ACTIVITIES

1. Choose One
Have each child choose and identify one flower using a wildflower guide, then draw and color the flower.

2. Adopt a Flower
Ask each child to adopt a flower and look at it daily, recording changes in size, color, and shape of the flower head. How do the seeds form and how long does it take before the seeds are ready to disperse?

3. Learn the Names
Together with the children, select ten common flowers, find out their names and learn them. (A local gardener or botanist might be able to help.) If they are *very common* wildflowers, they could be picked for display and labelling. Otherwise, discourage picking.

Skills

Science Process: Observing, Inferring, Brainstorming, Communicating, Comparing, Sorting and Classifying, Recording Data

Integrated Curriculum: Art, Drama, Reading, Writing, Language Arts, Math

Suggested Reading for Children:

Heller, Ruth. *The Reason for a Flower*. New York: Grosset & Dunlap, 1983. (y — wonderful illustrations, confusing format)

Johnson, Sylvia A. *Apple Trees*. Minneapolis, MN: Lerner Publication, 1983. (y/o — pollination, flowering, and more)

Selsam, Millicent E. *A First Look At Flowers*. New York: Walker, 1967. (y — good author)

_____. *Milkweed*. New York: William Morrow, 1967. (y/o — good author, one species' details)

CHAPTER IV — DESIGNS OF NATURE

Designs are evident everywhere in nature, from the shape of the scales on a cone to the concealing coloration of a caterpillar. Nature's designs may be beautiful in our eyes, but they contribute to a far greater cause, namely the survival of their owners.

Andreas Feininger, in a book called *The Anatomy of Nature*, gives the concept a special meaning as he describes a spider web he watched being built.

> Like any creation of nature, it is functional, designed for a definite purpose, constructed with marvelous economy to achieve maximum efficiency with a minimum expenditure of material and weight. It has clarity and symmetry of organization. And it derives from these basic qualities a particular kind of beauty which far surpasses that of man's ornamental design. (p. viii)

It is possible to appreciate designs of nature for their sheer beauty or for their functional efficiency. It is the purpose of the workshops in this concept to do both.

Webs and Their Weavers

Among nature's beautiful designs, few can surpass the intricate beauty of a spider web glistening with dew drops in the early morning sun. And few are so immediately and obviously functional. To watch a fly's unsuccessful twistings and turnings in the sticky strands of a web is to observe what an effective device a web can be for trapping food for its maker.

To many, the spider is far less worthy of admiration than its web, but, in fact, they are marvelous creatures. Although some people may think so, spiders are not insects. They are related in that they are both **arthropods**, and thus share jointed legs as well as external skeletons, but much of the similarity ends there. Spiders have eight legs, insects six; spiders lack both **antennae** and wings, both of which most insects possess; spiders have two body parts (**cephalothorax** and abdomen), and insects three (head, **thorax**, abdomen).

Spiders belong to the class Arachnida, as do mites and daddy longlegs (harvestmen). The scientific name is derived from the Greek word for spider, arachne, which commemorates the name of a legendary Greek maiden who challenged the Goddess Athena's spinning ability, and was turned into a spider.

The English word spider is a corruption of "spinder," one who spins. Almost all spiders can spin silk, and are able to do so from birth. The spinning organs are fingerlike projections called spinnerets that can be extended, withdrawn, compressed, and to some extent, aimed. They are located near the end of the abdomen on the undersurface. These spinnerets are tipped with many tiny spinning tubes as well as with "spigots" from which liquid silk comes. The silk, at least seven different kinds, is produced from glands within the abdomen. As soon as the fluid leaves the spider's body, it hardens quickly to form the familiar silken thread.

Spider silk has considerable strength and elasticity. A rope of spider's silk one inch thick would be stronger than a steel cable. Some of the threads will stretch one-half their length before they break. The thinnest lines are only one-millionth of an inch wide, and thus invisible to humans, but other lines are much heavier.

Not all spiders spin webs, but those that do, do so in order to catch insects. When an insect is caught in a web, the spider (often hiding off to the side) feels its struggles to escape. A spider can determine from the strength of the vibration whether prey has been caught, or a predator is approaching. If an insect is caught, the spider then rushes toward the prey, injects it with a poison that paralyzes it, and eventually ingests it. Spiders have small mouths and cannot eat solid food. They must either inject digestive fluids into the insect's body or secrete these fluids over it to dissolve the tissues, which they then suck in. Some spiders wrap the insect in silk and save it to eat later.

Webs vary greatly in complexity and structure, but there are a few fairly common and distinctive types.

Sheet webs are easily recognizable. The principal part of the web consists of a more or less closely woven sheet in a single, usually horizontal plane.

A funnel web is similar to a sheet web, the difference being that a funnel descends from it to the spider's hiding place.

The large conspicuous webs often seen on tall grass or suspended between dead tree branches during the summer are orb webs. They resemble a large wheel, sometimes with a zigzag band of silk running through the middle, which is thought to serve as a lure for flying insects. The characteristic design of this kind of web includes a number of supporting spokes made with dry and inelastic silk on which has been spun a sticky spiral elastic thread. The spider does not become entangled in its web because it steps only on the dry spokes and not on the sticky spiral lines.

One of the most familiar orb weavers is the black and yellow garden spider. Some species of orb spiders such as this one remain at the center of the web. Others hide in a nearby retreat where they can feel the vibrations of struggling prey along a so-called trap line that is stretched tightly from the center of the web to the den. The sensitivity of the spider to these vibrations, and its ability to interpret them, is remarkable.

During the late summer and early fall, spiders are apt to make a new web every twenty-four hours, as the large insects, once entangled, quickly destroy the webs. Most of this activity takes place around sundown.

Besides being used for webs, silk is also used for draglines. Wherever the spider goes, it always plays out a silken line that acts as a securing thread preventing falls and helping spiders to escape predators. Young spiders of most species (and adults of very small ones) spin unattached draglines in conditions of warm, fairly still air. The line is lifted by rising air currents and carries the young spider away with it. This is called ballooning and helps spiders reach new habitats.

Some spiders do not build webs, but instead stalk or ambush their prey. Wolf spiders, jumping spiders, and fishing spiders all go out and hunt their prey, whereas crab spiders wait in ambush for unsuspecting insects, capturing them without webs.

It would seem logical that spider silk, being so abundant, might be used commercially by humans. It is usable as fabric material in the same way as the silk of the silkworm. However, the practical difficulties of rearing and feeding large numbers of spiders are great because spiders are cannibalistic. Therefore, you will have to observe these wonderful silk creations and their creators in the natural world, or perhaps in your very own kitchen corner.

Suggested References:

Golden Nature Guide on *Spiders*. New York: Golden Press.

Gertsch, Willis J. *American Spiders*. Princeton, NJ: D. Van Nostrand, 1949.

Headstrom, Richard. *Spiders of the United States*. New York: A.S. Barnes, 1973.

Levi, Herbert W. and Lorna R. *Spiders and Their Kin*. New York: Golden Press, 1968.

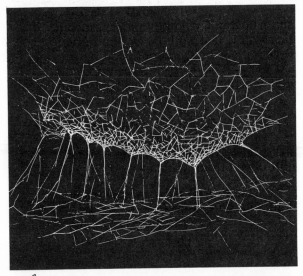

Sheet Web

Orb Weaver Web

Funnel Web

Focus: *Spider webs are beautifully designed to carry out their food-trapping functions, and so are the spiders that make them.*

ACTIVITIES	MATERIALS

Initial Question: Why do some spiders make webs?

SPIDER PUPPET SHOW

Objective: To introduce special characteristics of spiders and to point out some differences between spiders and insects.

Give the puppet show. Afterwards, discuss the differences between spiders and insects.

* *script, p.172*
* *puppets*

SPIDER SPYING

Objective: To give factual information through pictures and closer looks at live spiders.

Show pictures or read excerpts from the many excellent children's books and articles that illustrate spider webs and body parts. Pass around live spiders — one per jar — to look at closely. Use hand lenses. Notice the number of legs and eyes, body parts, hairiness. Look for silk in the jar, silk threads coming out of their spinnerets. Remember to release spiders back to where you found them.

Note: Some people are afraid of spiders. Encourage, but do not force children to hold a spider jar; perhaps you could hold it. If appropriate, discuss fears and explain that learning about something one fears often helps. Choose a couple of fears about spiders and explain the facts behind the scary looks or behaviors. If poisonous spiders live in your area, give the children information they should know.

* *pictures*
* *books about spiders*
* *hand lenses*
* *live spiders in jars* holes should be punched in the lid; try to pound out jagged edges

SPIDER SENSATIONS

Objective: To show how web-spinning spiders know by touch rather than by sight when they've captured prey in their webs.

Divide into groups of 6 and give each a wooden block, with yarn strands attached, to put on the floor. Designate one child to be the spider, crouched next to the block with eyes blindfolded, and the remaining 5 to be insects, who each take one strand of yarn and radiate out in all directions from the spider. The strands should be held taut, next to but not touching the ground. The spider's hands rest lightly on top of them in order to feel any vibrations. Leader points to one insect who plucks its strand once. The spider crawls to the end of the strand which moved, captures the insect, and then they change places. If the wrong insect was captured, the spider gets one more try.

Per Group:
* *block of wood* with 5 pieces of 6' yarn tied to large staple in center of block
* *1 blindfold*

ACTIVITIES	MATERIALS

SPIDER WEB RELAY

Objective: To illustrate through firsthand experience the process by which many spiders capture their food.

Divide the children into groups of 10. Arrange the groups in rows behind a starting line, each team facing a bicycle wheel "web." Leader passes out the relay props, explaining each child's task in the relay:

Child #1 gets spider to place on web

Child #2 gets fly to place on web

Child #3 pounces spider onto fly

Child #4 gets yarn to wrap up fly

Child #5 gets 2nd fly to place on web

Child #6 pounces spider onto fly

Child #7 gets yarn to wrap up fly

Child #8 gets 3rd fly to place on web

Child #9 pounces spider onto fly

Child #10 gets yarn to wrap up fly

At Go, the teams complete their ten tasks with each child returning to the starting line before the next child leaves. Leader may have to coach a little. Questions to ask at the end of the game might be, how did the spider know a fly landed? Why does it pounce on a trapped insect? Why does it wrap its food?

MATERIALS (for Spider Web Relay):
- *bicycle wheels*
  1 for each group with yarn woven in concentric circles through the spokes
- *spiders*
  1 per team made from pipe cleaners
- *flies*
  3 per team made from pipe cleaners
- *yarn strands*
  3 per team, 6-8" long

SPIDER HUNT

Objective: To encourage the children to notice as many different spiders and webs as possible.

Divide older children into pairs, younger children into small groups with a leader. Each group receives a Spider Hunt Card with the following list:

- A spider on a web.
- A spider not on a web (search flowers).
- An insect caught in a web.
- Part of a web that is sticky (look for liquid beads on the web, or lightly touch it).
- Part of a web not sticky.
- A web shaped like a sheet with a funnel on one side.
- A web near the ground.
- A web in the corner of a building.
- A web in a tree or bush.
- A web shaped like a wheel.
- A messy web.
- A spider egg case.

They should try to find as many items as possible, within set boundaries and a given time limit.

MATERIALS (for Spider Hunt):
- *Spider Hunt cards*
  one for each group

SHARING CIRCLE

Objective: To personalize each child's experience with spiders.

Sit in a large circle. Each child, in turn, completes this sentence: "One special thing about spiders is . . ."

SPIDER WEBS PUPPET SHOW

Characters: Bengi Bear
Charlotte Spider
Rhonda Robin

Bengi Bear: Ouch, Ouch!

Charlotte Spider: Hi, Bengi Bear. What's the matter?

Bengi: I'm pulling out bits of fur to make a cape to present to King Leo at the grand celebration.

Charlotte: What celebration?

Bengi: We're celebrating King Leo's return. All the animals of the woods are doing something special for him.

Charlotte: Great, what are the spiders doing?

Bengi: Well, all the insects will fly over the king and protect him from too much sun or rain.

Charlotte: Fly over the king! But spiders can't fly.

Bengi: Oh my, you can't, can you? I don't understand it. I thought all insects could fly.

Charlotte: But spiders aren't insects. Everyone thinks we are, but we're different from insects. Spiders are in a class all their own.

Bengi: I never knew that. I always thought you were insects.

Charlotte: No. We're really very different. Spiders have no antennae and no wings, and we have 8 legs. Insects only have 6 legs.

Bengi: Eight legs? Let's see if that's right (counts 7). (Charlotte protests) Let's count again. Will all of you help me count? (Counts 8) Goodness, you really are very different. I don't know what you spiders are supposed to do. If you've got no wings, you can't very well fly over the king.

Charlotte: You mean, no one has come up with anything special for the spiders to do? (almost crying)

Bengi: Well, uh . . .

Charlotte: Why does everyone forget about us spiders (crying)?

Bengi: It's not that we forgot about the spiders, Charlotte. We just thought you were insects.

Charlotte: Yes, that's the story of our lives. Everyone just thinks we're insects.

Bengi: Now don't cry, Charlotte. I'm sure we can think of something special for you spiders to do. What else can you tell me about spiders?

Charlotte: Well, we've got 8 eyes. How many animals do you know with 8 eyes?

Bengi: Eight eyes! I hope you never need glasses.

Charlotte: Well, it wouldn't matter so much if I did. We don't use our eyes as much as some other animals do.

Bengi: Oh, you mean you smell around for food.

Charlotte: No, not smell. We feel our food.

Bengi: Feel your food? But you must have to catch it before you feel it.

Charlotte: Oh, we do. We catch our food and we know we've caught it when we can feel it.

Bengi: Charlotte, I'm confused. What *are* you talking about?

Charlotte: We spin a web, a sticky silk web. Then we sit on or near the web and wait.

Bengi: Wait for what? Do any of you know what she waits for? (pause)

Charlotte: (That's right) we wait for little insects like flies and mosquitos to fly into the web and get caught. When we feel something moving, we rush out, bite whatever is caught, wrap some more silk around it, and eat it whenever we're hungry.

Bengi: Boy, you sure use a lot of silk. That must get expensive.

Charlotte: Expensive! Ha, ha, ha. We don't buy the silk, Bengi, we make it.

Bengi: Spiders can make silk? Wow, I wish I were a spider.

Charlotte: But don't forget. If you were a spider, everyone would be calling you an insect. Oh, it's so depressing. I guess I'll just stay at home in my web during the big celebration.
(leaves)

Bengi: Poor Charlotte. It's tough being a spider.
(Rhonda Robin appears)

Rhonda Robin: Bengi, Bengi, I'm glad I found you. I need your advice.

Bengi: What's the problem Rhonda?

Rhonda: I just spoke to King Leo's wife to find out what the king might like for a welcome home present. She said there was only one thing he wanted that he didn't have.

Bengi: Well, what's that? We'll get it for him.

Rhonda:	*Silk sheets.*
Bengi:	Silk sheets!
Rhonda:	Yes, silk sheets. Where are we ever going to get silk sheets?
Bengi:	Gosh, I don't know. Where are we going to get silk sheets? Do any of you in the audience know where we might get silk sheets? (Hopefully, they will suggest Charlotte Spider) That's a great idea. It will solve our problem and make Charlotte very happy. The spiders will have something special to do for the big celebration. (Rhonda Robin leaves; Charlotte walks across stage)
Bengi:	Charlotte, Charlotte, where are you going?
Charlotte:	The spiders just had a meeting. We can't stand the thought of a big celebration in which we have no part. So we've decided to move on to another forest. No one here will even miss us spiders.
Bengi:	But Charlotte, you can't leave. We *will* miss you, and besides, we do need you spiders. The spiders must make the gift that King Leo wants more than anything else in the world — silk sheets.
Charlotte:	Silk sheets! King Leo wants silk sheets? I've never slept on anything else myself. The spiders would be glad to make the king silk sheets, no problem at all. Bengi, this will make the spiders very happy. Thanks so much for thinking of us.
Bengi:	Oh, don't thank me. Thank the audience here. They're the ones that came up with the idea to ask you.
Charlotte:	Thanks everyone. You've made a lot of spiders very happy. We better go tell the others, Bengi, and then get right to work. Silk sheets for a lion could take a lot of time. Bye everyone, and thanks again.

FOLLOW-UP ACTIVITIES

1. Spider Web Spinning
Ask the children to each bring one wire coat hanger. Have the children "spin" webs around the hangers. Compare the different designs.

2. Read Aloud
Read *Charlotte's Web*, by E. B. White, aloud to the children.

3. Diary of a Spider
Suggest to the children that they find and watch one spider over a period of days or weeks and keep a journal of its activities.

Skills

Science Process: Observing, Inferring, Communicating, Predicting, Comparing, Recording Data

Integrated Curriculum: Art, Drama, Reading, Writing, Language Arts

Suggested Reading for Children:

Bason, Lillian. *Spiders*. Washington, DC: National Geographic Society, 1974. (y/o — excellent pictures)

Graham, Margaret B. *Be Nice To Spiders*. New York: Harper & Row, 1967. (y — charming story)

Lane, Margaret. *The Spider*. New York: Dial Press, 1983. (y — excellent photographs)

Oxford Scientific Films. *The Spider's Web*. New York: G. P. Putnam's Sons, 1978. (photographs)

Patent, Dorothy H. *Spider Magic*. New York: Holiday House, 1982. (o — photographs)

Rosen, Ellsworth. *Spiders Are Spinners*. Boston, MA: Houghton Mifflin, 1968. (y/o — illustrated poem)

Selsam, Millicent E. *A First Look At Spiders*. New York: Walker, 1983. (y — good author)

Walther, Tom. *A Spider Might*. New York: Scribner's (Sierra Club), 1978. (y/o — spiders' amazing feats)

White, E. B. *Charlotte's Web*. New York: Harper & Row, 1952. (o — classic story)

The Great Producers

Leaves come in a variety of sizes and shapes, but all share a common function; they manufacture food using a process called **photosynthesis**, which is unique to green plants.

This is how the process of photosynthesis works. Plants obtain water through their roots, from which it rises to the leaves. Here, in the presence of a green pigment called chlorophyll, and with energy provided by the sun, water is split into hydrogen and oxygen. At the same time, carbon dioxide is entering the leaf through leaf pores called **stomates**. Next, through some chemistry not yet fully understood, the hydrogen gas available from the splitting of the water is combined with the carbon dioxide. The result is sugar, a compound containing carbon, hydrogen, and oxygen. The leftover oxygen is released to the air, and helps replenish what we and all other animals need for breathing.

There are many adaptive designs that lend themselves to the efficiency of this photosynthetic process. Leaf size, even on the same plant, varies considerably. In general, leaves exposed to the full rays of the sun are smaller than those in the shade. The arrangement of leaves on a twig or stem usually takes advantage of the available sunlight.

Leaf shape varies considerably, from the needle-like leaves of the pines to the broad leaves of the maple. They can be nearly round, star-shaped or linear, but whatever their specific shape, the primary objective of leaves is to capture as much sunlight as possible in order to carry out photosynthesis as efficiently as possible. The total leaf surface exposed for light absorption is often amazing. An American beech tree fifteen inches in diameter was found to have 119,000 leaves with a total surface of about 3,000 square feet.

In addition, different shapes help to retain or remove water. Much of the water taken up by a plant for photosynthesis and for mineral nourishment is eventually **transpired** through the leaves of the plant. Some leaves, such as those of the American elm tree, are asymmetrical, in that the two sides are unequal. It is thought that this causes the leaves to tilt sideways in the rain allowing water to drain off quickly, which prevents bacterial infection. A majority of leaves have sharp points at their outer ends or along their margins. These "drip tips" also cause the water to flow off the leaf quickly. Rain water in drier areas evaporates rapidly, making these sharp tips unnecessary. Many leaves are lobed or divided, as are those of strawberry plants and ash trees. Divided leaves not only allow wind to pass through them without injuring them, but allow the leaf to transpire more water and take in carbon dioxide more efficiently. The fine teeth along the margins of many leaves act as emergency water pores allowing excess water to flow out of the leaf.

While green plants must have sunlight to live and manufacture food, the heat of the sun often causes them to lose too much moisture for proper functioning. They compensate for this with great efficiency. Leaves have many stomates, through which air passes inward, and water and gases escape. Most occur on the undersides of leaves. Cells on either side of each stomate expand and contract, controlling the water loss of the leaf. Desert plants have few stomates as they have to conserve what water is available. Willows on the other hand, thrive in moist habitats because they are unable to close their stomates completely, and thus cannot control moisture loss. Other adaptations that effectively conserve the water supply of plants include leaves turning on edge to avoid the hot sun, a thick outer leaf covering and temporary wilting.

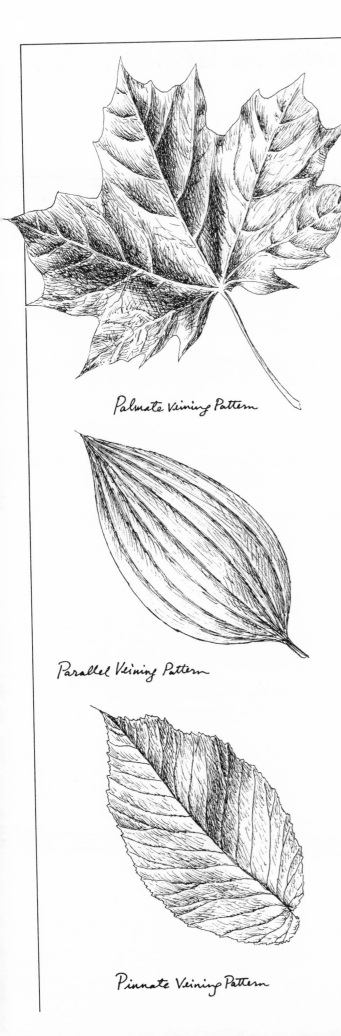

Palmate Veining Pattern

Parallel Veining Pattern

Pinnate Veining Pattern

Leaves are well designed for survival. Stems, or **petioles**, allow leaf blades to twist in the wind and rain, preventing the leaves from being torn to shreds. This movement also allows light to penetrate into the darker interior of the tree.

The design of leaves is not complete without mentioning the veins that extend through each leaf. Inside these veins are the ducts that carry water and minerals to the various parts of the leaf and carry manufactured sugars away. There are three common patterns — parallel, pinnate and palmate. Each species of plant has its own distinctive pattern of veins; most fit into one of the three categories.

Deciduous tree leaves demonstrate the ultimate efficiency of design, in that their very life span is determined by their usefulness to the tree. Chlorophyll, essential to photosynthesis, starts to disintegrate with shorter days and cooler temperatures in late summer, which allows hidden pigments such as xanthophyll (yellow) or carotene (orange or red) to be seen. Anthocyanin, another red pigment, is produced by the leaves when nights are cold and days are sunny. Brilliant fall foliage is the result. As the chlorophyll disappears, the leaves are no longer able to manufacture food for the tree. At this time about 90 percent of the minerals in the leaves are transported out of them and stored in the tree's tissues. A layer of corklike cells, the **abscission layer**, then gradually forms across the base of the leaf stem. The leaf soon breaks away and falls, exposing buds that, with the warmth of spring, will unfurl into next year's leaves.

Suggested References:

Brockman, Zim, Merlees. *Trees of North America.* New York: Golden Press, 1968.

Knobel, Edward. *Identify Trees and Shrubs by Their Leaves.* New York: Dover Publications, 1972.

Symonds, George W. D. *The Tree Identification Book.* New York: William Morrow, 1958.

Tolmie, Dr. Ghillean. Photos by Kjell Sandved. *Leaves.* New York: Crown, 1985.

Focus: *Leaves may vary in appearance and texture, but they are all designed to function as food producers for their plants.*

ACTIVITIES	MATERIALS

Initial Question: Why do plants have leaves?

TO EACH HIS OWN

Objective: To illustrate some differences among leaves.

Give each child a leaf to look at and study. Use hand lenses. After getting to know their leaves, all the children should put them in a pile, then find their own. After everyone has found the correct leaf, ask what were the unique characteristics of each. Point out the variety of shapes, sizes, textures, and patterns, and explain that these help serve important functions. Ask the children to look at their leaves and hold up the ones that:

1. catch the most sunlight — some trees have bigger leaves than others. When the leaves are small there are usually more of them.

2. are best protected from the wind — some leaves have flat stems (poplars) so they move easily in the wind rather than break; some have short stems, which hold them close to the twigs.

3. are designed so they won't become either too wet or too dry — some leaves have points on them or waxy coatings (oak leaves, pond lily leaves) so the water will drip off; others have rough or fuzzy coats to help keep moisture in.

Materials:
- *leaves*
  a few different kinds, 3 or 4 of each kind
  1 per each child
- *hand lenses*

LEAF RUBBING

Objective: To notice that the veins in different kinds of leaves look different.

Have each child keep the leaf from the previous activity. With the underside of the leaf up, place a piece of paper over the leaf and rub gently with a crayon to get a leaf rubbing. The most noticeable structures will be the veins. Try this again with other leaves. Discuss the three common veining patterns: parallel, palmate, and pinnate. Ask the children which kind they illustrated in their rubbings.

Materials:
- *paper*
- *crayons*
- *leaves*
- *diagram of 3 patterns*

ACTIVITIES	MATERIALS

LEAF LOOK

Objective: To look for and find an assortment of leaves outdoors.

Divide the children into small groups. Give each group a Leaf Look card with the following instructions:

Find a leaf:

- with 5 points
- with smooth edges; toothed edges
- with more than one color on it
- that is green; orange; brown; yellow; red
- on the ground, then try to find its parent plant
- that could catch a lot of sunlight
- whose stem is stiff; flexible
- that is waxy or rough

Find:

- 3 differently shaped leaves
- leaves with parallel veins
- leaves with palmate veins
- leaves with pinnate veins

Choose one leaf to collect and show to the others.

Tell them to look for the various leaves described. Afterwards, gather the groups together and have each show its special leaf. Why did they choose it?

Note: All kinds of leaves are appropriate, from blades of grass to palm fronds.

Materials:
- *Leaf Look cards*

PUPPET SHOW

Objective: To demonstrate the function of green leaves.

Explain that having seen the many different shapes and designs of leaves, the children are now going to find out what leaves do for a plant. Hang up poster with song words. Give the puppet show. Discuss why it is that leaves are sometimes called food factories and how all of us are dependent on plants for food.

Materials:
- *script, p. 178*
- *puppets*
- *poster with song words*

HAVE YOU THANKED A GREEN PLANT TODAY?

Objective: To become aware of our dependency on green plants.

Each child should tell his or her favorite food. (The leader writes the foods on a blackboard or newsprint.) When all have finished, trace a few of the foods back to their plant origins.

VARIATIONS ON A LEAF PUPPET SHOW

Characters: Farmer
Spouse
Goldie Goldenrod
Chlorophyll (green circle with pipe cleaner arms)

Props: CO_2 (blob with CO_2 label)
Water (drop)
Sunshine (yellow wedge)

Farmer: What's for dinner today, dear?

Spouse: Green beans.

Farmer: Beans again? We had beans last night.

Spouse: That was lima beans, tonight it's green beans.

Farmer: Green, lima, what's the difference? It's still beans, and I'm sick of beans.

Spouse: Well, food is so expensive now. We can't afford anything but beans.

Farmer: I'd rather stop eating if all I can eat are beans.

Spouse: Now don't be silly. You can't stop eating. All living things need some type of food.

Farmer: You know, you're right about that. Why, even plants need food. They're lucky though. They don't have to buy food, they make it. When was the last time you saw a plant going into a grocery store or stopping off at McDonalds?

Spouse: Hey, maybe we can make our own food. You know a lot about plants. Try to figure out how we can make food without buying anything. But hurry up, I'm getting hungry. (leaves)

Farmer: Hmmm. If I've got to figure out how plants make food, I'd better go talk to my friend Goldie Goldenrod. (Goldie appears; Farmer walks over to her) Hello, Goldie Goldenrod. How are you?

Goldie Goldenrod: I'm fine, enjoying the nice sunshine. I wish it would rain a little, though. The soil is getting awfully dry, and I do need water as well as sunshine.

Farmer: So water and sunshine are all you need to make food?

Goldie: Not exactly. I couldn't make food without the air around me and the chlorophyll in me.

Farmer: The *what* in you?

Goldie: Chlorophyll. Why chlorophyll's the most important thing we green plants have. Not only does it make us green, it helps us to make our food.

Farmer: Oh no, this sounds very confusing.

Goldie: A lot of people think it's confusing, but it's really not. That's why Mr. Chlorophyll wrote this little song and dance.

Farmer: What little song and dance?

Goldie: You ready Chlorophyll?

Chlorophyll: (from behind) I'm ready.

Goldie: A one, and a two, and hit it. (Chlorophyll appears)

Chlorophyll: Chlorophyll's the name, making food is the game.

(to the tune of "Oh My Darling")

First I take some carbon dioxide
Which I get straight from the air.
(CO_2 pops up)
And I mix it with some water
For the food I will prepare.
(water pops up)
Then I capture me some sunshine
(sun pops up)
And I mix the whole thing up.
And presto, there is plant food
Good for breakfast, lunch or sup.
So remember how important
These three friends all are to me.
With their help I find I'm able
To make plant food for Goldie.

Goldie and Farmer: Bravo, bravo!

Farmer: I'd like to hear that again.

Chlorophyll: Sure. But this time how about you and Goldie and anyone from the audience joining in?

Goldie: Great. A one, and a two, and hit it. (repeat song; hold up words on a large poster)

Goldie: You better go back now Chlorophyll. Thanks for the show.

Chlorophyll: Anytime, anytime. Hollywood, here I come. (leaves)

Farmer: That was great, Goldie. Now I know how you green plants make food. And I also know something else.

Goldie: What's that?

Farmer: Since I don't have any chlorophyll, I better start liking beans. (leaves)

Goldie: Liking beans? You know, sometimes I think plants are a lot easier to understand than people.

FOLLOW-UP ACTIVITIES

1. Spatter Prints

Have the children place leaves on paper and either shake paint off a paint brush or scratch paint with a toothbrush through window screening over them.

2. Celery Magic

Place fresh celery stalks upright in water that has been dyed different colors. Notice what happens to the celery. How long does it take?

3. Identification

Ask the children to choose 4 or 5 favorite, common tree leaves and look them up in a Tree Guide to find out what kind of tree they come from. Make a rubbing of each and write its name along with some of its special features beside the rubbing.

Skills

Science Process: Observing, Inferring, Communicating, Comparing, Sorting and Classifying

Integrated Curriculum: Art, Drama, Music, Social Studies, Reading, Writing, Language Arts, Math

Suggested Reading for Children:

Bancroft, Henrietta. *Down Come The Leaves*. New York: Crowell, 1961. (y — shapes, colors, purpose)

Caulfield, Peggy. *Leaves*. New York: Coward, 1962. (o — photographs, details, adult text)

Davis, Burke. *Biography of a Leaf*. New York: G. P. Putnam's Sons, 1972. (o — ecological role and life cycle)

Selsam, Millicent E. *First Look at Leaves*. New York: Walker, 1972. (y — questions to encourage observation)

Slender Stalks with Seeds That Nourish the World

easured in terms of geographic distribution and numbers of individual plants, the grass family is the most successful flowering plant family in the world. The almost 5,000 species, about one-third of which are found in North America, are distributed from tropic to tundra and from marsh to desert. Only the orchid and **composite** (for example, sunflowers, daisies; see p. 206) families have more species, but neither are as numerous in individual plants or grow in such diverse and widespread areas.

One key to the success of the grasses is the simplicity and adaptability of their basic design. The root system is dense and spreading, enabling the plants to utilize all available moisture, an important adaptation for plants that frequently grow in dry areas. This root mat also enables grasses to hold on to loose, sandy, or muddy soils such as marshes and sand dunes where they are often found.

Rhizomes, or underground stems, are an intricate part of the structure of many grasses. Like roots, rhizomes are important in that they help grasses hold on to soil. A second important function of rhizomes is propagation. These underground stems send up numerous shoots. If you have ever tried to eliminate witch grass from a garden, you are familiar with the white runners that send up what seems like endless plants. Rhizomes are an important design for the survival of grasses in areas that are burned frequently, such as prairies. While surface vegetation is burned, the underground stems are unharmed and quickly send up replacements. This adaptation is one of the factors that enable grasses to outcompete trees in prairie areas where lightning fires are common.

The stems of grasses are jointed with elongated round hollow sections interspersed with compact solid sections called **nodes**. Unlike most other plants, grass stems grow from the nodes, not from the tops or ends of branches — a necessity for a plant family that is browsed by a wide variety of animals. The nodes help provide additional rigidity for the plant as well as acting as points from which the leaves originate. The leaves encircle the stem, one above each node, in a sheath, and then protrude in different directions to provide for maximum exposure to the sun. Clasping the stem affords the long, narrow leaves much needed support. Some stems grow vertically; others may trail along the ground and root anew at each node.

Grasses are flowering plants and, as such, produce seeds. Unlike the general picture of a large colorful flower, grass flowers are small and easy to pass by. They are, however, extremely efficient at doing their job of making seeds. While many other flowers are **pollinated** by insects that must be attracted by either sight or scent, grass flowers are wind pollinated. This enables them to spend their energies producing prodigious amounts of pollen rather than showy flower parts. The pollen is tiny, allowing for easy transportation by the wind. The spring sufferings of hayfever victims is in part a testament to the pollen productivity of grass.

Seed dispersal is well developed and diverse in the grass family. Wind carries many grass seeds to new locations. These seeds are often equipped with fine hair-like structures similar to those found on dandelion seeds. Animals are also instrumental in spreading grass seeds. This can happen in many ways: by sticking to an animal's body as is the case with many barbed and pointed seeds, by being eaten and left in droppings, and by being stored for future use and forgotten. Still other grasses have seeds that are only lightly attached to the plant. These seeds are designed to be knocked to the ground by rain or passing animals. But whether intentionally or inadvertently, people have been the chief dispersers of grass seeds.

Grasses are the most important of plant families to people. Not only do we use grass for lawns and playing fields, we also use grass seeds as the basis of our diet. Wheat, rice, corn, oats, barley, rye, and sugar cane are all in the grass family. There would be little meat without grasses and their grains, which form the major component of both domestic and wild **herbivores'** diets.

Studying grasses is often intimidating to the inexperienced, because of uncertainty as to which plants are really grasses. If the stem has swollen nodes with each leaf starting its growth at a node, sheathing the stem before splitting to form a blade, then it almost certainly belongs to the grass family.

Take some time to look closely at and enjoy grasses. Their diversity and adaptability of design deserve our attention.

Suggested References:

Brown, Lauren. *Grasses Northeastern States.* Boston, MA: Houghton Mifflin, 1979.

Pohl, Richard W. *How to Know the Grasses.* Dubuque, IA: Wm. C. Brown, 1978.

Focus: *Grasses are uniquely designed to withstand challenges of weather and animals. Most members of the grass family produce grains that are a vital food source.*

ACTIVITIES	MATERIALS
Initial Question: How do grass plants look different from most other plants?	

FOCUS ON FEATURES

Objective: To notice firsthand some of the unique characteristics of grasses.

Gather in one or more circles, each with a leader. Pass a grass plant around each group. Each person, as they hold and examine it, should describe one characteristic. Make sure the following characteristics are noticed:

- The overall tall skinny shape of the plant
- The thick mat of roots
- The division of the stem into sections
- The way the leaves wrap around the stem before spreading open
- The long, narrow shape of the leaves
- The cluster(s) of flowers or seeds

Materials:
- *freshly picked grass plant* (a corn plant is good) with its roots and dirt clump still intact

GRASS MIX AND MATCH

Objective: To be able to distinguish different types of grasses by their seed heads.

Collect in advance 5 or 6 kinds of grasses, including seed heads, for each group. Use a photocopier to make a picture of each type of grass, or make a drawing that represents the overall shape and pattern of each seed head. Then, using a set of the same kinds of grasses that were photocopied or drawn, but *not* the same individual stems, have each small group of children choose one grass stalk and match it to the correct picture. Encourage the children to examine the grass with a hand lens and describe its unique features. Try to find matching grasses outdoors.

Materials:
- *sets of 5-6 kinds of grasses* (with seed heads) 1 for each group
- *sets of xeroxed pictures* or drawings of the same kinds of grasses 1 for each group
- *hand lenses*

STALK THE GRASS

Objective: To notice differences among grasses.

Divide into small groups and provide each group with a Stalk the Grass card with the following instructions on it.

Look for grasses with the following colors:
   green
   tan

Look for different sized grasses:
   taller than your hips
   shorter than your knees
   shorter than your feet
   the widest, skinniest, longest, shortest grass leaf that you can find

Materials:
- *Stalk the Grass cards*

ACTIVITIES	MATERIALS

Look for different textures:
   shiny
   hairy
   that tickles
   that is scratchy

Look for grass without seeds.

Look for grasses with different kinds of seed heads.

Look for a piece of grass:
   that has been partly eaten
   with an insect on it

Choose one grass stalk. With eyes closed, run your fingers up the stem from the ground to the tip. How many swollen joints (nodes) are there?

Send the children out to complete the hunt. Be clear about whether they should or should not pick specimens. They may want to *if* there are plenty and they need them for Nature Weaving.

NATURE WEAVING *(grades K-3)*

Objective: To create something beautiful or interesting with grasses.

- *sticks* forked or straight
- *string or twine*
- *grasses* and other natural materials

Start a square framework made of sticks and string or twine, or use a forked stick with strings stretched across the Y of the stick. Children can then weave their grasses and other finds into this framework.

BUILD A GRASS PLANT *(grades 4-6)*

Objective: To give the children firsthand experience with how a grass plant is made.

- *scissors*
- *tape*
- *string*
- *construction paper*

Divide the children into groups of three or four, giving each group the materials to build their plant. Have the children build plants illustrating the following grass characteristics.

1) a thick tangle of roots

2) a jointed stem (some grass stems may telescope — sections that fit into each other)

3) sword-shaped leaves with their bases sheathing the stem and their blades sticking out from it.

Have the children compare their plants and discuss what makes them grasses.

SNACK

Objective: To show how dependent humans are on some species of the grass family for food.

- *grains*

Pass out grains, which are actually grass seeds, for the children to eat. Discuss the fact that the children are eating grass seeds and that these make up a major portion of every person's diet. Easy to serve seeds include popcorn, puffed wheat, puffed rice, wheat chex, rice chex, and other breakfast cereals.

FOLLOW-UP ACTIVITIES

1. Watch It Grow
Encourage the children to mark off a small patch of grass and watch how fast it grows after cutting. Look for new blades of grass. They should try watering it, blocking out the sun, adding fertilizer. How does each affect the grass's growth? Record findings.

2. Other Uses
Discuss, or have the children research, the many other uses of grass around the world. They could draw pictures to illustrate their findings.

3. Word Games with Grains
a) Make up a crossword puzzle using foods made from grains.
b) Make up a word search in which children should circle grains and foods from them.
c) Post a list of foods that are made from grains along with a few "false" foods (grapenuts, grapes). Have the children discuss the list.

Skills

Science Process: Observing, Inferring, Brainstorming, Communicating, Comparing, Experimenting, Recording Data

Integrated Curriculum: Art, Social Studies, Reading, Writing, Language Arts

Suggested Books for Children:

Rinkoff, Barbara. *Guess What Grasses Do.* New York: Lothrop, Lee & Shepard, 1972. (y/o — uses of grasses)

Selsam, Millicent E. *Popcorn.* New York: Morrow, 1976. (o — good photographs, plant features)

Uhl, Melvin John. *All About Grasses, Grains and Canes.* Chicago, IL: Melmont, 1964. (o — uses of grasses)

SNOWFLAKES

Crystals in the Clouds

If you look very closely at a snowflake, you will quickly discover it is far from being just a small round speck of ice. It is usually an aggregate or collection of snow crystals. Although they begin as water vapor freezing around tiny, solid particles in the air, such as dust or salt, snow crystals take on beautiful shapes as they form. A crystal, by definition, is a regular and repeated arrangement of atomic particles. Based on similar geometric features, crystals can be grouped into one of six systems. Snow crystals fall into the hexagonal system, consisting of six-sided vertical or horizontal prisms. They are grouped according to their particular type of hexagonal crystal growth and its modifications. Some of the more common classifications are:

Hexagonal Plates: six-sided flat crystals with varying internal designs

Hexagonal Columns: six-sided cylinders with flat ends

Bullets: hexagonal columns with one conical end; sometimes a number of them grow outward from a common point to form a rosette

Capped Columns: hexagonal columns with hexagonal plates on either end

Needles: long slender six-sided columns looking like tiny bolts of lightning

Stellar Crystals or Dendrites: star-shaped with six branches having simple to elaborate designs radiating from the center

Spatial Dendrite: feathery stellar crystals with other branches projecting, usually at 90° angles from each of the six original branches

Graupel: small snow crystals that become coated with frozen droplets (rime) as they fall through moisture laden clouds

What determines which of these crystal formations will develop? The differences are due chiefly to the temperature and the amount of water vapor in the air in which the crystal grows and through which the crystal falls as a snowflake. When the temperature is very low, there is relatively little water vapor and the crystal growth will be relatively slow. Slow crystal growth results in small, simple snow crystals such as the columns and bullets, which form in high, wispy looking cirrus clouds. The low lying, heavier looking clouds, on the other hand, have a higher temperature, more water vapor, and thus a more rapid crystal growth. This yields the more complex varieties such as stellar crystals and spatial dendrites.

In addition to the varied crystal shapes, there is an even greater variety of designs within the crystal, formed by ridges, grooves, cavities, and water films. Ridges are thicker portions within the crystal, occurring along junctions of crystal segments. Grooves result where crystal segments, arms, or branches have only partially joined together. Most of the lines and dots on snow crystals are due to cavities, usually empty, but sometimes partially filled with water. Finally, the wavy scallops are caused by water films produced by slight melting. Along with diverse patterns, these formations also create varying degrees of brightness by the different ways in which they reflect or disperse light.

Snow is usually white because the crystals reflect and scatter all colors of the spectrum, leaving almost none to be absorbed. Occasionally, however, cold fluffy new snow has a bluish tinge, especially in the fresh cavities made while shovelling or playing in the snow. In the evening, snow sometimes reflects the sunset colors with a softer version of pinks and reds.

Since childhood, many of us have been told that no two snowflakes are alike. Probably this is true, though it would be impossible to prove. Looking at freshly fallen flakes through a hand lens one can see exquisite crystals, each one different: sturdy discs with scalloped edges, delicate stars, some with tiny stars attached, some icy looking. When it snows, pause to catch a snowflake and examine one of nature's most delicate designs.

Suggested References:

Bentley, W. A., and W. J. Humphreys. *Snow Crystals.* New York: Dover Publications, 1962.

Kirk, Ruth. *Snow.* New York: William Morrow, 1978.

LaChapelle. *Field Guide to Snow Crystals.* Seattle, WA: University of Washington Press, 1969.

Nakaya, Ukichiro. *Snow Crystals, Natural and Artificial.* Cambridge, MA: Harvard University Press, 1954.

Focus: *Snowflakes have beautiful designs and patterns caused by variations in temperature and moisture when they form.*

ACTIVITIES	MATERIALS

Initial Question: What do you know about snowflakes?

FLAKES ON FILM

Objective: To provide information about the main classifications of snowflakes.

Show pictures of snowflakes and discuss how the temperature and moisture content of the air influence the formation of different kinds of flakes. Name the basic classifications if appropriate to the age level.

- *photographs or drawings* of snowflakes (W. A. Bentley & Wm. Humphrey's *Snow Crystals*, Dover Publications)

SNOW MELT

Objective: To show how much of the volume of snow is actually occupied by air.

Give each group of children a clear plastic cup full of loose snow. Ask them to decide where they think the water level will be when the snow melts and to mark the spot with a colored rubber band. Set the cups in a warm place. Check in an hour — how close were the guesses? Discuss results.

- *cups of snow*
- *rubber bands* assorted colors

MAKE A FLAKE

Objective: To emphasize the six-sided structure of snowflakes and to create a winter snowstorm.

Give each child a square of paper. Follow the steps as illustrated. Cut out various shapes along edges EG and GF. Open up and you have a beautiful 6-pointed snowflake. Tape a piece of white thread to the snowflake (have varying lengths of thread), and tape the thread to the underside of the top of a large cardboard box. The front side of the box should be cut away and the bottom and back should be decorated as a winter scene.

- *white paper*
- *scissors*
- *thread*
- *tape*
- *winter scene* in an open-faced cardboard box

Note: For younger children, the folding can be done beforehand and just the cutting out left for them to do.

ACTIVITIES	MATERIALS

HIDDEN IMAGES

Objective: to look closely at the designs within a snowflake.

Give each pair of children a sheet of snowflake pictures to scrutinize for images within the snowflakes. When someone finds an image, describe it (e.g., I see what looks like 6 horses heads; these look like birds in flight). The others look for the snowflake with that image.

- *Snowflake pictures* enough copies for each pair of children

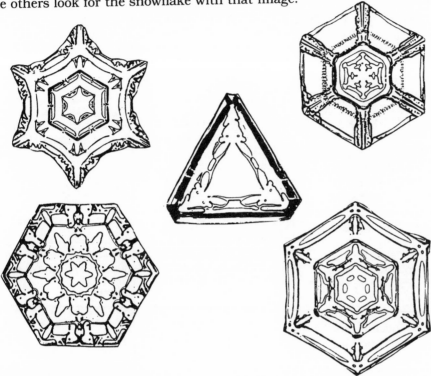

SNOW SHAKERS

Objective: To give the children a chance to make their own snow scenes.

Give each child a small glass jar with lid, a bit of florist clay, a small piece of styrofoam, and an evergreen twig. With the waterproof adhesive clay, stick the styrofoam to the inside of the lid. Then stick the twig into the styrofoam. Decorate, if you wish, with colored coding dots representing Christmas decorations or leaves. Fill the jar with "snowflake water," screw lid on tight, invert jar, and shake — a snowstorm!

- *small jars* with tight-fitting lids 1 per child
- *styrofoam*
- *clay* florist or waterproof adhesive
- *evergreen twigs*
- *colored dots*
- *snowflake water* — water with silver glitter added

SNOWFLAKE FANTASY

Objective: To develop a feeling for the creation and life of a snowflake.

Have the children find a quiet place where they can curl up with a jacket or sweater over their heads and with eyes closed. Read the fantasy and have them imagine that they are living it.

- *Snowflake Fantasy,* p. 188

FLAKES UP CLOSE

Objective: To notice the intricate designs of real snowflakes.

If it is snowing, take the children outside. Tape a small scrap of chilled dark material or dark construction paper onto the arm of each child, and give everyone a hand lens. Look closely at the snowflakes that fall onto the material. Share findings (who sees a star-shaped flake? a six-sided box? etc.).

- *dark material* small scrap for each child
- *tape*
- *hand lenses*

You are a tiny speck of dust, sitting on top of a dried-up weed in the middle of a big field. It is January and a cold, strong wind blows. Last fall, just when the children were going back to school, you landed on the weed while it was alive and green. Now you are wondering, will I ever become unstuck from this dried-up old weed?

The cold wind blows longer and harder, causing your weed stalk to shake back and forth. Suddenly you are thrown off of the weed and you are headed right for a grove of trees. The bare branches of the trees look closer and closer as the wind carries you toward them. Just at the last instant before you crash, you are lifted up over the tree tops and into the open sky.

As you rise higher and higher, you feel light as a feather. Down below, the field that you came from looks like a tiny speck on the earth. Just as you look up, the wind carries you into a dark gray cloud. Here, in the cloud, there are millions and billions of dust particles rushing around and bumping into one another. "Hey, watch it," you yell as a careless piece of dust bumps into you. "Ouch! It's too crowded in here."

It's also very wet and cold in the cloud and some water vapor begins to freeze onto you, forming tiny ice crystals on your side. More and more water vapor freezes onto you, and you begin to form little arms of feathery ice. You feel like a cold piece of white lace.

Now you have six beautiful arms growing longer and wider, so big that you become too heavy and start to fall. All around you thousands of other crystals are falling and floating down. Lower and lower you sink. Your arms stop growing and you look at them. You are now a tiny snowflake, a white, shining star falling to the earth. In every direction you look are other snowflakes and the whole world seems to be white.

You can't tell where you are going. You begin asking yourself, when will I ever land? Where will I be?

Have the children sit up. Ask them questions such as:
Where do you want to land? Why?
What do you want to become after you
    hit the ground?
What happens to snowflakes?

1. Record Snowfalls
Help the children keep a record of snowstorms. What type of flakes fell, and how many inches of snow in each?

2. Permanent Impressions
Show the children how to make snowflake imprints by catching falling flakes on chilled glass freshly sprayed with chilled hair spray.

3. Crystal Gazing
Invite the children to examine other frost crystals with a hand lens, such as window frost, crystals on plants, frost in a deep freeze. Notice similarities and/or differences.

Skills

Science Process: Observing, Brainstorming, Communicating, Predicting, Comparing, Measuring

Integrated Curriculum: Art, Drama, Reading, Writing, Language Arts, Math

Suggested Reading for Children:

Bell, Thelma Harrington. *Snow.* New York: Viking, 1954. (o)

Bentley, W. A., and W. J. Humphreys. *Snow Crystals.* New York: Dover Publications, 1962. (y/o — photographs of real snowflakes, adult text)

Branley, Franklyn M. *Snow is Falling.* New York: Thomas Y. Crowell, 1963. (y — general look at snow)

Busch, Phyllis S. *A Walk in the Snow.* Scranton, PA: Lippincott Jr. Books, 1971. (y — photos, sensory exploration)

Nestor, William P. *Into Winter — Discovering a Season.* Boston, MA: Houghton Mifflin, 1982. (o — lots of information)

Webster, David. *Snow Stumpers.* Garden City, NY: The Natural History Press, 1968. (y/o — snow and ice mysteries)

Williams, Terry, and Ted Naylor. *Secret Language of Snow.* New York: (Sierra Club) Pantheon, 1984. (o — snow around the world)

TRACKS AND TRACES

Clues That Tell a Tale

To discover animal tracks in the snow or to come across footprints along the muddy edge of a pond is almost as exciting as seeing the creatures that made them. In fact, it may be more so, because unless you are lucky, or very well concealed, an animal will flee at the first hint of your presence.

Tracks, on the other hand, remain waiting to be examined, measured, and followed. Infrequent glimpses of an animal cannot tell you much about its habits and behavior; tracks can.

The immediate impulse upon finding a track is to ask what made it. However, there are many questions to ask, even if one can identify the tracks, because knowledge about any animal increases with observations about where it's been, what it's been doing, and where it's going.

One of the first questions has to do with habitat — is the track near a pond? a stream? in the middle of a field? deep in the woods? The answer eliminates some track-maker possibilities. You would not expect to find a beaver track in the center of a field any more than a squirrel track in the middle of an iced-over lake.

How big is the print and how deeply embedded? Sometimes, in deep snow especially, it is unclear whether a print was made by a single foot, or by all four feet landing together. At this point it is necessary to decide whether you are looking at one large footprint, like that of a dog, or a pattern of footprints like those of a squirrel in which all four feet land quite close together. Once the relative size of the footprints is determined, one can guess the approximate size of their owner.

Individual footprints can quickly settle the mystery of who made them if the prints are clear. They rarely are, because melting, freezing, rain, snow, and wind tend to blur distinct features. Sometimes the prints are obliterated by excited trackers; remind children to step carefully. Details to notice that will help identify the track include shape, length, width, number of toes, presence or absence of toenail marks, and even the shape and number of pads.

As habitat, size of track, and footprint are being examined, so too should the pattern of the track. For many trackers, this is the single most important clue. Although any animal may speed up or slow down, which can alter its track pattern, most animals typically fit into one of 4 distinct ways of moving: walking/trotting, galloping, bounding, waddling (see page 190).

Once you have determined the pattern, it's time to measure the tracks. The distance between footprints (as in the walkers) or between sets of footprints (as in the gallopers) is called the **stride**.

The width of the track from the outer edge of one print to the outer edge of the next print (illustration) or across the set of prints (illustration) is called the **straddle**. Size of animals can vary, as can their speed and thus the size of their leaps, but if one knows the pattern, the stride, the straddle, and the dimensions of at least one footprint, one can usually figure out the track with the help of a good track book.

Identifying the tracks gives great satisfaction, but following them reveals a chapter in the animal's life otherwise closed to most of us. Does the path follow a fairly straight route toward some seen or unseen destination, and are the tracks evenly spaced? If so, the animal was probably neither pursuing nor being pursued. Does the animal go under low branches, around them, or step over them? (A hint as to its height.) Do the tracks end at a tree? Does the pattern and spacing suddenly extend, showing that the animal speeded up?

Animals move about for three main reasons. They are probably looking for food, for shelter, or for mates. Nibbled branches, cone scales, bits of fur or feathers and blood indicate three quite different eaters: a deer or rabbit may nibble branches, a squirrel peals off cone scales to get at its seeds, and a predator, like a fox or a hawk, might account for remnants of hair or feathers. Holes in the snow or well-trodden paths leading to hollow trees or evergreen groves can indicate a shelter or home. A ruffed grouse will dive into soft snow on cold nights to take advantage of the snow's insulation. Porcupines and deer reuse paths to and from their sheltered spots. In the spring, tracks of animals that usually appear alone, like fox tracks, are often paired.

Tracking may leave its followers with more questions asked than answers found, but there is no better way to learn about the secretive world of wild creatures without interfering in their lives.

Suggested References:

Brown, Tom Jr., and William Jon Watkins. *The Tracker*. Englewood Cliffs, NJ: Prentice-Hall, 1978.

Ennion, E. A. R., and N. Tinbergen. *Tracks*. London, England: Oxford University Press, 1967.

Headstrom, Richard. *Whose Track Is It?*. New York: Ives Washburn, 1971.

Murie, Olaus. *Field Guide to Animal Tracks*. Cambridge, MA: Houghton Mifflin, 1954.

Stokes, Donald. *A Guide to Nature in Winter*. Boston, MA: Little, Brown, 1976.

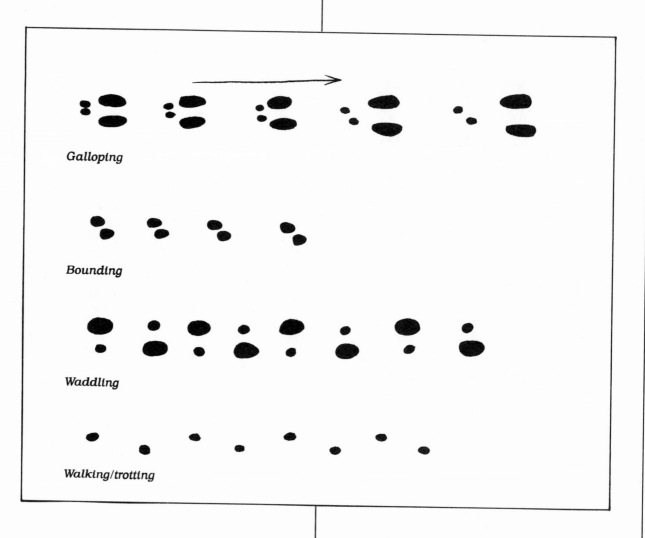

Galloping

Bounding

Waddling

Walking/trotting

Focus: *Tracks can provide a glimpse into the lives of animals whose actions are otherwise hidden from us.*

ACTIVITIES	MATERIALS
Initial Question: How do tracks of different animals look different?	
## PUPPET SHOW	
Objective: To introduce children to some differences in animal track patterns and reasons for their differences.	• *script, p.193* • *puppets* • *pattern drawings*
Perform, or have the children perform, the puppet show. Review the animals in the puppet show, how they move, and what their track patterns look like.	
## FOLLOW THE FOOTPRINTS	
Objective: To show how track patterns help us identify which animals made them.	• *pattern chart* • *generic footprints* • *tape*
Using the track pattern chart, discuss the four types of patterns and which groups of animals make them. Enlarging the scale to suit the size of the children, tape circular pieces of paper to the floor in each of the 4 track patterns. Then have the children try to follow each set of footprints on hands and feet. (It's not easy!) Discuss how an animal's shape and way of moving relate to the track it leaves.	
## WINDOW SHADE STORY	
Objective: To have the children figure out this series of events.	• *window shade story*
Gradually unroll the window shade to show the story in stages and have the children figure out what happened.	

Story: A fox trots to a hen house and grabs a hen. Someone lets the dog out of the house. It chases the fox. The fox runs off, having dropped the hen, which runs back to the hen house. The dog trots along for a way. He then confronts a skunk, which turns tail and sprays. The dog runs home to his dog house.

Hen house

Home

| ACTIVITIES | MATERIALS |

PRINTS AND PATTERNS

Objective: To illustrate that characteristics of both prints and patterns can help in identifying the track-maker and what it was doing.

• *brooms*

Divide into small groups with even numbers. Assemble each group near a different patch of clear snow or dirt. (Use broom to clear away footprints, if necessary.) This could also be done on a cement walk with wet footprints.

Prints — Divide the group into pairs. Have the tracking partners face away with eyes closed, while the print-making partners take a few steps. The print-makers' boots or shoe soles are then shown so that the tracking partners can identify the correct tracks. Next, switch roles and try it again.

Patterns — While everyone in the group is facing away with eyes closed, the leader silently chooses one child to walk, skip, jump, roll, or hop (the possibilities are endless) across the clear area. The others then look at the pattern and try to guess what movement caused that track. Now try it with another child and movement. Children may have fun making up their own movements.

Note: For younger children, demonstrate this *first* with all watching, so they can see what movement makes what track.

TRACK DETECTIVES

Objective: To find tracks and traces of animals, and, by noticing the location, size, shape, and pattern, try to determine what animals made them and what they were doing.

• *track books* or track chart
• *rulers*

Lead the children in small groups to areas where you have previously found tracks or animal signs. Have them comment on all the characteristics they notice about the tracks, and together try to discover as much as possible about the track-maker and what it was doing. With older children, measure the prints and patterns, and check the track chart or track book for identification.

TRACK STORIES

Objective: To reconstruct the story children "read" outside or to invent a story and tell it with tracks.

• *sponge tracks* or
• *stencils* of a dog family, deer, rabbit, and mouse print
• *water based paint* (for sponge tracks)
• *shelf paper*
• *crayons*

Divide the children into small groups and give each a section of shelf paper. Each group should first decide on a story, either one they have seen outside or a made-up one. After sketching and coloring in the habitat, they use sponge tracks, or stencils which you have previously made, to print their story. It works well to have each child take one set of tracks. The groups then take turns holding up their track story and having the other groups try to interpret it.

TRACKS AND TRACES
PUPPET SHOW

Characters: Henry
Mouse
Porcupine
Mink

Props: track pattern signs:
1. Walker/Trotter 2. Galloper
3. Waddler 4. Bounder

Henry: Mom, have you seen Woof? I've called and called, and he hasn't come home. It's his dinner time.

Mother: (from backstage) No, dear, but that dog of yours is always hungry for his supper. He should be home soon.

Henry: Well, I'm going to go look for him. I don't want him lost in this cold snow.

Mother: (backstage) Dress warmly, dear. Don't forget your boots. And don't be gone too long or Woof will get home before you do. (Henry leaves; returns dressed for cold)

Henry: (whistling, calling Woof) Where could that dog be? Hey! There are his tracks (walk/trot track pattern sign held up briefly). I can see his toenail marks. Guess I'll follow them. Hmm. Looks like he's following these other little tracks. (galloper track pattern sign appears; Mouse appears out of breath)

Mouse: You bet he was following those tracks. They were mine and I was scared to death hearing that loud sniffy nose, and feeling the snow shake with those big, clumsy feet.

Henry: I am sorry, Mouse. Your tracks are so tiny, he probably had to use his nose to follow you. But I can see your tracks clearly — four prints, then a space, then four more prints.

Mouse: Yes, I may be little, but I can move pretty fast. I'm a galloper you see, sort of like a horse. My strong back legs push off and I land on my front feet; my back feet land ahead of my front feet and push off again. I have to move along quickly so I won't get caught and eaten by dogs, or owls, or whatever. Speaking of moving along, I better go. Goodbye. (galloper prints down; Mouse gallops off)

Henry: I'm glad that mouse went back under the snow before Woof got him. (walks along, then stops; waddler track pattern sign appears) What tracks did Woof follow here? That's a pretty wide path, with a footprint on one side, then on the other. Looks like the animal wasn't in much of a hurry. (Porcupine appears)

Porcupine: (grumpy) Are you talking about me young man?

Henry: Uh, well, uh, I'm not sure. Do you leave a wide path in the snow when you walk?

Porcupine: Yes I do. Good thing too, makes it a lot easier to get around, following my own trail in the snow.

Henry: You go pretty slowly.

Porcupine: No need to hurry with these quills of mine to protect me. Some folks call me a waddler because I walk along flat-footed and slowly, but I usually get where I'm going (heads towards Henry who moves aside). If you'll excuse me, I'll be on my way.

Henry: (backing up) Certainly, certainly. Don't let me hold you up. (waddler pattern down; Porcupine leaves) Whew! When I find Woof I'm going to tell him to stay away from that track. It's getting late, I better hurry. (back and forth across the stage) Wow! What are these tracks Woof found? (bounder track pattern sign appears) Looks like somebody doing a whole bunch of broad jumps. (Mink appears)

Mink: (cheerfully) Did you say broad jumps? Ha, ha, ha. I never thought of it that way. I think of myself as a bounder.

Henry: A bounder?

Mink: Well, look how I'm built, long and skinny, with short legs. It's easiest for me to spring forward, land on my front feet, and have my back feet follow into my front footsteps. My back arches up when I run that way.

Henry: You mean sort of like a slinky coming down the stairs?

Mink: Slinky minky. Ha, ha, that's a good one. Yes, I guess that's a good way to describe us. Well, I can't stand around chatting all day, I've got some hunting to do. (bounder pattern down; Mink leaves)

Henry: Speaking of dinner, I'm hungry. From Woof's tracks, it looks like maybe he is too. (trotting track pattern appears briefly) He is trotting right along towards home. (hurries across stage and leaves)

Henry: (on stage, warm clothes off; calls towards offstage) Hey, Mom, you were right. Woof got home before I did. Thanks for feeding him.

Mother: (offstage) You're welcome dear. What took you so long? Woof's been home for half an hour.

Henry: Well, one thing led to another, and . . .

Mother: (offstage; interrupting) That's nice dear. Supper's ready.

Henry: (leaving) Hey Mom, did you know a mouse gallops?

193

FOLLOW-UP ACTIVITIES

1. Home Track Detectives
Ask the children to check outside their houses every morning for tracks. Can they tell which person, car, or animal was there?

3. Track Scouts
Suggest to the children that they go for a walk with their parents and look for tracks. Follow some and try to figure out what the animal was doing.

3. Creative Writing
Have the children write a story in which following tracks is an important part of the story.

Skills
Science Process: Observing, Inferring, Brainstorming, Communicating, Predicting, Comparing, Sorting and Classifying, Measuring

Integrated Curriculum: Art, Drama, Reading, Writing, Language Arts, Math

Suggested Reading for Children:

Arnosky, Jim. *Crinkleroot's Book of Animals Tracks and Wildlife Signs*. New York: G. P. Putnam's Sons, 1979. (y/o — fun introduction to tracking)

Ennion, E. A. R., and N. Tinbergen. *Tracks*. London: Oxford University Press, 1967. (y/o — track mysteries)

George, Jean Craighead. *Snow Tracks*. New York: Dutton, 1958. (y)

Mason, George. *Animal Tracks*. New York: William Morrow, 1943. (o — field guide format)

Selsam, Millicent E. *How to be a Nature Detective*. New York: Harper & Row, 1966. (y/o — ideas for projects)

Webster, David. *Track Watching*. New York: Franklin Watts, 1972. (o — projects and activities)

CONES

Cradles for the Conifers

Cones are among the beautiful designs of nature that often go unnoticed, hanging as they usually do high in trees, out of reach. But those who find them, or use cones for wreathes and arrangements, can admire the shapes and textures that together create effective cradles for their seeds.

For many people the term pine cone is the generic name for a cone from any evergreen tree. However, there are many different kinds of cones. Trees that bear cones, pines, spruces, firs, hemlocks, and cedars are called **conifers**, which means cone bearers. Their cones take on the name of the parent tree, such as spruce cone or hemlock cone.

A cone consists of a woody stalk with stiff leaf-like scales growing from it. Each scale is designed especially to cradle its seeds during infancy and to shield them until the opportune time for dispersal. Each cone is composed of many overlapping scales, like shingles on a roof; if you look closely you can see the spiral arrangement that, especially on cones of the white pine, make parallel diagonal patterns up the sides of the cone. Most ripened cones hang upside down from the tree, and when the seeds are fully mature, their scales separate slightly allowing the seeds to fall out. If you've ever made a pine cone wreath, you may have started with cones whose scales were closed. After a few days in a heated house, however, the scales begin to separate and the cones seem to enlarge. This is part of the natural process for releasing seeds.

The production of seeds by conifers is considered a somewhat primitive process compared with the process used by flowering plants. Conifer seeds are described as naked seeds (**gymnosperm**, the name given to the class of plants that includes conifers, means "naked seed") because they develop in an exposed position on top of the scales and are not enclosed by fruit when

mature, as are the seeds of apples, for instance. With a wing-like membrane attached, they rest lightly on the scales until they fall or are shaken or taken out.

Much research has been done on the life cycle of pines, probably because they are such a valuable timber resource in this country. A description of the development of pine cones and seeds will serve to illustrate the process, although not necessarily the timetable, by which all conifer seeds and cones are formed. In the spring when pine buds begin to swell, the first parts to emerge are the new pollen "cones," which are clustered at the base of the new growing twig. (Even in winter you can find dried clusters of last year's pollen cones which look a little like wispy shavings at the base of last year's new twig.) The twig elongates, sprouting needles along its length, until finally in late spring, the new seed cones appear on some of the most vigorous branches, standing straight up at the tips of the twigs. These gumdrop sized cones are soft and green when they first appear.

When the **pollen** grains have ripened, the pollen cones elongate, thereby separating the pollen sacs and exposing them to the air. Drying then causes them to split open and release clouds of yellow pollen, often seen as yellow dust floating in ponds and lakes or covering cars, usually in late May or early June. At this time, the scales of the seed cones, each of which has two **ovules** at the base of its upper surface, separate slightly to allow the pollen grains to drift down between them. To further insure successful **pollination**, each ovule secretes a small drop of sticky fluid which traps the landed pollen grains and draws them into the pollination chamber. Once the seed cone has been pollinated, the stalk of the cone begins to bend, and the scales enlarge and harden, so that by the end of the first summer the cones are tightly sealed and hanging upside down. With pollen in place and ovules enlarged, the seed cone rests through the winter.

In pines, it is not until the second spring that fertilization actually takes place, when the sperm from the pollen reaches the ovule. Then development and growth begin in earnest, so that a white pine seed cone that is three-quarters of an inch long at the end of its first summer grows to a length of four to eight inches by the end of its second summer. After being fertilized, the two ovules at the base of the once tiny scales enlarge and mature to become two seeds approximately three-quarters of an inch long resting on scales approximately one inch long.

Some seeds disperse from the hanging cone; others hitch a ride to the ground with the falling cone where, as in the case of jack pines and western lodgepole pines, they may rest for years until fire opens the closed cones to release the seeds. This remarkable adaptation allows these trees to colonize newly opened areas.

Pine cones take two seasons to mature. Cones from other conifers take only one season, even though there is still an interval between pollination (when the pollen lands) and fertilization (when the sperm reaches the ovule).

Cones have been successful for millions of years in fulfilling their roles as efficient seed nurseries and effective seed dispensers. With their overlapping arrangement of scales, their unique variations of scale shapes, and the delicate color pattern and shading of each individual scale, cones are among the most artistic and functional designs of nature.

Suggested References:

Brockman, Zim, Merdees. *Trees of North America.* New York: Golden Press.

Dodd, John D. *Course Book in General Botany.* Iowa: Iowa State University Press, 1977.

Harlow, William M. *Trees of the Eastern and Central United States and Canada.* New York: Dover Publications, 1957.

_____. *Fruit Key and Twig Key to Trees and Shrubs.* New York: Dover Publications, 1959.

Symonds, George W. D. *The Tree Identification Book.* New York: William Morrow, 1958.

Focus: *Cones are beautifully designed with series of overlapping scales to hold and protect their seeds until dispersal.*

ACTIVITIES	MATERIALS
Initial Question: Why do some trees have cones?	
## PUPPET SHOW	
Objective: To introduce the function of cones as seed bearing organs.	• *script*, p. 199 • *puppets*
Perform, or have the children perform, the puppet show.	
## PINE CONE PATTERNS	
Objective: To see where seeds are located within a cone and to find some seeds if possible.	• *pine cones* enough for each child if possible
Divide into groups. Give each child a cone. Ask them to look for seeds on top of the opened scales. Shake out or take out a seed and examine it. Can they see the indentations where the seeds rested? Discuss with the children how seeds are formed. While still in small groups, ask the children to examine their cones from the following different angles and, in turn, to tell the colors, shapes, and patterns they see:	
1) with the bottom or stem end towards them	
2) horizontally, with the cone on its side	
3) with the top pointing diagonally up so that the bases of the scales are visible	
4) with the top pointing straight towards them	
## TO EACH HIS OWN	
Objective: To see differences among the same kind of cones.	
Using the cones from the preceding activity, have the children study their cones closely enough to be able to recognize them. Put all the cones in a pile from which the children should find their own. When all cones are found, each child should point out his or her cone's special identifying features.	

ACTIVITIES	MATERIALS

SPIN THE CONE

Objective: To make children aware that different kinds of cones come from different kinds of trees.

Divide the children into groups, and give them 5 or 6 different kinds of cones with clues taped to them describing the branches to which they belong. Display branches to match the kinds of cones you have collected. Place a spinner in the center of each group of cones. At a signal from the leader, one child in each group turns the spinner, reads the clue taped to the appointed cone, and affixes it to the appropriate branch. Another child from each group spins and the whole process repeats. Every child should have a turn. The following cone clues can serve as examples.

- cones and branches from 5-6 different kinds of conifers 1 set for each group
- *clues* taped to cones
- *large cone for spinner*

1) clusters of 5 needles (white pine)

2) flat, individual needles approximately ½", with white stripes on underside and tiny stem (hemlock)

3) short, 4-sided, somewhat prickly needles which grow all around the branch (spruce)

4) flat, individual needles approximately ¾", with white stripes on underside and no stem; wonderful smell when crushed. (balsam fir)

WHERE'S MY TWIN

Objective: To match cones of the same species through a sense of touch.

Put out matching sets of cones plus one central grab-pile. Each child should choose a partner; one of the partners will be blindfolded. Three or four pairs of children gather around a matching set of cones. Each sighted partner hands a cone from the grab-pile to the blindfolded partner who then feels among the matching set of cones to find the twin cone. Others in the group watch, awaiting their turns. Partners switch blindfolds and repeat.

- *blindfolds* for half the children
- *matching sets of cones* 5 or 6 different kinds of cones in each set (a sample set and a grab-pile set)

CONE HUNT

Objective: To find a variety of cones outdoors.

Divide into small groups and give each a pencil and a Cone Hunt card with the following items on it:

- Cone Hunt cards
- *pencils*

Find:

a cone that hangs upside down
a cone that sticks straight up
a cone that is twice as long as it is wide
a cone smaller than your thumb
a cone with seeds still inside it
a cone that hasn't opened up
a cone with no seeds left inside
a cone with sap on it
a cone that has fallen to the ground
a cone that's been partly eaten
a scale from a cone
a seed from a cone

Check off items as they're found. Gather together at the end to share findings.

CONES PUPPET SHOW

Characters: Penny Pine Cone (pine cone with closed scales)
Paula Pine Cone (pine cone with closed scales)
Carol Cone (pine cone hanging so the *open* scales face down)

Penny Pine Cone: Oh my, I'm so upset. Summer has come and gone, winter is here and still not a flower, fruit, or seed on this whole pine tree.

Paula Pine Cone: But Penny, you know from living on a pine tree, pine trees don't have flowers or fruits. At least I've never seen any.

Penny: That's what I'm worried about. Apple trees have beautiful blossoms in the spring and apples in the fall. The apples hold the seeds to make more apple trees. But what about us pines? If we really don't have any fruit or flowers, we must not have any seeds.

Paula: And without seeds, no more pine trees can grow.

Penny: Exactly. Why, we might be the last grove of pine trees ever.

Paula: Oh my, you're right. We do have something to be upset about.

Penny: Look, here comes Carol Cone. She's a big cone. Maybe she'll know the answer.

Paula: I don't know. She's been acting awfully strange lately, hanging from her branch head down, with her scales sticking out. Not closed like us.

Penny: Well, let's ask her anyway. (Carol Cone enters) Carol Cone, we've got some questions for you.

Paula: Yeah, like how come you've been hanging upside down for so long?

Penny: And how come your scales are open and our scales are closed?

Paula: And how come pine trees don't make any seeds?

Carol Cone: Questions, questions, questions. Well, there's one very simple answer to all your questions.

Penny & Paula: There is?

Carol: The answer is, pine trees *do* make seeds.

Penny: They do?

Paula: But that doesn't answer all our questions. We still don't even know *where* pine trees make seeds.

Carol: Well, if you figure out where pine trees make seeds, you'll figure out all the answers.

Penny: I know! They make seeds in their roots.

Carol: No.

Paula: They make them in their twigs.

Carol: No.

Penny: They make them in their needles.

Carol: No.

Paula: Well, the only parts left to the tree are us cones . . . ahh, I wonder. What do you think Penny? You think we pine cones have the seeds?

Penny: I don't know. What do you think audience? Do you think the seeds to the pine tree come from us pine cones? (pause)

Carol: There's only one way to find out. Why don't you take a close look at me? (Both gather around Carol)

Paula: Wow!

Penny: Wow, wow!

Penny & Paula: There are seeds in there.

Paula: Right there on the scales.

Carol: Right. And now do you know why you're *not* opened up and hanging upside down?

Paula: 'Cause we're not old enough and our seeds aren't ready to come out.

Carol: That's right.

Penny: Wow, if I hadn't seen those seeds, I would have never believed that seeds come from us pine cones.

Paula: Now I know why I'm growing so fast. I wonder what it will be like hanging upside down.

Penny: We'll know soon enough. You know there's one thing that bothers me a little.

Carol: What is that?

Penny: The audience didn't get to see any seeds yet.

Carol: Well come on. We'll have to take care of that!
(all three leave)

1. Cone Creatures

Let each child choose a cone(s), collect some construction scraps, and make a cone "creature" or cone "person." Place the creatures in a pre-designed diorama.

Materials needed: *cones, pipe cleaners, bits of dried winter weeds, twigs, scraps of cloth or leather, glue and tape, diorama box with evergreen forest.*

2. Cone Bird Feeders

Give the children a mixture of peanut butter and bird seed to spread on pine cones. Hang out for the birds.

3. Cone Display

Invite the children to bring in different kinds of cones, find and identify them in a guide book, and set up a display with labels.

4. Cone Mobiles

Using hangers or branches and assorted cones, the children could make cone mobiles.

Skills

Science Process: Observing, Inferring, Communicating, Comparing, Sorting and Classifying, Measuring

Integrated Curriculum: Art, Drama, Reading, Writing, Language Arts, Math

CAMOUFLAGE

Designed to Conceal

The ability not to be noticed has saved the lives of many animals, **predator** and **prey** alike. A predator whose food supply depends on its skill as a hunter can get much closer to its prey before attacking if its coloration blends with the surrounding habitat. And prey have a safety advantage if their skin covering and shape render them inconspicuous. The coats and coverings of many animals are so well designed to match their surroundings that they are almost impossible to see: a motionless green frog at the edge of a pond, a ruffed grouse nesting on the forest floor.

Camouflage is a relatively new word to describe an age old phenomenon. The word comes from two French words, "camouflet" meaning puff of smoke and "moufler," to cover up. It came into common usage during World War I when armies had to disguise their men and operations from aerial reconnaisance. In current usage, camouflage has broadened its meaning to describe disguises of color, pattern, and shape.

To escape notice is the prime adaptive function of camouflage. But no matter how effective the disguise of a creature may look, it is only successful relative to the creature's ability to **freeze**, to remain absolutely motionless. A spotted fawn lies still when danger is near; cats crouch motionless in between advances toward their prey. Anyone who birdwatches in the spring knows that spotting a sudden movement in the newly leafed trees is the only way to catch a glimpse of an elusive warbler.

Matching color is the most common and obvious disguise, where the color of skin covering approximates the color of the environment, such as a lion on the African plains or a polar bear on the Arctic ice cap. The chameleon is perhaps the most famous camouflaged creature, changing color within minutes to match its surroundings. This color change occurs as the top layer of pigment cells expands or contracts to reveal or conceal the under layers of pigment cells. Some animals have evolved to the point where they change color in order to match their surroundings: the snowshoe hare becomes white in winter, as do weasels in the north; the deer's winter coat is darker with more brown-grey tones. The process of shedding and growing in different colored coats is triggered by the shortening and lengthening daylight hours.

Unless observed in its own habitat, one would hardly think of a spotted giraffe or a copperhead snake with its distinctive hourglass pattern as camouflaged. But these coats exhibit disruptive coloration, a series of patterns, spots or stripes, which against partially sunlit background, eliminates sharp outlines of body shape and thus causes the animal to blend into the surroundings. Patterns combined with special colors have evolved on certain creatures to blend with specific backgrounds. The birch moth's white and gray lined wings make it unnoticeable on a birch tree.

Shape and texture have been copied to provide near invisibility. The walking stick, when motionless on a branch, is almost impossible to see, and his cousin the water scorpion looks just like a floating twig. An inchworm camouflages itself by grasping the twig on which it is climbing with its hind appendages and holding the rest of its body rigidly at an angle. In experimental tests, even hungry blue jays have overlooked this juicy morsel, mistaking it for just another twig.

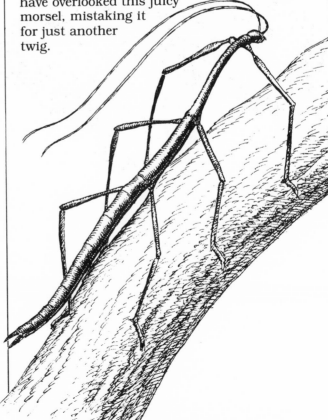

The effect of light and shadow has been used to advantage by some. Many birds have light bellies which show up poorly against the light sky and dark backs which, from above, blend with the dark earth. This light against light and dark against dark is called countershading. It gives a two-dimensional effect which tends to flatten the shape of the bird. Fish also are often light on their bellies and dark on their backs; a motionless trout is nearly impossible to spot. Shadows can also be a give away, and there are creatures who try to eliminate their shadows. Polar bears lie flat to avoid casting a shadow; moths with their horizontal wings can lie almost flush against a surface. And one amazing bird, the Australian nightjar, turns with the sun so that its long tail casts the least possible shadow.

Camouflage for animals, as for humans, can be created by devising a disguise from available materials. This is called masking. The caddisfly larva, for instance, creates a tube-like shelter from available twigs, pebbles, or reeds on the bottom of the pond or stream. By using materials from its own habitat, its shelter is unnoticeable to the untrained eye. Likewise, spider crabs stick bits of sea vegetation to their shells and end up looking just like the bottom of a tide pool. Even bird nests are constructed with materials that blend with the shrubs, trees, or ground where they're built.

Not all coloration contributes to disguise. In fact, certain colors and patterns are very noticeable, and this phenomenon is called warning coloration. The creatures that exhibit this either smell or taste bad or inflict pain. Skunks are the best known mammals with warning coloration. A young, inexperienced predator might well attack a skunk, but once that spray has hit, the receiver is not likely to forget the black and white striped creature that emitted the odor. Monarch butterflies apparently carry a residue of toxin from the milkweed plants they ate as caterpillars. Birds, after one taste, recognize and avoid them. The viceroy butterfly takes advantage of this with its similar orange and black striped pattern. This protective mimicry keeps the birds away from them also.

There's one other common trick — looking scary. Among insects, an effective scare tactic is the sudden appearance of large staring owl-like "eyes," a device used by both the caligo and polyphemous moths. These "eyes" are normally hidden on the underwings, but when they sense danger, these moths can suddenly spread their wings and startle the would-be attacker.

As a design for survival, camouflage in all its varied forms is extremely effective. And it is a self-correcting adaptation because those creatures with the best camouflage live to breed and pass on successful characteristics. Those whose coloration has not adapted to a changing environment fail to escape notice and are less likely to survive.

Suggested References:

Cott, H. B. *Adaptive Coloration in Animals*. London, England: Metheun, 1966.

Fogden, Michael, and Patricia Fogden, *Animals and Their Colors*. New York: Crown, 1974.

McClung, Robert. *How Animals Hide*. Washington, DC: National Geographic Society, 1973.

Focus: *A surprising number of creatures are shaped or colored to blend into their surroundings. The many forms of camouflage are among nature's most creative designs for survival.*

ACTIVITIES	MATERIALS
Initial Question: Why is it helpful for some animals to blend into their surroundings?	

HARD TO SEE

Objective: To introduce the concept of camouflage.

Show pictures of animals in their normal habitats exhibiting different types of camouflage. Discuss the differences and which would be hardest to see.

- *pictures of animals to illustrate different types of camouflage*

SECRET SHAPES

Objective: To show how difficult it can be to see the outline of camouflaged animals.

Divide the children into groups of 4 or 5. Have each group choose a background piece of wallpaper. From different wallpaper scraps, have the children design and cut out secret shapes (at least as big as a thumbnail) and glue them onto their background sheet. Have each group hold up their wallpaper, telling how many secret shapes to look for. Let the other children point out all they can find.

- *wallpaper samples 8" x 11" pieces and scraps*
- *glue*
- *scissors*

A BIRD'S EYE VIEW

Objective: To demonstrate how matching color is an effective camouflage.

Before the workshop, scatter colored pieces of yarn on a small area of grass (if bad weather, colored hole punch dots may be used on patterned rug or cloth). Tell children that they are hungry birds looking for caterpillars to eat (pieces of yarn represent caterpillars). When leader says Go, children pick up as many caterpillars as possible. Allow a few seconds and then call Stop. Tell children that there were 10 pieces of each color. Which colors were easiest, hardest to find? Look for remaining pieces of yarn; they may be difficult to find, demonstrating how effective camouflage is. Older children may graph the results or discuss them using percentages.

- *two-inch pieces of colored yarn (green, brown, red, etc.) 10 pieces of each color*

ACTIVITIES	MATERIALS

HIDDEN IN PLAIN SIGHT

Objective: To illustrate how difficult it is to see unexpected objects outdoors if their shape, color, or texture blend in with the environment.

Before the workshop, place 10 man-made objects on a 30' section of trail. Keep the objects secret. With the children in a line spread apart somewhat, have them walk silently along the trail trying to spot and count (but not pick up or point at) as many objects as they can. A leader at the end of the trail should ask each child to whisper how many objects were seen. If time permits, children can be told how many objects *are* on the trail and given a chance to go back to look again. Wrap-up discussion should include which objects were easiest to see and why. Can the children think of any animals that are colored or shaped similarly? (Don't forget to collect the objects before leaving the trail.)

- *10 man-made objects some should stand out brightly and some should blend in with their surroundings*

CAMOUFLAGED CRITTERS

Objective: To give the children a chance to build a creature that will be correctly camouflaged for a specific habitat.

Assign a micro-habitat (a shrub, a small area of grass, a tree, a stone wall) to each small group of children. Have the children each make one or two creatures to fit into the assigned habitats and place their critters in that habitat (no fair hiding them under anything). All groups should then visit each micro-habitat and try to find the critters. Critter creators should point out their creatures if they are not found within a reasonable amount of time (but hands behind backs until then). Which were easiest to find? Which were most difficult? Why?

- *sticks*
- *leather and cloth scraps*
- *pipe cleaners*
- *paper*
- *tape*
- *glue*
- *scissors*

FOLLOW-UP ACTIVITIES

1. Be a Designer

Challenge the children to design camouflage outfits for the following (include appropriate backgrounds): skydiver, underwater swimmer, cowboy, lion tamer, school teacher, gardener, skier, lumberjack, mountain climber, football player, hunter, coal miner.

2. Color Me a Survivor

Have children draw a picture of different animals and color their pictures as accurately as possible, being mindful of how each animal uses its coloration to survive. Then draw in the appropriate habitat.

3. Invisible for a Day

Ask the children to pretend they are so well camouflaged for one day that they can move around without being seen. Write a story about what might happen.

Skills

Science Process: Observing, Inferring, Brainstorming, Communicating, Comparing

Integrated Curriculum: Art, Social Studies, Reading, Writing, Language Arts, Math

Suggested Reading for Children:

Hess, Lilo. *Animals That Hide, Imitate or Bluff.* New York: Charles Scribner's Sons, 1970. (y/o — good photographs)

McClung, Robert M. *How Animals Hide.* Washington, DC: National Geographic Society, 1973. (y/o — excellent photographs)

Selsam, Millicent E. *Hidden Animals.* New York: Harper & Row, 1969. (y — involves in search)

Selsam, Millicent E., and Ronald Goor. *Backyard Insects.* New York: Four Winds Press, 1981. (y/o — good photographs, camouflage and coloring)

Survivors in a Challenging World

Dandelion!
You'd make a dandy lion
With your fuzzy yellow ruff.
But when you're old
You're not so bold.
You're gone with just one puff.

Dandelions may well be the first flowers that many of us learned to call by name. Their abundance, their relatively early blooming, and their use/nuisance reputations bring them to the attention of children and adults alike. The name dandelion is also easy to remember, especially if you know its derivation, "dents de lion" or teeth of a lion.

Dandelions are members of the **composite** family, which gives them a number of famous relations, such as daisies, hawkweed, sunflowers, chicory, goldenrod, burdock, and aster to name a few. Among flowering plants, the composites are second only to the orchid family in number of species, with something over 13,000 species. The dictionary defines composite as being made up of distinct components. This relates closely to the botanical meaning of the word composite which describes flowerheads composed of many tiny individual flowers; when you pick one dandelion flower, you actually pick approximately 300 dandelion flowers or florets.

People familiar with dandelions probably recognize the long, narrow, deeply indented or toothed leaves, the round, compact, fuzzy-textured yellow head, and the ball-shaped, white, symmetrical seed head. How do these three familiar parts connect with one another to create a successful plant? During the first year the leaves, which grow in a circular pattern close to the ground, are the only visible part of the plant. These first year leaves make food that is stored in the long carrot-shaped root, thus enabling the plant to get a head start for the second and succeeding years in making flowers.

One dandelion plant can produce many flower heads at a time and in rapid succession. The unopened flowerhead is protected by green **bracts** folded up around it; these same bracts curl down when the flowers emerge, but are ready to shutter in the flowers on rainy, cloudy days and at night. When a dandelion flowerhead blossoms, the individual florets, each a complete miniature flower, mature in circular rows starting at the outside rim. First, **pollen** is produced from the **anthers** which are fused together in a tube-like formation around the **stigma** (this is very hard to see, even with a hand lens). Then the female part, the stigma, pushes up through the pollen, carrying pollen grains with it.

Dandelions are rarely pollinated by insects, as one might think; the many insects that visit dandelions gather pollen, but they only cross-pollinate one in ten thousand dandelions. Rather than forming as a result of **pollination**, dandelion seeds usually form from a part of the parent plant. Dandelions are one of the few plants in which seeds can form without pollination occurring; in effect, many dandelions are thus clones of their parent plant. One can see variations in dandelions, but those growing close together look very much alike.

If a flowering dandelion head were bisected, one could see rows of tiny seeds-to-be nestled on a concave, saucer-like receptacle, each with a miniscule stem topped with a fringe of white hairs that lead up to the yellow tube-like floret. When all florets have matured, the bracts once again close, temporarily, around the flowerhead. At this time it is easy to mistake the closed green head for an unopened bud. One clue as to its age is the yellowish fluff at the top, the no longer needed flower parts. Gradually the seeds enlarge, the seed stems elongate, the receptacle swells into a convex platform that separates the seeds, and the white fluffy hairs become parachutes ready to carry the seeds away. While the seeds are thus preparing for flight, the stalk of the flowerhead grows rapidly, perhaps to provide a raised launching platform easily accessible to the wind.

After studying dandelions, it's hard not to admire them. Humans, however, have very mixed feelings about the plant. On the positive side of the ledger, new spring dandelion greens are delicious and nutritious, the blossoms make tasty wine, and, to some, green fields blanketed with yellow dandelions are one of May's most beautiful sights.

Those who prefer only grass in their lawns and only planted vegetables in their gardens may well have a legitimate complaint against dandelions; they are hard to battle and nearly impossible to conquer. Why? One, the long central taproot, which can reach scarce water and nutrients, can't be pulled up; it must be dug up. This is easier said than done because of its length and because of the tiny secondary roots which grow out from it and help anchor it to the soil. If any fragment of the root is left behind, it can give rise to another entire plant. Two, the leaves, being flattened to the ground and somewhat bitter from the white latex in their juices, repel both mowers and grazers. Three, dandelions produce flowers from April into November (few actually blossom in mid-summer). These flowers produce seeds with little regard for weather or insect pollination because they can be either self-fertilized or not fertilized at all and still produce viable seeds. And four, once formed, the seeds are great travellers, relatively unparticular about where they land because they can germinate in a great variety of habitats. No wonder dandelions are so successful.

Suggested References:

Dowden, Ann Ophelia T. *Look at a Flower.* New York: Thomas Y. Crowell, 1963.

Sire, Marcel. *Secrets of Plant Life.* New York: Viking Press, 1969.

Focus: *The amazing ability of dandelions to survive is the result of their efficient and rugged design.*

ACTIVITIES	MATERIALS
Initial Question: Why are there so many dandelions, even though people sometimes try to get rid of them?	
## PUPPET SHOW	
Objective: To introduce some of the dandelion's survival adaptations. Give the puppet show.	• *script, p. 210* • *puppets*
## DANDELION DETAILS	
Objective: To see the whole plant and to learn how each part relates to the rest. Divide into groups of between 6 and 10. Give each group a whole dandelion plant. Pass the plant around the circle. As each person receives it, he or she should notice, and tell or ask, something about some part of the plant. No repeats. Count the buds and blossoms.	• *whole dandelion plants* (washed) enough for each group
## TO EACH HIS OWN	
Objective: To take a close look at a flowerhead and see what its component parts are. Give each person a dandelion flower and, if possible, a hand lens to study the flower until it becomes familiar. Place all flowers in a central pile. Each person finds his/her own flower. When all flowers have been chosen, explain the particular characteristics that made each dandelion unique. **Note:** Explain: 1) that each flower is actually made of numerous tiny complete flowers called florets; 2) that the florets mature from the outer rim toward the center; 3) the protruding, forked stems are the pistils, one per floret. Have the children pull off one floret, with help if necessary, and examine with hand lenses.	• *dandelion flowers* enough for each child • *hand lenses*
## BEAUTY BEFORE AGE	
Objective: To recognize different stages of flowering and to realize that seed development is the flower's primary function. With the help of pictures or live dandelions, explain the different stages. Closed bud — notice the bracts tightly surrounding the bud, then layering down as the flower opens. Open flower — cut a flower in half to show the tiny seeds forming, the miniscule stem, and the white hairs which will become the parachute. Closed up old flower — show the bracts up around the flower again, the brownish-yellow petals pushed up, the white fluff visible. Cut the flower in half and notice the enlarged seeds and stems. Mature seed head — comment on how long the stems on each seed are, how the platform for the seeds has swollen to help separate the seeds, and how the white fluff has expanded.	• *dandelions* in various stages or • *pictures*

Arrange some of the dandelions from previous activities in order of age.

ACTIVITIES	MATERIALS

DANDELION HUNT

Objective: To notice dandelions outdoors.

Give each group of children a Dandelion Hunt card with the following instructions on it:

Find a dandelion with ready-to-blow seeds. Blow the seeds off and follow the last one. See if you can find it on the ground.

Look for: 1) the longest flower stalk, 2) the broadest plant, 3) the plant with most buds and flowers, 4) a plant with no buds and flowers.

Rub or trace dandelion leaf (leaves) on paper and make a smudge of yellow using a flowerhead.

Dig up a dandelion plant without breaking the root.

Where are the most dandelions (name one place)?

Each child pick one flower (if there are enough).

At the end of a specified time, compare findings.

Materials:
- *Dandelion Hunt cards*
- *paper*
- *trowels* or weed forks

DANDY LION

Objective: To enjoy the color and texture of dandelions while learning how they got their name.

Either play "pin the mane on the lion," blindfolding the children and having them pin their dandelions onto an outlined lion head, *or* have them arrange their dandelion heads on the outlined lion's head. Add "teeth" by gluing on toothed dandelion leaves. Discuss how dandelion got its name.

Materials:
- *pins*
- *drawing of lion head on cardboard*
- *dandelion blossoms and leaves*
- *pins*
- *glue*

SHARING CIRCLE

Objective: To encourage personal thoughts about dandelions.

Passing around either a dandelion plant or a blossom, each person should say "I like dandelions because . . ." or "I don't like dandelions because . . ."

DANDELIONS PUPPET SHOW

Characters: Dandy Dandelion (use a real plant for the puppet and have one as a spare)
Spring King
Harry Horse
Lucy (little girl)

Props: lawnmower silhouette for Lucy to push
4 signs: Danger #1; Danger #2; Danger #3; Danger #4

Dandy Dandelion: (sing) Hail to the king with the golden crown.
(say) Hail to the king with the golden crown.
(growl) Hail to the king with the golden crown.

Spring King: What are you saying? What's this I hear? I am the King, the Spring King.

Dandy: I was just practicing, sir, in case you wanted to share your title. I'd even be willing to prove I'm good enough to share it.

Spring King: Humph! I doubt you could. I have very high standards. But if you can live through four dangers, Dandy Dandelion, I might consider allowing you to keep the name of King with the Golden Crown.

Dandy: I'm ready. When do we start?

Spring King: Sooner than you think. Goodbye for now.
(leaves; sign saying Danger #1 pops up for a second; Harry Horse appears)

Harry Horse: I'm hungry after eating hay all winter. This fresh green grass will be delicious. Chomp, chomp. (nibbles dandelion) Splew! That tastes terrible, and I didn't even get a big mouthful.
(leaves)

Dandy: Boy, that was close. Danger #1 nearly finished me, nearly chopped me into digested horse food. It sure is lucky my leaves grow flat against the ground so the horse couldn't get much of a hold on me, and I'm glad I taste so bitter. I wonder what's next. Oh dear, what is that awful noise? Cover your ears and duck your heads friends, here comes trouble.
(Danger #2 sign pops up and down; Lucy appears)

Lucy: Vroom, vroom! This lawn mower sure can go fast. (She races back and forth vrooming.) Oh boy, I'll get these dandelions. My father says they're a nuisance and ugly. Vroom, vroom.

Dandy: Dear heavens, danger #2 sounds horrible. Here it comes. I better duck (bends over, straightens again). Am I really still alive after that horrible machine ran over me?

Lucy: Whoops, the lawn mower just pushed over that one. Too bad, but I'm in a rush to finish this lawn.
(vrooms her way off stage)

Dandy: I'm glad our flower stalks can bend so easily. Aha! Here comes Spring King. I bet he'll be surprised to find me in such good shape.
(Spring King appears)

Spring King: So Dandy, you've managed to survive the first two dangers. Well done, but aren't you a little thirsty?
(Danger #3 sign pops up and down)

Dandy: As a matter of fact, I am thirsty, and it hasn't rained for days. All my neighbors look droopy and some seem to be dying. Spring King did you send this drought as my third danger?

Spring King: Of course I sent it. Drying out, Dandy Dandelion, might finish your dreams of being king.

Dandy: I may be thirsty, but that doesn't mean I can't find a drink of water. You don't realize I have a long, long root under me (lift puppet gradually higher to show long carrot type root) that can reach down to where the water is. (slurp) Even a *little* moisture helps. Mmmm. I feel better now.

Spring King: Humph, I guess that challenge didn't defeat your dream of being king. Well this last danger is the worst of all; you'll wonder why you ever challenged my title. (leaves)

Dandy: Oh dear. It sounds like I'll really need one of my special, secret, super-duper body designs to get me through.
(Danger #4 sign pops up and down)
Uh-oh. Here comes that wild little girl again. I wonder what terrible treat she has in store for me this time. (Lucy appears singing)

Lucy: "La la la flowers for my ma"
"rat tat tat, flowers for my hat."
(she picks off the flower from Dandy Dandelion) My mother will be so happy when I bring her flowers to make dandelion wine. And I'm going to make a gorgeous hat for myself. I need lots and lots. I'm going to pick every single one. (leaves)

Dandy:	(stripped of blossoms) Well, this is the worst. Spring King thought this would finish me off, but he doesn't know how many other buds I have and how quickly I can grow new flowers. Sooner than anyone thinks there'll be more yellow blossoms for my golden crown. (leaves; new dandelion with flowers appears) See what I mean? It looks like I survived all four dangers. (Spring King appears)
Spring King:	Well Dandy, you sure passed the test. It all happened so fast I can't remember what happened. Audience, you were watching, weren't you? How did he do it? Why didn't Harry Horse gobble him up? (answer: leaves close to ground and bitter). And how come he didn't die of thirst?
Dandy:	(pause for answer) This long root of mine can almost always reach water.
Spring King:	And when she yanked off all your flowers? Audience, tell me how he survived that one. (answer: grows new flowers quickly) Well, Dandy, you deserve to share my title, in fact to have your own title. Hail to the King with the Golden Crown. Audience, say it with me, Hail to the King with the Golden Crown.

FOLLOW-UP ACTIVITIES

1. Dandelion Diary
Have the children mark a dandelion bud and predict how long it will take before it goes through all its stages and finally loses its seeds. Watch it daily; measure and record its growth.

2. Dandelion Delectables
Work together with the children to find recipes for dandelion greens, jelly, and try them.

3. Dandelion Dyeing
Many dandelion parts will make natural dyes. Find a book with instructions, and try dyeing wool yarn or T shirts with the children.

Skills
Science Process: Observing, Inferring, Brainstorming, Communicating, Predicting, Comparing, Sorting and Classifying, Measuring, Recording Data

Integrated Curriculum: Art, Social Studies, Reading, Writing, Language Arts, Math

Suggested Reading for Children:

Busch, Phyllis. *Lions in the Grass*. New York: World, 1958. (y — photos, a dandelion story)

Selsam, Millicent E., and Jerome Wexler. *The Amazing Dandelion*. New York: Morrow, 1977. (y/o — photographs, many details)

Welch, Martha McKeon. *Sunflower*. New York: Dodd, Mead, 1980. (y/o — photos, detail composite flower growth)

Hives and Honey: A Lifetime of Work

Honeybees are amazing insects. Imagine making 60,000 flights to gather nectar for one teaspoon of honey or constructing such perfectly designed cells that architects, the world over, marvel at their strength and their economy. Bees lives, like their hives, appear complex at first. But efficiency is nature's way, and the confusing, bustling activity of a beehive breaks down into a simple series of tasks, with both bees and hives designed to ensure the successful completion of those tasks.

Three different types of bees perform all the jobs within a hive: the queen, female workers, and male **drones**. The queen is a special female from the start. While all **larvae** receive royal jelly (a substance produced by the bees from **pollen** and honey) for the first three days of their development, a larva chosen by the worker bees to be a queen gets royal jelly throughout her 16 day development period. Having been reared in an enlarged cell and fed a special diet, the queen grows to be much larger than the workers and longer and slimmer than the drones.

A newly emerged queen will attack other new queens or rip open and destroy unhatched queen cells to try to attain supremacy within the hive. Once her supremacy is established, she moves around over the combs for about a week, then ventures out on her mating flights where she will mate with as many as eight to ten drones, usually from other hives. A few days later the queen starts laying eggs. In theory, she can lay 3,000 eggs per day, but she does not keep this pace up at all times. She lays from early spring to late autumn for as many as five years. Female workers develop from fertilized eggs. Unfertilized eggs develop into drones.

Worker bees emerge as adults in twenty-one days and live for four to six weeks. Only the last brood of the summer lives through the winter. It takes three days for the eggs to hatch. The new larva is fed royal jelly for three days and bee bread (pollen and nectar) and honey for three more days. The larva then spins a cocoon and pupates for twelve days, finally emerging as a sterile female.

The life of a worker changes with age. She is involved in hive duties for the first three weeks of her life, producing royal jelly, then wax, packing pollen in cells, cleaning house, helping with repairs, and guarding the entrance of the hive. Then she starts taking short scouting trips out of the hive, and spends her final weeks as a field bee.

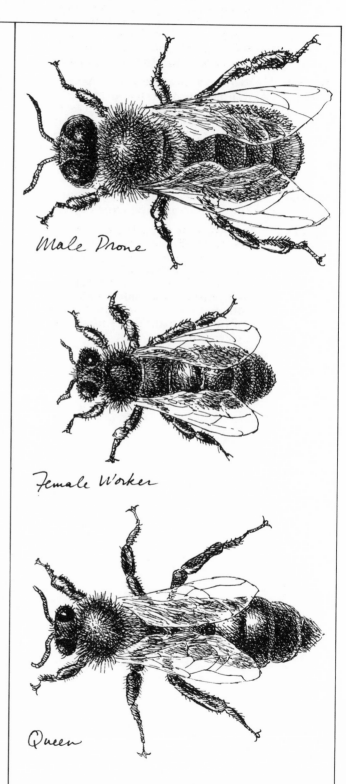

Male Drone

Female Worker

Queen

Male bees serve only one function: to fertilize the queen. In autumn, drones are forced out of the hive by the worker bees to face certain death. Males will be produced again in the spring.

In order to perform its complicated tasks, a bee's body must be very specialized, both internally and externally.

1. **Antennae** — Contain many smell-sensitive pits, giving the bee a keen sense of smell

2. **Compound Eyes** — Can differentiate colors except red and black

3. **Mandibles** — Gather pollen and mold wax

4. **Tongue** — Collects nectar and passes it on to the honey stomach

5. **Wings** — Two pairs of delicate wings that lock together with fine hooks, enabling the bee to fly distances up to eight miles

Legs — Three pairs of specialized legs:

6. *First pair* — each leg has a comb for removing pollen and other materials from the antennae and a pollen brush to gather pollen from the foreparts of the body

7. *Second pair* — each leg has a pollen brush to remove pollen from the first legs and other body parts, and a spur to pick up wax

8. *Third pair* — each leg has a pollen basket for carrying pollen, pollen brush, and pollen comb for cleaning its body and collecting pollen; the wax gland is located just behind this pair of legs

9. **Stinger** — Connected to a gland that secretes stinging fluid; when used, it and other parts of internal organs are pulled out of the bee, causing its death.

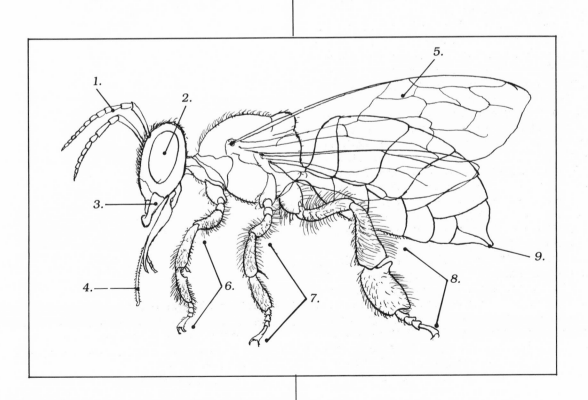

A honeybee's success depends not only on the functional design of its body but also on its ability to carry out its tasks efficiently. The honeybees' system of communicating their knowledge of a good source of nectar or pollen to field bees in their hive contributes to their efficiency. A food source less than 100 yards away from the hive is communicated through a round dance. When a field bee comes back to the hive, it starts dancing in a small circle, going first one way and then the other. Bees follow close behind this bee with their **antennae** touching her to pick up its scent. Soon thereafter they leave the hive to find the source.

When the nectar is farther away than 100 yards, the scout bee does a wagging dance. This is a flattened figure eight, with the bee wagging on the center junction of the 8; the more rapid the wags, the closer the nectar. A bee uses the angle of the sun in relation to her flight path to indicate the direction of the feeding source to the other bees. On a vertical comb, it is as though the sun were straight up. The bee wags directly up if the food source is towards the sun, or if not, to the right or left at an angle commensurate with the angle between the correct flight path and the sun. By following her and touching her, the field bees learn the direction, the distance, and the specific scent of the nectar. The nectar collected by the field bees is taken by worker bees in the hive, which pass it back and forth until enough of the excess moisture evaporates for it to be deposited into storage cells. Evaporation continues until the honey is the right consistency, and then the bees seal the cell.

Honeybees did not always build their hives in the wooden boxes we see today; many still don't. Their original dwelling places were the hollow trunks of dead trees. People now use wooden hives with frames to facilitate harvest of the honey. For the combs, the bees themselves produce flakes of wax from abdominal glands. They then mold the wax with their **mandibles** to prepare it for use as a building material.

The cells are used for raising young as well as for storage of honey and pollen. The structure of the cells is remarkably efficient. Each cell tilts in such a way that the honey does not trickle out and the larva is easier to feed. The shape is hexagonal, with cells sharing mutual walls, which provides the most efficient use of building materials and space. Square cells would waste space in the corners and would be harder to clean; round cells could not share common walls.

Whether learning about the design of their hives or their bodies or studying their importance as pollinators, wax manufacturers, and honey makers, those who get to know honeybees agree that they are truly amazing insects.

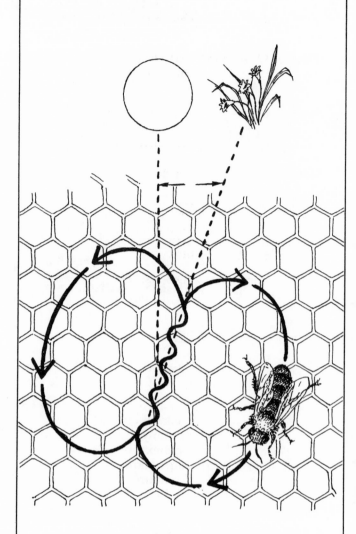

Suggested References:

Frisch, Karl von. *Animal Architecture*. New York: Harcourt Brace & World, 1974.

_____. *The Dancing Bees*. New York: Harcourt Brace & World, 1953.

Any Field Guide to Insects.

Focus: *Honeybees are fascinating insects whose uniquely designed social and physical structures contribute to their success and survival.*

ACTIVITIES	MATERIALS
Initial Question: What do you know about honeybees?	
## PUPPET SHOW	
Objective: To learn about the lives of worker bees, plus the functions of the queen and drone bees in the hive.	• *script, p. 217* • *puppets*
Give the puppet show. Discuss the roles of each kind of bee. Explain the life cycles of bees.	
## COMB SHAPES	
Objective: To understand why the design of beehive cells is so efficient in terms of space and strength.	Per Group: • *2 sheets of paper 8½" x 11"* • *20 circles 2¼" diameter* • *20 hexagons 2¼" between opposite points (not between opposite straight edges)*
Divide into groups of 3 or 4. Give each group 2 pieces of paper, 20 circles, and 20 hexagons, and ask which shape will fit the most pieces onto the paper. Tell them to fit as many circles as possible within the edges of one piece of paper, as many hexagons as possible within the other. Without overlapping, which shape allows the greatest number of pieces? Which shape leaves the least amount of open space on the paper? What other advantages are there to hexagonal comb shapes?	
## A CLOSER LOOK	
Objective: To give the children a chance to examine some actual cells and bees.	• *dead honeybees (beekeepers could supply them)* • *beehive or honeycomb cells* • *hand lenses* • *diagram of a honeybee*
Divide the children into groups. Give each group some honeycomb or beehive cells and some dead honeybees to pass around. Ask the children to examine them carefully with their hand lenses. Discuss the shape, size, and texture of the cells. Then ask the children to describe what they notice about the bee. Use a diagram of a honeybee to point out the important design features of the bee's anatomy, then give the children another chance to examine the bees.	
## DANCE OF THE BEES	
Objective: To understand how a bee communicates to other bees where the pollen and nectar may be found.	• *honey and crackers*
Explain that bees communicate the whereabouts of nectar and pollen by "dancing": a circle dance when the source is close, a figure 8 dance when it is distant. Have the children perform both types of dances by following the leader. Then the leader should dance the figure 8 dance with the center line of the dance pointing towards a prehidden snack of honey and crackers. Children follow after the leader in the figure 8 dance to learn the direction and then take off on their own and make a beeline for the snack.	

ACTIVITIES	MATERIALS

SNIFF AND SCOUT (Grades 3-6)

Objective: To see how important the sense of smell is to bees for identifying a preselected food source.

Divide the group into partners. One partner (a scout bee) takes two different scented cotton balls and hides them within a designated boundary while the other partner (a field bee) waits, with eyes closed, until the scout returns. When the scout returns, she picks up one duplicate scented ball and does a figure 8 dance for her partner, to communicate the whereabouts of the hidden cotton balls. She then gives the duplicate scented ball to the field bee, who must fly to and find the hidden cotton balls, and then choose the one with the correct scent. Repeat with roles of finder and hider reversed.

- *cotton balls*
- *different scents*
  at least 3

HONEYBEE HAUNTS

Objective: To see where honeybees get their nectar and pollen, and to notice if there are honeybees in your area.

The children should visit distinctly different types and colors of flowers (e.g., clovers, goldenrods) to see if honeybees are seen at each kind. Notice visits by insects other than bees. Have children guess why different flowers (note shape, size, color, etc.) would attract different types of insects. Children should stand or sit quietly at each spot for a couple of minutes. Record findings on a simple chart.

- *pencils*
- *charts*

Flower	Honeybee	Other Insects
White		
Yellow		
Pink		
Red		
Blue		
Other		

SHARING CIRCLE

Objective: To wrap up and personalize the complexities of a honeybee's life.

Sitting in a circle, have each child finish the sentence, "I'd like to be a queen, or worker, or drone because . . ."

HONEYBEES PUPPET SHOW

Characters: Mother
Helen as Girl
Helen as a Bee
Fairy
2-3 Worker Bees
Queen Bee (much larger)

Mother: Helen, Helen. Where are you?

Helen: Yes, Mom, I'm right here.

Mother: Since tomorrow is your birthday, I was wondering what you'd like me to fix you for your birthday supper.

Helen: Birthday supper! You mean I can have anything I want?

Mother: You name it, I'll make it.

Helen: Well, I'll start off with some honey and cracker appetizers. Then for the main course I'd like a honeyburger, a carrot and honey salad, mashed potatoes with butter, sour cream, and honey, and honey-glazed cauliflower. For dessert I'll just have a honey pound cake and honey ice cream, with honey syrup topping.

Mother: Helen, all you want is honey this or honey that. Why don't I just get you a big jar of honey and a spoon and let you eat away?

Helen: Sure, that would be fine with me.

Mother: Helen, you must like other things besides honey.

Helen: Well, I do, kind of. But honey is my favorite food. I could eat honey all day.

Mother: You better be careful. Before you know it you'll have turned into a honeybee.

Helen: You mean honeybees eat honey all day?

Mother: Well, not exactly. They have to spend an awful lot of time making honey before they can eat it.

Helen: Gosh, I would love to spend time making honey. How do they make it?

Mother: Well, first they fly out and get nectar from the flowers. Then they go back to the beehive and put the nectar into the hive.

Helen: But then all they have is nectar. I thought they ate honey.

Mother: They do eat honey. Once the nectar is in the beehive, all the bees work on it and change it into honey.

Helen: You mean if I got nectar from a flower, I couldn't just change it to honey?

Mother: It would be pretty hard, unless you were a honeybee of course. Well, enough talk. I've got to go find a recipe for honeyburgers.
(Mother leaves)

Helen: Wow, I would love to be a honeybee, making and eating honey all day. It sounds wonderful!
(Birthday Fairy comes flying in)

Helen: Who are you?

Fairy: I'm your Birthday Fairy. I'm the one who makes your birthday wishes come true.

Helen: You mean I can have any wish in the whole world?

Fairy: Yes, but I hope you're not thinking of wishing to be a honeybee.

Helen: That's exactly what I'm thinking. Please won't you turn me into a honeybee?

Fairy: Being a honeybee is a lot of work. I'm not so sure you'll like it much.

Helen: But making and eating honey all day, what could be better?

Fairy: If that's what you wish. But don't say I didn't warn you. If you should change your mind once you're a honeybee, just call out zzub zzub, and I'll change you back to a person.

Helen: Zzub, zzub. What kind of magic word is that?

Fairy: Zzub is just buzz backwards.

Helen: Oh, then zzub it is, but I'm sure I'll want to be a honeybee for a long time.

Fairy: Well, here goes. I've never turned anyone into a honeybee before. Maybe if the audience helps me it will be easier. Just say the magic words after me.
   Abra Cadabra (Abra Cadabra)
   Fiddle-de-fee (Fiddle-de-fee)
   You will become (You will become)
   A honeybee (A honeybee)
(old Helen disappears; new Honeybee Helen appears)

Fairy: It worked. Thanks for the help boys and girls.

Helen: Hey, I'm a bee. I'm a bee! This is so exciting. What do I do first?

Fairy: You better go to your new beehive home. It's over in that hole in the big oak tree. The queen bee will put you to work.

Helen: Queen bee! There's a queen bee?

Fairy: Oh, yes. The queen bee is like the head of all the other bees in the hive. She doesn't do any of the housework.

Helen: No work. Then what does she do?

Fairy: The queen bee mates with the boy bees and lays eggs, which become baby bees.

Helen: You mean the boy bees and other girl bees do all the work while the queen bee just lays eggs?

Fairy: Well, that's almost right. Except, the boy bees don't do any work either. All they do is wait around hoping to mate with the queen bee.

Helen: You mean the girl bees are the only ones that do any work?

Fairy: That's right. That's why girl bees are called the workers. They do all the work.

Helen: Oh, no. Since I was a girl-person, does that mean I'm a girl bee too?

Fairy: It sure does. A girl bee is a worker bee, so you're a worker.

Helen: I'm not sure I'll know exactly what to do.

Fairy: Well, just go to that beehive in the oak tree. The queen bee there is Queen Bee-a-trice. Tell her I sent you. She'll explain to you what you have to do. Bye, bye.
(Fairy leaves)

Helen: I guess I better fly to that oak tree and get to work. I hope I like being a honeybee. (flies around) Here's the oak tree and here's the beehive. Boy, I sure hope I recognize Queen Bee-a-trice. I could use your help boys and girls. Let me know if you see a bee that could be the queen bee. I think the queen bee is bigger than the rest. (bees come out and leave again) I don't see any bee that's bigger. How am I ever going to . . . (much larger bee comes out) (hopefully, children will shout out that she's the queen bee.) You're right. That must be Queen Bee-a-trice. Let's call her to get her attention. Queen Bee-a-trice, Queen Bee-a-trice. (have children help call.)

Queen: Yes, yes, were you calling me? I'm very bizzzzy so make it quick. I've got lots of eggs to lay.

Helen: I was sent by the Birthday Fairy. I'm a girl bee so that means I'm a worker.

Queen: It sure does. You've got a lot of work to catch up on.

Helen: You mean I have to start going out and collecting nectar to make honey?

Queen: That's what you do when you get a little bit older. Young worker bees first start off by cleaning cells in the beehive and feeding the baby bees.

Helen: Cleaning and feeding the bees!

Queen: Next, you'll start building new parts to the hive.

Helen: You mean first I have to clean the cells in the beehive, then I have to feed the baby bees, then I build cells, and finally I get to go out, get nectar, and make honey for me to eat?

Queen: That's right. But most of the nectar you collect won't be for honey for you to eat. It will be for honey for *all* of us bees to eat.

Helen: *All* of us. Even the bees that didn't collect any nectar?

Queen: Right again. All honey that's made is shared by everyone.

Helen: Wow, that sounds like an awful lot of work for not much honey.

Queen: The life of a worker honeybee is not easy. You better get started right away. (leaves)

Helen: Gosh, it sounds like I could get a lot more honey if I were a person instead of a honeybee. Do you think I should go back to being a person, children? I think I will. Now what were the magic words the Birthday Fairy told me to say? Oh, yes, zzub, zzub. Children help me, zzub, zzub. (Helen turns back to a person) Hey, it worked. Thanks for the help, everyone. I better hurry and get back home. Otherwise, I'll miss my honeyburger birthday dinner.

FOLLOW-UP ACTIVITIES

1. Read Aloud
Read the account of Winnie the Pooh's solution for getting some honey. *The World of Pooh*, A. A. Milne (New York: E.P. Dutton, 1957) pp. 8-23.

2. Beekeeper Visit
Invite a beekeeper to visit the classroom, bringing the equipment needed to keep bees.

3. Demonstration Beehive
Visit a demonstration beehive, one with glass walls so the children can find the queen, worker, and drone bees, watch the dances, and notice the cells with honey and with baby bees. The apiarist at the State Department of Agriculture could give advice on setting up a demonstration beehive.

Skills
Science Process: Observing, Inferring, Brainstorming, Communicating, Predicting, Comparing, Recording Data

Integrated Curriculum: Drama, Social Studies, Language Arts, Reading, Math

Suggested Reading for Children:

Dickson, Naida. *The Biography of a Honeybee.* Minneapolis, MN: Lerner Publications, 1974. (o — a great deal of information)

Foster, Virgil E. *Close-up of the Honey Bee.* New York: Young Scott, 1960. (excellent photos, adaptations, beekeeping)

Hawes, Judy. *Bees and Beelines.* New York: Thomas Crowell, 1964. (y/o — simple, information)

_____. *Watch Honeybees With Me.* New York: Thomas Crowell, 1964. (y — good information on bees, jobs, beekeeping)

Hogan, Ray. *The Honeybee.* Milwaukee, WI: Raintree, 1979. (y)

Lecht, Jane. *Honeybees.* Washington, DC: National Geographic Society, 1973. (excellent photos, clear, simple text)

Lewellen, John B. *The True Book of Honeybees.* Chicago, IL: Children's Press, 1953. (o)

Oxford Scientific Films. *Bees and Honey.* New York: G. P. Putnam's Sons, 1977. (y/o — good photos, confusing information)

Shuttlesworth, Dorothy E. *All Kinds of Bees.* New York: Random House, 1967. (y/o — structure, life cycle)

APPENDIX A

ELF—Vermont's *Environmental Learning* for the *Future* Program

The enthusiasm for the Vermont Institute of Natural Science ELF Program in Vermont elementary schools and the success with which it has introduced many thousands of adults and children to the natural world not only encouraged, but almost compelled us to publish this book. The urge to share was very strong.

One of the first decisions we had to make was whether to emphasize the hands-on activities or the strategy of using volunteers to teach ELF. We opted for the activities but consider our system for disseminating ELF to be unique and highly effective. This is how it works.

With very limited funds, it has been necessary from the beginning to make optimum use of community resources. ELF therefore relies on volunteers, the nearby natural world, local expertise, and whatever other helpful resources, collections, exhibits, or examples can be procured.

In 1985-86 the equivalent of two full-time Vermont Institute of Natural Science staff disseminated effective hands-on natural science to more than 4300 children in thirty-two schools each month. This was accomplished by a simple system, used by VINS for more than a decade. VINS staff travel throughout the state teaching monthly ELF training workshops to volunteers at the local elementary school (or sometimes a nearby church, fire station, or house) during school hours. These workshops are attended by a variety of community people, curious to learn for themselves and willing to volunteer their time to share their learning and their love for nature with children. These volunteers are led through the month's workshop, activity by activity, indoors and outdoors, as described in the chapters of this book. In effect, they are treated like both adults and children as they watch the teaching being role-modeled, while becoming involved as participants. They learn firsthand how to teach the children and what it feels like to do the activities. How confusing is it to make a snowflake? What are the sensations of being blindfolded?

After the workshop, volunteers gather into classroom teams to plan their presentation to the children, deciding whether to include all activities, who's going to introduce and explain each activity, what materials are needed, and so on. The assembling of materials takes some organizing. Non-expendable materials, such as puppets or murals, are usually made by one person or group for use by everyone; slides or collections are borrowed from state fish and wildlife departments or from more local sources; common school supplies are provided by the schools; and everyday objects like winter weeds or shoeboxes are brought from home.

The time actually spent with the children varies greatly among and within schools; it ranges from an hour to an entire day. The role of the classroom teacher varies too. Some get release time to attend the training workshops, some just help the volunteers when they get there, and others do not participate at all.

Review and evaluation of the success of ELF with the children is incorporated into the training workshop by devoting the first half hour of it to feedback from the volunteers. This is extremely valuable, raising issues of teaching techniques, discipline, environmental ethics, and effectiveness of the activities. It also brings forth hilarious stories and helps create a close feeling within the group. (To encourage a friendly atmosphere, we limit numbers to twenty-five participants per training workshop.)

The mechanics of setting up an ELF Project are available in detail from VINS, Church Hill Road, Woodstock, Vermont 05091. The issues to consider include funding, volunteer numbers, and the attitude of the school toward the program. It is also important to have a good volunteer coordinator who is responsible for finding volunteers, for organizing the program, and for acting as liaison between the professional ELF teaching staff and the school.

The positive aspects of the ELF Program as described above are many. It reaches a broad range of people in each community, increasing their knowledge about the natural world and their awareness of environmental issues. Many volunteers admit that their excitement about what they learn is their prime motivation for becoming an ELF volunteer. It is good for school-community relations, bringing as it does so many community people into the school. It gives children the important message that many adults care about them and about their learning, that nature and science are not confined to a textbook or a classroom, nor dependent on special equipment, experts, and faraway field trips.

While Vermont has some special features that make its system for teaching *Hands-On Nature* both possible and necessary, it is our hope that other regions will be able to adapt the ELF Program for their use.

APPENDIX B

Equipment — Where to Get It or How to Make It

The emphasis throughout this book is on simple, inexpensive materials and equipment that are readily available or easy to locate. A shelf full of arts and crafts or stationary supplies will meet the requirements of most activities. However, there are some shortcuts to making or finding the more complicated and specific items. Hopefully, the following hints will save time and frustration.

Animal Parts (skull, antlers, etc.) — Fish and Wildlife Department, local game warden, school and university biology departments, local collectors.

Bags, Expedition — plastic bags with locking plastic handles are useful for outdoor packets of scavenger hunt supplies. Ask a distributor or manufacturer for a donation.

Bags, Mystery — old flannel "silver" bags or sewn 8" (length) x 6" (width) dark cloth bags with draw strings.

Bicycle Wheels — bicycle repair shop.

Bingo Cards — simple drawings or pictures of animals (2" x 2¾") glued onto 8" x 11" paper, 4 across and 4 down. Make as many copies as needed. Cut the copies into individual pictures and glue onto 8" x 11" cardboards, varying the order.

Binoculars — write BIRDING, P.O. Box 5, Amsterdam, NY 12010 (or call 518-842-0863) for catalogue of good binoculars at discount prices.

Blindfolds — felt squares folded in thirds with elastic head bands attached.

Boxes, Bug — order from Nature Shop, 185 Willow St., P.O. Box 315, Mystic, CT 06355.

Boxes, Shoe (for dioramas, etc.) — shoe store or sports store. Stationary boxes also work well. Ask any office for empty letterhead boxes.

Cards, Paint Chip — hardware or paint store.

Cards, Task — index cards, with written instructions, then covered with clear contact paper. Add a strip of masking tape on one edge if listed items need to be checked as accomplished. Replace tape after each activity.

Discs (for clocks, spin the dial games, etc.) — pizza cardboards or heavy-duty paper plates.

Feathers — poultry farm, or from someone who raises chickens.

Felt Board — cardboard or other solid, lightweight board covered with felt.

Felt Board Cut-outs — felt cut-outs don't work over an extended period. Oak-tag or heavy paper cut-outs with scotch tape on back side work well. Use masking tape circles (circle of tape with sticky side out) stuck onto scotch tape for attaching to feltboard.

Hand Lenses — order from Delta Education, Box M, Building 4, Factory St., Nashua, NH 03061. Add neck strings before using.

Jars (for snowflakes, insects and spiders, etc.) — save small jars with lids. Collect baby food jars. Punch holes in lids if live creatures are to be housed.

Mural for easy transporting — white window shade (has added advantage of being unaffected by tape). For permanent display — large piece of cardboard, scene covered with clear contact paper.

Mural Cut-outs — see Felt Board Cut-outs.

Pictures (of animals, plants) — old nature magazines. Senior center visitors or nursing home residents are often willing to cut out pictures. National Wildlife Federation Stamps.

Pond/Stream Nets — 6" or 8" kitchen strainers.

Pond/Stream Pans — (for temporary holding of creatures) white plastic dishpans. For individual children — cottage cheese containers.

Puppets — we use *simple* drawings on oaktag, mounted on paint stirrer sticks or dowels (2 drawings glued back-to-back so either side can face the audience).

Puppet Stage — an overturned table, a bookcase, anywhere that hides the puppeteer and can hold a taped-up script.

Puzzles — mount the full picture on cardboard, cover with contact paper, then cut out pieces.

Scents (for smelling games) — for lasting, but not sickening or toxic, scents, flavorings work the best (such as peppermint, lemon, maple).

Slides — (to borrow) Fish and Wildlife Departments; schools and universities; local nature lovers and travellers. (To buy) birds: Laboratory of Ornithology, Cornell University, Ithaca, NY; mammals: Mammal Slide Library, Department of Zoology, American Society of Mammalogists, SUNY, Oswego, NY 13126

Specimens (mounted animals or insects, nests, nature collectables) — schools and universities; local persons who have collections (advertise to find them).

Thermometers — check with hardware store for simple aluminum thermometers with °F and °C, or write Carolina Biological Supply Co., Burlington, No. Carolina 27215 for catalogue.

Track Prints (for track stories) — Dr. Scholl footpads cut to shape with correct number of toes or footprint outline — glued onto plastic or wooden blocks.

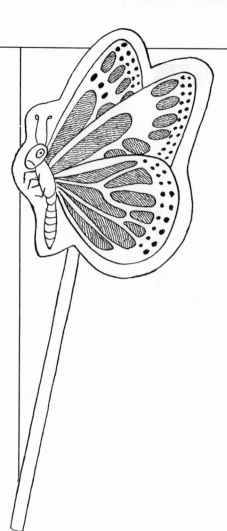

GLOSSARY

abscission layer   a zone of thin-walled cells that forms across the base of leaf stems and causes them to fall

alternate   bud or leaf arrangement on a plant in which there is only one bud or leaf at a node so that the leaves grow on alternating sides of the stem

amphibian   any member of the class of cold-blooded vertebrate animals that includes frogs, toads, and salamanders, and is characterized by eggs laid in water that hatch into gill-breathing larvae and metamorphose into lung-breathing adults

angiosperm   a plant with seeds enclosed in a mature ovary (fruit)

antenna   a jointed appendage, usually occurring in pairs on arthropods; used as a sensory receptor

anther   the upper portion of the stamen containing the pollen grains

arthropod   an invertebrate with a segmented external skeleton and jointed legs; examples include insects, spiders, ticks, millipedes, centipedes, and crustaceans

bird of prey   any member of a group of birds that kill and eat other animals for their food, and are characterized by a sharp, hooked beak and strong, sharp talons, as in hawks and owls

bract   a specialized leaf or leaf-like structure on a plant, usually found at the base of a flower

cambium   a layer of tissue in woody plants, from which new bark and new wood originate

canines   the four pointed teeth occurring at the front corners of the upper and lower jaws of flesh-eating mammals, used for gripping and tearing flesh

carnivore   an animal that consumes meat

cephalothorax   a body division with the head and thorax combined, as in spiders

chitin   the primary component of arthropod skeletons, which is tough, flexible, and resistant to most chemicals, including water

chlorophyll   the green pigment found in plants that is necessary for the process of photosynthesis

chrysalis   the pupa of a butterfly

composite   one of a family of flowering plants that produce many small flowers closely grouped into compact heads, such as dandelions, goldenrods, and sunflowers

compound eye   an eye composed of many individual facets, each capable of sight; common to insects

conifer   a cone-bearing plant such as pine, fir, spruce, hemlock, cedar, and redwood

consumer, primary   an animal that eats plants

consumer, secondary   an animal that eats other animals

deciduous   trees and shrubs that lose their annual growth of leaves each autumn

decomposer   an organism (chiefly bacteria and fungi) that causes the mechanical and chemical breakdown of dead plants and animals

decomposition   the process of rotting and decay which causes the complex organic materials in plants and animals to break down into simple inorganic elements which can be returned to the atmosphere and soil

dormancy   a temporary state of inactivity for a plant or animal that enables it to endure a period of environmental stress such as extreme heat, cold, or scarcity of food

drone   the male of the honeybee and other bees

223

ecosystem — a basic functional unit consisting of complex interactions between plants and animals and the physical and chemical components of their environment, varying in size from a small field to the entire earth.

emergent — an aquatic plant that is rooted in a pond or stream bottom and has stems and leaves above the surface, such as grasses, sedges, rushes, and cattails

food chain — the transfer of food energy in sequence from plants to animals that eat plants to animals that eat other animals

food web — a network of interconnected food chains within a community

freeze — to become absolutely motionless, either through fear or caution, in order to escape detection by another animal

frost line — the maximum depth to which water penetrates the pore spaces between soil particles and freezes during the winter

fungi — a group of plants including mushrooms, molds, and mildews that lack chlorophyll and subsist upon dead or living organic matter

gymnosperm — a plant such as a pine or spruce with seeds that are not enclosed in an ovary

herbaceous — referring to any nonwoody plant

herbivore — an animal that eats plant material

hibernation — a prolonged state of sleep or torpor by which some animals escape stresses of winter

incisors — teeth in the front part of the lower and upper jaws of mammals, adapted for cutting

insectivore — an animal, such as moles and shrews, that characteristically feeds on insects

invertebrate — an animal that has no backbone, but uses some other form of support such as a shell or exoskeleton

keratin — a protein that is very resistant to physical wear and chemical disintegration; the primary component of horns, feathers, hairs, and nails

larva — an immature and usually active feeding stage of an animal, unlike the adult in form

lateral bud — a bud that grows out from the side of a stem or twig

lenticels — small structures on the bark of a shrub or tree, usually in the form of horizontal slits or pores, which permit the exchange of gases

mandible — in birds, the lower part of the beak; in insects one half of a pair of mouth appendages

metamorphosis — a process by which an immature animal transforms to an adult through a series of developmental changes

metamorphosis, complete — the four-stage development of insects which includes egg, larva, pupa, and adult

metamorphosis, incomplete — the three-stage development of insects which includes egg, nymph, and adult

micro-habitat — a small, specialized home within a larger habitat, such as under a rock

molars — in mammals, the back, permanent teeth which have surfaces adapted for grinding

niche — the unique function or role of a given species within a community

node — the region of a plant stem where one or more leaves arise

nymph — the immature stage of an insect that undergoes incomplete metamorphosis

omnivore — an animal that eats both plant and animal foods, such as raccoons, skunks, and humans

opposite — leaf or bud arrangement on a plant in which two buds or leaves arise opposite each other at a node

ovipositor — an egg-laying structure on the rear abdominal body segment of a female insect

ovule — a rudimentary seed of a plant that develops into a seed after fertilization

petiole — the slender stalk by which a leaf is attached to the stem of a plant

phloem — the conducting tissue in a plant that transports food produced in the leaf to all other parts of the plant

photosynthesis — the production of sugars, by plants, from carbon dioxide and water in the presence of chlorophyll using sunlight as the source of energy

pistil — the central organ of a flower which contains the female parts: stigma, style and ovary

pollen — fine, yellowish powder-like grains which contain the male germ cells of a plant

pollination — the transfer of pollen from the anther (male) to the stigma (female) of a plant for fertilization

predator — an animal that hunts, kills, and eats other animals

prey — an animal hunted for food

producer — an organism that produces its own food (plants)

pupa — the third stage of complete metamorphosis in insects during which a larva transforms into an adult

reptile — a member of the class of cold-blooded vertebrate animals including lizards, snakes, turtles, and alligators, characterized by dry, scaly skin and eggs suited for development on land with membranes and shells to protect the embryo

rhizome — an elongated, underground, horizontal stem which usually produces roots and sends up shoots

ruminant — an herbaceous land animal with a compartmentalized stomach that allows progressive digestion as partially digested food (cud) is regurgitated, chewed, and reswallowed, such as cattle, sheep, goats, deer, moose, and caribou

scavenger — an animal that feeds on dead organic matter, either plant or animal

spiracles — external openings in insects through which air enters the respiratory system

spore — a tiny reproductive cell as in the mosses, ferns and fungi

stamen — the male organ of the flower consisting of anther and filament, which produces the pollen

stigma — the most elevated part of a flower's pistil which receives the pollen

stomates — minute openings in the outer surface of leaves and stems of plants, through which water vapor and gases pass

straddle — the width of an animal's track, the distance between the outside edges of opposing feet

stride — the distance between the prints of a walking animal, or the distance between track patterns of a running animal

style — a slender column of tissue that connects the ovary and the stigma of a flower pistil

submergent — an aquatic plant that is rooted in a pond or stream bottom, with completely submerged stems and leaves

subnivean — under the snow

surface tension — a property of liquid in which the surface layer has a stretched, elastic character that offers some resistance to penetration

terminal bud — a bud at the end of a plant stem or twig

thorax — the group of body segments between the head and the abdomen of an insect

transpire — to give off water vapor, as from the surface of leaves and other plant parts

vertebrate — an animal having a segmental backbone or vertebral column; bony fishes, amphibians, reptiles, birds, and mammals

whorled — bud or leaf arrangement on a plant in which three or more buds, or leaves arise at a single node, surrounding the stem

xylem — the vascular tissues that transport water throughout the plant

225

GENERAL BIBLIOGRAPHY

Environmental Education Books

Allman, A. S., and O. W. Kopp. *Environmental Education: Guideline Activities for Children and Youth.* Columbus, OH: Charles E. Merrill, 1976.

American Geological Institute. *Environmental Studies Packets.* Olympia, WA: Essentia, Evergreen State College. (Six different packets, n.d.).

Baker Science Packets. *Baker Nature Study Packet.* Holland, MI: 1961. Grades 1-9.

Busch, Phyllis. *Urban Discovery Manual. 75 Stimulating Ideas for Investigating Some Common Urban Resources.* Columbus, OH: ERIC/SMEAC, 1969.

Cornell, Joseph Bharat. *Sharing Nature with Children.* Nevada City, CA: Ananda Publications. 1979.

Gross, Phyllis, and Esther P. Railton. *Teaching Science in an Outdoor Environment.* Berkeley, CA: University of California Press, 1972.

Hammerman, Donald R., and William M. Hammerman. *Teaching in the Outdoors.* Minneapolis, MN: Burgess, 1973.

Hug, John W., and Phyllis J. Wilson. *Curriculum Enrichment Outdoors.* New York: Harper & Row, 1965. (Out of print, but a good reference).

Jorgensen, Eric, Trout Black, and Mary Hallesy. *Manure to Meadow to Milkshake.* Los Altos, CA: Hidden Villa, 1978.

Minnesota Environmental Sciences Foundation. *Environmental Discovery Units* (Transect Studies and Vacant Lot Studies). Washington, DC: National Wildlife Federation, 1412 16th St. NW 20036, 1971.

Nickelsburg, Janet. *Nature Activities for Early Childhood.* Reading, MA: Addison-Wesley, 1976.

Outdoor Biological Instructional Strategies (OBIS). Berkeley, CA: Lawrence Hall of Science, 1974-1979. (Four volumes).

Peck, Ruth L. *Art Lessons That Teach Children About Their Natural Environment.* West Nyack, NY: Parker, 1973.

Pringle, Laurence P., ed. *Discovering the Outdoors.* Garden City, NY: Natural History Press, 1969.

Project KARE. *A Curriculum Activities Guide to Interdisciplinary Environmental Studies.* U.S. Education Resources Information Center, ERIC Document ED 157 682, 1976.

Project Learning Tree. Supplementary Activity Guide. The American Forest Institute, Inc., 1977.

Project WILD. Conservation education activities for elementary and secondary educators. Western Regional Environmental Education Council, Project WILD, Salina Star Route, Boulder, CO 80302, 1983.

Robinson, Barbara, and Evelyn Wolfson. *Environmental Education: A Manual for Elementary Educators.* New York: Teachers College, Columbia University, 1982.

Roth, Charles E., and Linda G. Lockwood. *Strategies and Activities for Using Local Communities as Environmental Education Sites.* Columbus, OH: ERIC/SMEAC, December 1979.

Russell, Helen Ross. *Ten-Minute Field Trips.* Chicago: J. G. Ferguson Publishing Co., 1973.

Schults, Beth, and Phyllis Marcuccio. *A Guide to Learning.* Columbus, OH: Charles E. Merrill, 1972 (includes activities and skill cards).

Science 5/13. *McDonald Educational Series.* School Council Publications, Milwaukee: McDonald Raintree, 1973.

Science and Children. Elementary education curriculum materials. National Science Teachers Association, 1742 Connecticut Ave. NW, Washington, DC 20009 (published eight times a year).

SCIS (Science Curriculum Improvement Study). Elementary education curriculum materials. Delta Education, P.O. Box M, Nashua, NH 03061-6012.

Sisson, Edith. *Nature With Children of All Ages: Activities and Adventures for Exploring, Learning, and Enjoying the World Around Us.* Massachusetts Audubon Society. Englewood Cliffs, NJ: Prentice-Hall, 1982.

Swan, Malcolm D., ed. *Tips and Tricks in Outdoor Education.* 2nd ed. Danville, IL: Interstate Press, 1978.

University of the State of New York. *Living Within Our Means: Energy and Scarcity; Environmental Education Instructional Activities.* Albany, NY, n.d.. (two volumes).

VanderSmissen, Betty, and Oswald Goering. *Leader's Guide to Nature-oriented Activities.* 3rd ed. Ames, IA: Iowa State University, 1977.

Van Matre, Steve. *Acclimatization.* Martinsville, IN: America Camping Association, 1972.

————. 1974. *Acclimatizing.*

————. 1979. *Sunship Earth.*

Vinal, William Gould. *Nature Recreation.* New York: Dover, 1963.

Wensburg, Katherine. *Experiences with Living Things.* Boston, MA: Beacon, 1966.

Wentworth, Daniel F. et al. *Examining Your Environment*. Series. Toronto, Montreal, Canada: Holt, Rinehart and Winston of Canada Ltd., 1972.

Wheatley, John H., and Herbert L. Coon. *One Hundred Teaching Activities in Environmental Education*. Columbus, OH: ERIC/SMEAC, 1974.

Natural History Books

Encyclopedias

The Audubon Nature Encyclopedia. Vol. 10. Philadelphia, PA: The Curtis Publishing Company, 1971.

The Golden Book Encyclopedia of Natural Science. New York: Golden Press, 1962.

Series

Audubon Aids in Natural Science. New York: National Audubon Society, Educational Services Divn., 950 Third Ave., 10022.

Cornell Science Leaflets. Ithaca, NY: New York State College of Agriculture, Cornell University. (published 4 times a year).

Doubleday Nature Guides. New York: Doubleday.

Golden Field Guides. Racine, WI: Western Publishing Co.

Golden Nature Guides. New York: Golden Press. (paperback series).

How to Know Series. Dubuque, IA: William C. Brown.

Life Nature Library. New York: Time-Life Books.

Nature Scope. Washington, DC: National Wildlife Federation

Our Living World of Nature. New York: McGraw-Hill, in cooperation with World Book Encyclopedia, 1967.

Peterson Field Guides, ed. Peterson, Roger Tory. Boston, MA: Houghton Mifflin Co.

Books

Brown, Vinson. *The Amateur Naturalists Handbook*. Englewood Cliffs, NJ: Prentice-Hall, 1980.

Buchsbaum, R., and M. Buchsbaum. *Basic Ecology*. Pittsburgh, PA: Boxwood Press, 1957.

Chinery, Michael. *Enjoying Nature With Your Family*. New York: Crown Publishers, Inc., 1977.

Comstock, Anne B. *Handbook of Nature Study*. Ithaca, NY: Cornell University Press, 1967.

Eckert, Allan. *The Wild Season*. Boston: Little, Brown & Co., 1967.

Godin, Alfred. *Wild Mammals of New England*. Baltimore, MD: The John Hopkins University Press, 1977.

Headstrom, Richard. *Nature in Miniature*. New York: A. A. Knopf, 1968.

Laurence, Gale. *The Beginning Naturalist*. Shelburne, VT: New England Press, 1979.

Palmer, E. Lawrence, and Seymour H. Fowler. *Fieldbook of Natural History*. New York: McGraw-Hill, 1975.

Stokes, Donald. *A Guide to Nature in Winter*. Boston, MA: Little, Brown & Co., 1976.

Storer, John H. *The Web of Life*. New York: Devin-Adair Co., 1953.

Worthley, Jean Reese. *The Complete Family Nature Guide*. New York: Avon, 1976.

Children's Books

Arnosky, Jim. *Secrets of a Wildlife Watcher*. New York: Lothrop, Lee & Shepard Books, 1983. (o — detailed illustration, natural history observation techniques)

Borland, Hal. *This World of Wonder*. Philadelphia, PA: J. B. Lippincott Co., 1973. (o — monthly topics, few illustrations)

Dr. Suess. *The Lorax*. New York: Random House, 1971. (y/o — story with message)

Mitchell, John, and Massachusetts Audubon Society. *The Curious Naturalist*. New Jersey: Prentice-Hall, 1980. (y/o — pictures, activity ideas, brief info.)

Selsam, Millicent E. *How to Be a Nature Detective*. New York: Harper & Row, 1966. (y/o — ideas for projects)

Smith, George. *Woodland Animals*. New York: Abeland-Schuman, 1970. (o — field guide format)

Wong, Herbert, and Matthew F. Vessell. *Animal Habitats: Where Can Red-Winged Blackbirds Live?* Reading, MA: Addison-Wesley, 1970. (y — compares habitats)

INDEX

NOTES

J enepher Lingelbach, editor of *Hands-On Nature*, has been active in the VINS ELF program since its inception, designing activities, researching background information, and teaching both adults and children. She is presently Director of Education at VINS. With an AB from Vassar College, elementary teaching certification from Dartmouth College, selection to attend the 1985 NSF Honors Workshop for Elementary Science Teachers, and recognition by the Vermont Department of Education in 1986 as an Outstanding Teacher, Ms. Lingelbach has helped to awaken a curiosity and caring about the natural world in people of all ages.

Vermont Institute of Natural Science

Hands-On Nature comes from the Vermont Institute of Natural Science in Woodstock, Vermont. Its activities have been used with great success statewide since 1972 in the ELF (Environmental Learning for the Future) program for elementary school children.

The Vermont Institute of Natural Science is a non-profit membership organization dedicated to protecting Vermont's environmental quality of life through education and research. Outreach programs are conducted for audiences of all ages throughout Vermont, while at the 77 acre VINS preserve in Woodstock, Vermont, members and visitors are welcome to visit the Vermont Raptor Center, and to walk the self-guided nature trails.

Design: The Laughing Bear Associates